英语畅谈中国文化风俗

Album of Culture and Conventions in China

赵 嚚 蔡新芝 编著

科 学 出 版 社
北 京

图书在版编目(CIP)数据

英语畅谈中国文化风俗：汉英对照/赵嚚，蔡新芝编著. —北京：科学出版社，2011.5
ISBN 978-7-03-030779-8

I. ①英… II. ①赵… ②蔡… III. ①中华文化-介绍-英、汉 IV. ①K203

中国版本图书馆 CIP 数据核字(2011)第 070800 号

责任编辑：阎　莉 / 责任校对：刘小梅
责任印制：李　彤 / 封面设计：无极书装

联系电话：010-6403 0529　电子邮箱 yanli@mail.sciencep.com

科学出版社 出版
北京东黄城根北街 16 号
邮政编码：100717
http://www.sciencep.com
涿州市般润文化传播有限公司 印刷
科学出版社编务公司排版制作
科学出版社发行　各地新华书店经销
*
2011 年 5 月第　一　版　开本：B5 (720×1000)
2023 年 8 月第九次印刷　印张：22
字数：520 000

定价：65.00 元
(如有印装质量问题，我社负责调换)

Preface

前　言

在世界经济全球化的进程中，改革开放后的中国在世界经贸、科技创新、和平共处等方面起着越来越重要的作用。大量的中国人走出国门去学习和工作，来自世界各地的友人也涌向中国，他们在中国积极开拓业务的同时，也对中国悠久的历史和文化风俗充满好奇和向往。跨文化的互动与交流日益频繁，而整个世界都面临着文化差异所带来的变化和巨大挑战。风俗习惯、思维方式、社会背景等方面的不同往往会造成不可回避的交往障碍和冲突。在多年的英语教学工作中，我们经常看到很多优秀的英语学习者，尽管通过了大学英语六级，甚至英语专业八级等考试，但他们在涉外活动中却不能用适当、得体的英语向外国友人介绍中国的风俗习惯，以及由几千年历史沉淀而来的思想、艺术。对此，我们感到无限的自责和巨大压力。为了弘扬中国民族文化，为了让世界更好地了解中国，我们试图利用英语这一国际化语言，把我国璀璨辉煌的民族文化和源远流长的历史文化风俗向世界传播。

本书旨在让世界上说英语的人了解地道的中国文化，也能给那些希望向世界介绍中国文化的国人提供一定的英语素材，同时还能为很多没有时间系统钻研本土文化的研习者提供学习和了解本国民族文化风俗的另一个平台。本书也可作为英语学习者提高英语水平、拓展知识范围和增强文化底蕴的读物或教科书。

由于中国文化博大精深，涉及的方面极其广泛，而编著者水平有限，书中不免会有一些错漏之处，恳请广大读者和有关专家批评指正。同时也非常感谢美籍教师 Nicholas John O'shen 先生对本书的认真修改和润色。

赵　罱　蔡新芝

2011 年 1 月 10 日

Contents

目 录

UNIT 1

Chinese Dragon Culture

龙文化

题记

中国人的先祖和世界上其他民族一样，都经历了氏族公社时期。黄帝和炎帝是当时最著名的两个部落首领，属华夏集团。由于黄帝、炎帝在部落联盟时期的重要位置，其后人被称为“炎黄子孙”，他们也自称为“龙的传人”。神秘的龙文化一直延续至今。

The ancestors of the Chinese people like other nations experienced a clan commune period. At that time Yandi and Huangdi were leaders of the two most famous tribes, belonging to the Huaxia. Since Yandi and Huangdi played an important role in the tribal alliance period, the later generations were known as the descendants of them. But they also called themselves the descendants of the dragon, and the mysterious dragon culture still continues today.

Many Chinese people like to sing a song: “There is a dragon in the ancient orient whose name is China. There is a group of ancient oriental people there too, who are all the descendants of the dragon…” Here the word “dragon” is the symbol of Chinese nation. Many foreigners call China the “oriental dragon”. Chinese people also like to call themselves the “descendants of the dragon”.

In fact, "dragon" is only a kind of mythological animal in legend. No one has ever seen the flying dragon winding through the clouds in China or anywhere else. It is the mysterious dragon worship, especially the worship of the snake totem that causes Chinese to think of themselves as the descendants of the dragon.

Researchers believed that dragon worship was formed after the tribe that took snakes as totems combined with the tribes that took horses, fish, deer, camels, turtles, eagles, cattle and tigers as totems. That is why the new totemism—dragon has deer's horns, camel's head, tortoise's eyes, snake's neck, the scales of fish, the claws of eagle, the palms of tiger, and the ears of cattle. It is said that dragons can fly, swim, gather clouds to pour down rain and change into different forms.

Since the beginning of the Xia Dynasty, the Chinese have worshiped the dragon. The concept of dragons has already infiltrated every part of society. In ancient people's beliefs "dragon" was a symbol of the power and gods, so the Chinese emperors were thought of as dragons. In the past, everything related to the Chinese emperor was connected with the "dragon", therefore the emperor was called "the real dragon and the son of heaven"; the illness of the emperor meant "The dragon's body is not very well."; when the emperor rewarded someone, the person would say "Thank dragon"; the imperial chariot was called "dragon's chariot"; emperor's clothes are called "dragon robes", and so on.

In Chinese language, people always show their love and respect to the dragon. For example, they use "Hidden dragons and crouching tigers" to describe the talented or outstanding people who remain obscure to the untrained eye; "Long to see one's son become a dragon", means to hope that one's child will have a bright future. The person who is full of vim and vigor is called "doughty as a dragon and lively as a tiger". "Fighting between a tiger and a dragon" is used to describe the fierce struggle between well-matched opponents. From the above we can see the great vitality of ancient dragon culture in China.

段落译文

很多中国人爱唱这样一首歌:"古老的东方有一条龙，它的名字就叫中国；古老的东方有一群人，他们全是龙的传人……" 这里所说的"龙"是中华民族的象征。很多外国人也称中国为"东方巨龙"。中国人更喜欢称自己为"龙的传人"。

实际上,"龙"只是一种传说中的虚构动物。在当今世界，没有人见过蜿蜒飞舞的龙，在中国，也从来没有人目睹过腾云驾雾的龙。中国人自称龙的传人，是与神秘的龙崇拜有关，尤其与对蛇的图腾崇拜有关。

研究者认为，以蛇为图腾的部落在与以马、鱼、鹿、骆驼、龟、鹰、牛、虎等为图腾的部落融合后，形成了新的崇拜对象 "龙"，其角似鹿，头似骆驼，眼似龟，颈似蛇，鳞似鱼，爪似鹰，掌似虎，耳似牛。传说中的龙能飞，能游水，能兴云雨，善变化，充满神秘感。

自夏朝开始，中国人对龙的崇拜经久不衰。龙的观念，龙的形象已渗透到社会的各个角落。在古代人们的信仰中"龙"是神灵和权威的象征，后来他们把皇帝和龙归为一体，使帝王更具威严、更神化。因此中国皇帝的一切都与"龙"有关。他们被称为"真龙天子"；皇帝有病要说"龙体欠安"；皇帝给赏赐，大臣口称"谢龙恩"；皇帝所乘的车叫"龙舆"，皇帝的衣服被称为"龙袍"，等等。

在帝王的宫殿里，到处可见龙的图案。例如，北京的故宫是龙图案最多的地方。皇帝的龙椅上，雕有一条巨大的蟠龙和 16 条小金龙。故宫的正门——天安门城楼上有 932 条彩绘金龙，其大殿的天花板上有千姿百态的卧龙、飞龙、盘龙 1700 多条，可谓是名副其实的“龙楼”。天安门前的华表上也盘着汉白玉雕龙。

民间以龙为主题的风俗也很多。在中国的农历里，几乎每个月都有与龙有关的节日或庙会。例如，农历正月，很多地区都有“龙灯会”，也称为“闹龙灯”。正月初五是云南瑶族的传统节日——“龙头节”。当地群众在这一天用各种供品祭祀龙王。正月十三至十五是湖北武昌的“祭龙节”，人们的庆祝形式有舞龙、烧龙、拔河比赛等。二月初二是“龙抬头节”，有些地方的人们吃油煎食品来庆祝，有些人吃“龙须面”，而且面越长越好，象征吉祥。五月端午节前后，江苏、广东、湖南、湖北、贵州、四川等地都会有“龙船赛会”，因此五月节也被称为“龙舟节”或“龙船节”。六月六为“晒龙袍日”，等等。

在语言方面，中国人也时常流露出对龙的热爱和崇敬。例如，“人才辈出”称为“藏龙卧虎”；希望孩子有出息，成为有用的人才，是“望子成龙”；身体健康，精神旺盛的人被说成是“生龙活虎”；还可以用“龙争虎斗”来形容强手之间的争斗。从中可以看出在中国古老的龙文化一直保持着旺盛的生命力。

实用词汇

龙 dragon

龙的传人 the descendants of the dragon

炎黄子孙 descendents of Yandi and Huangdi ; descendents of the Yan and Huang Emperors

华夏民族 Huaxia nationality; the Chinese nationality; the Huaxia

图腾 totem

图腾崇拜 totemism

真龙天子 the real dragon and the son of the heaven
龙子龙孙 dragon sons and dragon grandsons
龙袍 dragon robes
龙椅 dragon seat; throne
龙宫 dragon palace
龙王 the king of the water/dragon
龙灯会 dragon lantern festival
舞龙 perform the dragon dance
华表 cloud pillar; ornamental columns
汉白玉雕龙 white marble dragon
庙会 temple fair
龙须面 dragon whiskers noodles; long, thin noodles

名言俗语

画蛇添足。

Draw a snake with feet added to it.

画龙点睛。

To dot the eyeballs while painting a dragon; to bring the painted dragon to life by putting the pupils into its eyes.

龙游浅滩遭虾戏，虎落平阳被犬欺。

A dragon will be teased by a shrimp in a shoal water; a tiger will be bullied by a dog on a treeless plain.

欲擒龙王，先得下海。

He who would catch fish must not mind getting wet

在家一条龙，在外一条虫。

A lion at home, a mouse abroad.

龙生龙，凤生凤。

A man that begets a barren cannot have a grand child.

国家兴亡，匹夫有责。

Every man has a share of responsibility for the fate of his country.

龙飞凤舞。

Like dragons flying and phoenixes dancing, which means lively and vigorous flourishes in calligraphy.

龙凤呈祥。

The dragon and the phoenix bringing prosperity, which means to exercise good fortune.

龙驹凤雏。

The dragon colt or young phoenix—a brilliant young man.

群龙无首。

A host of dragons without a head, which means a group without a leader.

龙争虎斗。

The fighting between a tiger and a dragon; a fierce struggle between well-matched opponents.

生龙活虎。

Doughty as a dragon and lively as a tiger; full of vim and vigor.

词语注解

画蛇添足：画蛇添上脚，比喻做多余的事，反而不恰当。

Draw a snake with feet added to it: this idiom is frequently quoted to depict any act which ruins the effect by adding what is superfluous.

画龙点睛：原意是为画好的龙画上眼睛，使其附有生命。现在经常用来比喻写文章或说话时在关键地方加上精辟的语句，使内容更加生动传神。

It means to bring the painted dragon to life by putting the pupils into its eyes. The literal translation of it means to dot the eyeballs while painting a dragon. But now this saying is widely quoted to refer to adding the crucial touch to a work of art that brings it to life or putting in the word or two that clinches the point.

叶公好龙：传说有位叶公，非常爱好龙。真龙知道了，就到叶公家看他，叶公吓得面如土色，拔腿就跑。比喻某人说是爱好某事物，其实并不是真爱好。

Lord Ye's love of the dragon turns into his worst fear: It is often cited to depict the professed love of what one really fears.

藏龙卧虎：比喻潜藏着的杰出人才。

Hidden dragons and crouching tigers which means talented or outstanding people who remains obscure to the undiscovering eye.

望子成龙：希望儿子能成为出人头地或有作为的人。

Long to see one's son become a dragon, which really means to hope that one's children will have a bright future.

中西合璧

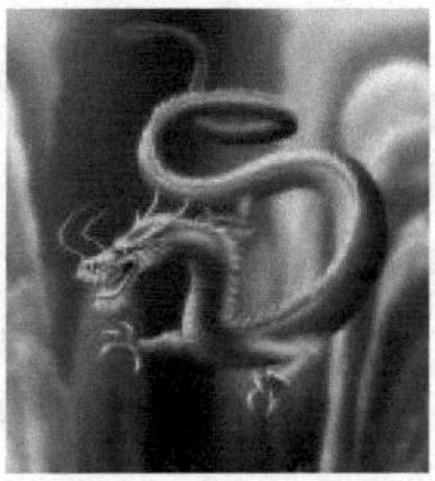

值得说明的是，中国的“龙”与西方传说中的“龙”的含义完全不同。在西方“龙”被描绘成一种长着翅膀、能喷火、邪恶并凶猛的动物，而中国的“龙”则是威严、高贵、权利的象征。

尽管西方人认为龙是一种凶暴的动物，但是法国还是有一个与龙有关的节日。该龙节是在每年 6 月底举行，为期 4 天，纪念传说中的圣女马尔泰战胜一条巨龙的事迹。龙节有好多庆祝活动，其中舞龙游行与中国舞龙灯很相近。

It is worth saying that there are some complete differences between the Chinese dragons and western dragons in the legend. In the west, "dragon" was portrayed as an evil and ferocious animal with wings and could be able to breathe fire. In china, dragon is a symbol of dignity and power.

Although Westerners think that the dragon is a violent animal, there is a dragon festival in France, which portrays a different idea. This four-day festival is held each year at the end of June to commemorate Joan Marthe who, as the legend goes, conquered a dragon. There are a lot of activities during the festival, among which a procession of dragon dancing is similar to the Chinese dragon lantern dancing.

UNIT 2

Mountains and Rivers in China

名山大川

题记

中国幅员辽阔，地理结构复杂。陆地面积约占 960 万平方公里，仅次于俄罗斯和加拿大，是世界第三大国家。中国有很多的名山大川，其中最著名的要数“三山五岳”及包括长江在内的“七大水系”。

China has a vast territory with complicated geographical structure. Its land is about 9.6 million square kilometers, and it is the third largest country in the world, only next to Russia and Canada. There are many great mountains and rivers in China. The most famous ones must be "Sanshanwuyue", and seven major rivers, including the Yangtze River.

When it comes to mountains, Chinese people will mention "Sanshanwuyue", which means three great mountains and the five sacred mountains in China. Initially, the three great mountains referred to the three mountains of immortals—Penglai, Fangzhang and Ying Chow, which were not real mountains though described as very beautiful scenery. Now the three great mountains refer to Mount Huang in Anhui province, Mount Lu in Jiangxi and

Mount Yandang in Zhejiang. The five sacred mountains are the Eastern Mountain—Mount Tai, the Western Mountain—Mount Hua, the Northern Mountain—Mount Heng in Shanxi, the Central Mountain—Mount Song, and the Southern Mountain—Mount Heng in Hunan. It is said that these mountains were all granted additional titles by many emperors in the ancient times. Although they are not the highest and the most precipitous ones, they appear particularly high and steep for they are located in plain or basin.

Mount Huang is located in the south of Anhui Province, which is famous for its pines, rocks, seas of clouds and hot springs. It is a botanical garden with a lot of flowers, ancient trees, rare birds and animals. Mount Lu is in Jiu Jiang City, Jiangxi province, and is celebrated for the tall and graceful peaks, the unpredictable sea of clouds, magical scene at the spring waterfall, as well as many historic sites. It is a world-renowned summer resort too. Mount Yandang is located in Yueqing County, Zhejiang Province. Because of the lake on the top of the peak and dense reeds where the wild geese are fond of staying during their migration, it is called Mount Yandang which means Wild Goose Mountain. There are many waterfalls there, the most famous ones are "big dragon pond", "small dragon pond" and "Sanzhepu".

Mount Tai is located in Shandong Province. It has many unique stones, pine trees, clouds and magnificent natural landscape. It is called "the number one mountain in China". It is also said that in ancient times, many emperors worshiped it when they ascended the throne or during peacetime. In 1987, Mount Tai was listed as the cultural and national heritage of the world by

UNESCO.

The Western Mountain—Mount Hua is 2,200 meters above sea level and located in Shanxi Province, which is the highest mountain among the five sacred mountains and its natural landscape is peculiar and full of rocks, precipitous cliffs, deep valleys and dangerous paths. It is known as the most dangerous mountain. That is why a great number of people are attracted to climbing it every year.

The Southern Mountain—Mount Heng is located in the middle of Hunan province. Hengshan's natural scenery is very beautiful and its exuberant forest is green and full of fragrant flowers all year round. It is a sacred site of Buddhism and there are many temples, including the magnificent Nanyue Temple, which covers nearly 100 thousands square meters.

The Northern Mountain—Mount Heng in Shanxi is famous for Taoism. It is said that it is where Guolao Zhang, one of the Eight Immortals in Chinese mythology once lived. There are a lot of cultural relics and historic sites, such as the Hanging Temple, Buddha wooden pagoda, Yuanjue Temple pagoda and so on, in which the structure, shape, decoration, sculpture, and painting play an important part of Chinese architectural history.

The Central Mountain—Mount Song is in Henan province. Among the 36 peaks, Junji is the main peak, 1492 meters above sea level. It has many historical monuments and the most famous ones are Shaolin Temple, Songshan Temple, three carved stones of the Han Dynasty, Zhong Yuemiao temple, and Huishan Temple, and so on.

The most famous Seven Rivers in China are Yangtze River, Yellow River, Huaihe River, Pearl River, Haihe River, Songhua River and Liaohe River. The Yangtze River is the longest river in China, 6300 kilometers in length. It covers 11 provinces and autonomous regions. It ranks the third in the world after the Nile in Africa and the Amazon in South America. The Yellow River, with length of 5464 kilometers is the second largest river in China, the cradle of Chinese culture, and the mother river of the Chinese people. The Yellow River is a world famous multi-sediment-laden river. Huaihe River is between the Yangtze River and Yellow River, whose branches densely cover four provinces—Henan, Anhui, Jiangsu and Shandong. The Pearl River is the fourth largest river in China with a total length of 2215.8 kilometers, and a small part of it is in Vietnam. Haihe River is the largest river in North China. The Songhua River, 1927 kilometres long moistens the vast Sanjiang Plain. The 1430-kilometre-long Liaohe River flows past Inner Mongolia and Liaoning province.

Other relatively well-known rivers are the 2137-kilometer Tarim River which is the largest inland river in China and Qiantang River which is famous for its high tide. China also has the world's longest man-made canal—the Beijing-Hangzhou Grand Canal. It is the largest water conservancy project in ancient China, it is 1764 kilometer long and flows past Beijing, Tianjin, Hebei, Shandong, Jiangsu, Zhejiang, six provinces and cities, and link five great rivers such as Haihe River, Huanghe River, Huaihe River, the Yangtze River, and Qiantang River.

段落译文

一谈到山，中国人就会提到“三山五岳”。最初的“三山”是指神话中传说的蓬莱、方丈、瀛洲三个仙山。它们虽然被描绘得风光绮丽，却不是真实的山。而现在的“三山”是指安徽的黄山、江西的庐山和浙江的雁荡山。“五岳”是中国五大名山的总称，它们是东岳泰山、西岳华山、北岳恒山、中岳嵩山及南岳衡山。据说这些

山都是古代帝王加封的。五岳虽然不是中国最高、最险峻的山峰，但是由于他们都是高耸在平原或盆地，因此显得格外高峻。

位于安徽省南部的黄山是以奇松、怪石、云海、温泉“四绝”闻名于天下。黄山有很多的名花古木、珍禽异兽，是一座天然的动、植物园。在江西省九江市的庐山有雄奇挺秀的山峰、变幻莫测的云海、神奇多姿的泉水瀑布，以及很多历史悠久的古迹。庐山还是中外闻名的避暑胜地。雁荡山位于浙江省乐清县，因山顶有湖，芦苇茂密，南归秋雁喜欢在此停留，故名雁荡山。雁荡山瀑布众多，其中最著名的是大龙湫、小龙湫和三折瀑。

泰山——五岳之首，位于山东省。泰山具有独特的苍松巨石，云烟岚光，自然景观雄伟壮丽。在中国有“天下第一山”之称。据说古时候历代帝王登基时或太平年岁，都会到此朝拜。1987年，泰山被联合国教科文组织世界遗产委员会列为世界文化、自然双重遗产。

西岳华山位于陕西省，海拔 2200 米，是五岳中最高的山。华山自然景观奇特而壮美、奇岩危崖、山高壁峭、幽谷险道。自古以来就被称为“奇险天下第一山”。正因为如此，华山每年都会吸引很多不畏险阻攀登的勇敢者。

南岳衡山位于湖南省中部。衡山自然景色非常秀丽，林木茂盛，终年翠绿；奇花异草，四季飘香。衡山还是佛教圣地，当地有很多的寺庙，其中南岳大庙气势宏伟，占地近 10 万平方米。

位于山西省的北岳恒山以道教闻名。传说中国神话中的八仙之一张果老就是在此隐居修行的。恒山文物古迹，星罗棋布，例如悬空寺、释迦木塔、圆觉寺砖塔等。它们的结构、造型、装饰、雕刻、彩画等方面都在中国的建筑史上有着重要的地位和价值。

中岳嵩山位于河南省。嵩山共有 36 峰，峻极峰为主峰，海拔 1492 米。嵩山拥有众多的历史遗迹，其中著名的有少林寺、嵩山寺塔、汉代三阙、中岳庙、会善寺等。

中国最著名的七大水系是指长江、黄河、淮河、珠江、海河、松花江及辽河。长江是我国第一大河，全长 6300 公里，流经 11 个省、自治区，居世界第三位，仅次于非洲的尼罗河和南美洲的亚马逊河。

黄河长为 5464 公里，是中国第二大河、中华文化的发祥地，也是中国的母亲河。黄河的含沙量极大，是举世闻名的多沙河流。淮河位于长江和黄河之间，其支流密布在河南、安徽、江苏、山东四省。珠江是中国第四大河流，总长 2215 公里。其中有一小部分在越南境内。海河是中国华北地区最大的水系。松花江全长 1927 公里，滋润着广阔的三江平原。辽河全长 1430 公里，地跨内蒙古、辽宁两个省份。

另外比较出名的河流还有全长 2137 公里的塔里木河 ——中国最大的内陆河及以潮水闻名的钱塘江等。中国有世界最长的人工运河——京杭大运河。京杭大运河全长 1764 公里，流经北京、天津、河北、山东、江苏和浙江六个省市，连接了海河、黄河、淮河、长江和钱塘江五大河流，是中国古代最大的水利工程。

实用词汇

名山大川 famous mountains and great rivers
黄山 Mount Huang
庐山 Mount Lu
五岳 the five sacred mountains; the five great mountains
东岳泰山 the Eastern Mount / Mountain—Mount Tai
西岳华山 the Western Mount / Mountain—Mount Hua
北岳恒山 the Northern Mount / Mountain—Mount Heng in Shanxi
中岳嵩山 the Central Mount / Mountain—Mount Song
南岳衡山 the Southern Mount / Mountain—Mount Heng in Hunan
仙山 the mountain of immortals
云海 sea of clouds; stretch of clouds that look like a sea from far above
奇峰 vagarious mountain peak
瀑布 waterfall
悬空寺 the Hanging Temple; Suspending Temple; Mid-Air Temple
木塔 wooden pagoda
世界文化遗产 world cultural Heritage

世界文化自然遗产 world cultural and national heritage
平原 plain
盆地 basin
青海高原 Qinghai-Tibetan Plateau
避暑胜地 summer resort
长江 Yangtze River
黄河 Yellow River
多沙河流 river of mud
珠江 Pearl River
黑龙江 Heilongjiang River
松花江 Songhuajiang River
淮河 Huaihe River
内陆河 inland river
钱塘大潮 spring tide of Qiantang River
京杭大运河 the Beijing-Hangzhou Grand Canal

名言俗语

海纳百川
All rivers run into the sea. / The sea refuses no river.
江山易改，本性难移。
You cannot make a crab walk straight.
山清水秀
Green hills and limpid water; picture-perfect scenery
江山如此多娇
Land with such superb beauty and grandeur
打江山
Fight for supreme power.

词语注解

长江不拒细流，泰山不择土石。可以比喻虚心接受他人的建议和忠告。

The Yangtze refuses no water from tributaries; Mount Tai discriminates no dirt from other rocks. It really means that one who likes to learn never refuses suggestions and advices from others.

江河日下：原指江河水天天向下流。比喻情况一天天坏下去。

Rivers flowing downstream on a daily basis, which also means going from bad to worse.

愚公移山：讲的是一位 90 岁的老人，想把家门前的两座大山搬走。所以率领子孙每天挖山不止，最后感动了天帝，他派了一个神仙把山背走了。“愚公移山”告诉人们有志者竟事成的精神。

Old man Yu Gong moved mountains: A 90-year-old man, whose name was Yu Gong, wanted to move away the two mountains which were located in front of his house. He worked with his sons and grandchildren everyday. Later, the Heaven God was moved by the old man's determination and sent another god to take the two high mountains away. It tells people that so long as one is determined and sticks to it long enough, anything can be done, no matter how difficult it is.

山盟海誓：男女相爱时所立的誓言和盟约，表示爱情要像山和大海一样永恒不变。

Couple's pledge of love as long-lasting as mountains and the sea; a solemn pledge of love.

山穷水尽：山和水都到了尽头，前面再没有路可走了。比喻陷入绝境。

Where the hills and streams end, often means at the end of one's hope.

中西合璧

众所周知，世界第一高峰是珠穆朗玛峰，海拔 8844.43 米。最长的河流是尼罗河，全长 6695 公里。最长的内流河是欧洲的伏尔加河，全长 3690 公里；最大的淡水湖是北美的苏必利尔湖，面积达 82400 平方公里。最深的湖泊是贝加尔湖，水深达 1940 米。最出名的运河是苏伊士运河及巴拿马运河。世界各国都有各自的名山大川。例如，阿尔卑斯山是欧洲最高大的山脉，其主峰海拔 4810 米。美国最高的山峰是 6194 米的麦金利山。

It is well known that the world's highest peak of Mount Everest, is 8844.43 meters above sea level; the longest river is the Nile, the length of 6695 kilometers; the longest inland river in Europe, is 3690-kilometer-long Volga River; the largest freshwater lake is Lake Superior in North America with an area of 82.4 thousand square kilometers. The deepest lake is Lake Baikal about 1940 meters deep. Suez Canal and Panama Canal are the most well known canals. All the countries have their own famous mountains and great rivers. For example, the Alps is the tallest mountain range in Europe and its highest peak is 4810 meters. The tallest mountain in the United States is Mount McKinley, which is 6194 meters high.

UNIT 3

Religion

宗教文化

题记

在中国古代文化中，宗教文化是中国的精髓。封建社会时期，宗教作为统治阶级统治工具的同时也承担了发扬中国文化的重任。

Religion is the essence of Chinese culture. It was a tool of ruling class in feudal society, and assumed the responsibility of promoting Chinese culture.

China has many religions and Chinese citizens can choose and express their Religious beliefs, and show their religious status freely. According to incomplete statistics, there are now more than 100,000 religious activities in China, with more than 300,000 clerics from all religions, more than 3,000 national and local religious communities, and more than 70 religious schools. Various religions publish their scriptures, religious books and journals in China, of which 20 million copies are of the Bible.

The early religious beliefs in China originated from primitive society, and the production of primitive religions took the values of God as a symbol. Based

on archaeological discoveries and documents, there were four religious forms popular in China during ancient times. They were nature worship, ancestor worship, totem worship, and reproduction worship. The first one included the worship of nature and natural phenomena, such as astrological phenomena. In ancient times, people were quite unable to do anything with natural phenomena (e.g. wind, rain, thunder, and lightning), so that they worshipped all as celestial beings, especially full of awe to the God of Thunder. The second one came from people's mystical understanding of their own life. They thought that experience and wisdom and authority of ancestors would exist with the souls forever, which could be the supernatural power to protect the tribal members. With the inheritance of ancestors' worship customs, the earliest national ancestors became the symbol of national caste. They then were cherished as the man of God or the sage by apotheosis of ancient history, such as Yu in Xia Dynasty, Qi in Shang Dynasty, and Houji in Zhou Dynasty. The third one, which was the combination of nature worship and ancestor worship, was a clan badge, meaning its consanguinity, such as Nvwa with the head of a woman and reptilian body, Emperor Yan and Shennong with the head of a cow and human body. The last one was the worship of reproduction based on the importance to reproduction of population in a clan or tribe.

Taoism, which belongs to the Chinese native religions, was formed in the late Han Dynasty two thousand years ago. Its essence was a people's belief in immortals, and treating immortality as the purpose of life were taking Taiping Taoism and Five Pecks of Rice Taoism (Grains of Rice Daoist Sect) which was respectively created by Zhang Jiao and Zhang Daoling as symbols. Taoism integrated fairy legend with necromancer and necromancy, blending the theory of Yin and Yang and five elements. Depending primarily on the learning about the Emperor Huang, which showed the characteristics of Chinese national culture. The basic belief of Taoist Scriptures was Dao, considering it as the origin and the master of the universe. Taoist Immortal belief declared war against the fate of death that could not be avoided, and on the natural irresistible power of aliens. It also directly denied the death of human being itself and hoped the human body could become a spirit, attempting to possess the ability of creation of the heaven and the earth by manpower and natural and supernatural power. In Taoists' opinion, their lifelong business was to be immortals. Taoism had a profound effect on Chinese culture (e.g. medicine, music, architecture, and painting, etc.). In the process of its development, Taoist medicine enriched the treasure house of traditional Chinese medicine in both theory and practice. In addition, Four Great Inventions of ancient China had contributed greatly to the scientific development of the world, of which black powder and the compass are closely related with Taoism.

Chinese Buddhism refers to particular form of Buddhism in China. Buddhism was introduced to the mainland of China from Western Regions during the Western and Eastern Han Dynasties, with its development period being from the late Eastern Han Dynasty to Wei, Jin, Southern and Northern Dynasties. The teachings of Buddha thought that all things and phenomena were vanity. Later, based on the studies of Niepan, Buddhism focused on how and why to become a Buddha, and the stages of being a Buddha. Chinese Buddhism had a major influence on all classes of feudal society in its long years of development. Furthermore, its outward dissemination promoted cultural exchanges among China, its neighboring countries and the world.

As a carrier of social culture, Chinese religion played an active role in Chinese traditional scientific knowledge production, accumulation and development.

段落译文

中国是个多宗教的国家。中国公民可以自由地选择、表达自己的信仰和表明宗教身份。据不完全统计，中国现有宗教活动场所10万余处，各种宗教教职人员约30万人，全国性和地方性宗教团体3000多个，70多所宗教院校。各教都自己出版经典、书刊，其中仅《圣经》的印数即达3000万册。

我国早期的宗教信仰起源于原始社会，以神灵观念为标志。根据考古发现和文献记载，中国在远古时期流行有自然崇拜、祖灵崇拜、图腾崇拜、生殖崇拜等原始宗教形式。自然崇拜包括对自然物和自然现象的崇拜，如天象崇拜。远古时人们对自然现象(风、雨、雷、电)束手无策。因此就有了诸位天神，其中雷公最受人敬畏。祖灵崇拜的产生是因为人对自身生命的神秘理解。对他们来说，祖先所代表的经验、智慧和权威，将随其灵魂而永存，成为一种超自然的力量而护佑氏族成员。随着祖先崇拜习俗的传承，民族始祖成为民族的象征，他们经古史传说的神化，被奉为神人或圣人，如夏族的禹、商族的契、周族的后稷都是原始民族的始祖。自然崇拜和祖先崇拜经结合而产生图腾崇拜。“图腾”是族徽标记，意思是他们的亲族，如女娲的头像人，身体像蛇，炎帝、神农的头像牛，身体是人。生殖崇拜是基于重视氏族或部落的人口繁衍而产生的对生殖力的崇拜。

道教是中国本土产生的宗教，形成于汉代后期，迄今有两千年的历史了。道教以神仙信仰为核心、以长生视为人生目的，由张角、张道陵分别创立的太平道和五斗米道是道教形成的标志。道教综合了上古时代的神仙传说和和方士方术；融合了阴阳五行学说；以道家黄老之学为主要依据而形成，具有鲜明的中华民族文化色彩。道教的经典都成其根本信仰是“道”，认为“道”是宇宙的本源和主宰者。道教的神仙信仰是向人所无法摆脱的生老病死的命运和无法抗拒的外在异己的自然力量宣战，直接否定人自身的死亡，追求肉体成仙，试图通过人力，借助自然和超自然的力量夺天地造化之功，把得道成仙当做人生的事业。道教在发展的历史过程中对我国文化(如医学、音乐、建筑、绘画等)产生了深远的影响。其中道教医学从理论和实践两个方面，丰富了中国传统医学的宝库。中国古代的四大发明为世界科学发展做出了重要贡献，而其中黑火药和指南针的发明就与道教有着密切的关系。

中国佛教是指佛教在中国的发展的特殊形式或中国化的佛教。佛教于两汉之际由西域传入中国内地，东汉末到魏晋南北朝是佛教在中国的发展时期。其教义认为一切事物和现象都是空幻不实的；后期以涅槃学为主，主要讲如何成佛、成佛的理据以及成佛的阶段等。中国佛教经历了漫长的发展岁月，在封建社会各阶层中曾有过广泛的影响，是中国传统文化的组成部分。其向外的传播则推进了我国与邻国及世界各国的文化交流。

中国宗教作为一种社会文化载体，曾经为中国传统科学知识的产生、积累和发展发挥了积极作用。

实用词汇

宗教文化 religious culture
自然崇拜 nature worship
祖灵崇拜 ancestor worship
图腾崇拜 totem worship
生殖崇拜 reproduction worship
道教 Taoism
八卦 the Eight Trigrams
白莲教 White Lotus Society (a secret religious society active during the Yuan, Ming and Qing Dynasties, which was often used as a cover of peasant rebellions)
宗教信仰 religious belief
太平道 Taiping Taoism
五斗米道 Five Pecks of Rice Taoism

阴阳五行学说 the theory of Yin and Yang and five elements

黄老之学 the learning about the Emperor Huang

佛教 Buddhism

佛教教义 the teachings of Buddha

比丘 monk

比丘尼 nun

出家 become a monk or a nun

出家人 Buddhist or Taoist priest

道德经 The Classic of the Virtue of the Tao

神仙 supernatural being; person who has the power of clairvoyance; person not encumbered with worldly cares

十重戒 Ten Unpardonable Sins

受符 Shou-fu（transmission of the art of tailsmanic figures）

土地庙 tiny temple housing the village god

金童玉女 the Golden Boy and the Jade Maiden（attendants of the Taoist immortals）

灶神 Kitchen God

土地神 gnome kobold

财神 mammon

门神 door-god

炼丹术 alchemy

老道 Taoist priest

老庄学派 school of thought represented by Lao Zi and Zhuang Zi

莲台 a Buddha's seat in the form of a lotus flower

炼丹 （try to）make pills of immortality（as a Taoist practice）

炼度 prayer for the dead

庙号 temple title

名教 Confucian ethical code

极乐世界 Land of Ultimate Bliss

极天际地 reach the high heavens and pervade the earth—fairly enormous

即身成佛 attain Buddhahood in the present body

急来抱佛脚 clasp Buddha's feet when in trouble—seek help at the last moment

借花献佛 present Buddha with flowers given by another—make a gift of sth. given by another

金刚界 diamond element

活佛 Living Buddha; (in classical novels) Buddhist monk or the person who assists people in distress and saves people from danger

名言俗语

一盘棋下完，国王与小卒都放在同一个盒子里。/人生如戏，到头来总要落幕。

After the game, the king and the pawn go into the same box.

上教堂的人未必个个都是圣人。

All are not saints that go to church.

我为人人，人人为我。

One for all and all for one.

有所舍，方能有所得。

All gains are made at some sacrifice.

除了上帝，万物皆有祈愿。

All things have a beginning, God excepted.

愤怒的人不适合祈祷。

An angry man is not fit to pray.

泥菩萨过江，自身难保。

A clay idol of bodhisattva fording a river can hardly save itself, let alone anyone else.

穿袈裟的不一定是和尚。

The cowl / hood does not make the monk.

善有善报，恶有恶报。

Do good, reap good; do evil, reap evil. / Do well and have well.

拜金的人多过拜神的人。

Gold has more worshippers than God。

离教堂越近，离上帝越远。

The nearer the church, the farther from God.

俗语注解

白莲教：活跃在元、明、清时期的一个秘密宗教团体

White Lotus Society: a secret religious society active during the Yuan, Ming and Qing dynasties

半路出家：意指没有接受过训练就改换做一种新的工作

turn to be a Buddhist late in life—change to a new profession for which one has received no previous training

不看僧面看佛面：出于对某人的尊重做某事

do something not for the monk's sake, but for the Buddhist's—do sth. out of consideration for sb. else

慧根：对佛教的彻底理解

(Buddhism) talent to thoroughly comprehend Buddhist teachings

慧眼：洞察过去、将来的能力

(Buddhism) mind which perceives both past and future; mental discernment; insight; acumen

舍利：佛死后尸体遗留下的部分，作为佛教徒珍藏的遗留物

sarira, remains from cremation of Buddha's body, regarded as most treasured Buddhist relics

禅宗为中国佛教所独创，被视为佛教中国化的典型，故禅宗又被称为“中国禅”。禅是“禅那”的简称，汉译为“静虑”，意思是静中思虑，一般叫“禅定”。禅宗的创始人是惠能。

Zen, which was original created by Chinese Buddhism, was considered as a Buddhism which was sinicized typically. Thus, Zen was also called Chinese Zen, a short form of "Chan Na", meaning "静虑" in Chinese. It means to think over in silence, calling "Chan Ding". The founder of Zen is Huineng.

中西合璧

中国宗教和世界宗教有着共性和差异，中国宗教有它独特的发展历程，尤其是道教对中国科技的发展有重要贡献。中国宗教只是局限于汉民族范围，主要指佛道两教和民间信仰；西方宗教指基督宗教，包括天主教、新教、东正教。在信仰特征上，中国宗教的大众信仰具有多元化的特征，西方宗教的群体信仰则具有一元化特征。在信仰意识上，中国宗教的大众信仰以现世功利意识为主体，西方宗教的群体信仰以教义意识为主体。从教派关系上来比较，中国宗教的信仰社会是以皇权为主体的共处相争的方式来求得发展，而西方宗教的信仰社会是以教权为主体的相互排他的方式来求得发展。中国宗教，属于弥散式的信仰模式。西方宗教，属于凝聚式的信仰模式。中国佛教既承袭了印度佛教戒律中所包含的伦理精神，又逐步接受源于儒学的忠孝仁义等道德价值取向，从而丰富了中华道德规范：一是孝道论；二是慈悲观；三是善恶观；四是因果报应。

Similarities and discrepancies exist between Chinese religion and world religion. It has its own unique developing process, especially Taoism which makes great contributions to Chinese science and technology. However, it is just restricted to the Han Nationality, mainly referring to Taoism, Buddhism and folk belief, while western religion refers to Christian faith, including Catholicism, Protestantism, and the Eastern Orthodox Church. These two religions have the following differences: Firstly, in terms of the characteristics, mass belief of Chinese religion is diversified, but group belief of western religion is unified. Secondly, in terms of consciousness, the former is mainly based on the earthly utility, while the latter on the teachings of its religion. Thirdly, in terms of relationship of religious dominations, Chinese religion develops itself, based on imperial power, while western religion develops itself based on religious power by the way of exclusion. Lastly, religious belief in China is dispersive, but it is united in western countries.

Chinese Buddhism not only inherited moral spirit included in religious discipline of Indian Buddhism, but also gradually accepted moral values orientation originated from Confucianism, such as loyalty, filial piety, benevolence, and righteousness, etc. Hence, it enriched Chinese moral norms: doctrine of piety, view of compassion, view of Good and Evil, and retribution for sin.

UNIT 4

Chinese Etiquette

中国礼仪

题记

中国享有“文明古国”、“礼仪之邦”等美誉之称。在其五千年的历史演变发展过程中，中国礼仪文化深刻地影响和制约着中国人的思想言论及行动。“从一定意义上说，一部中国文化史，即是一部礼的发生及发展史。”

Known as “ancient civilization” and “courtesy of the nation”, Chinese cultural ceremony has influenced and restricted Chinese thoughts, words and behaviors profoundly for over five thousand years of historical development. “In a sense, the history of Chinese culture is the history of its development of etiquette.”

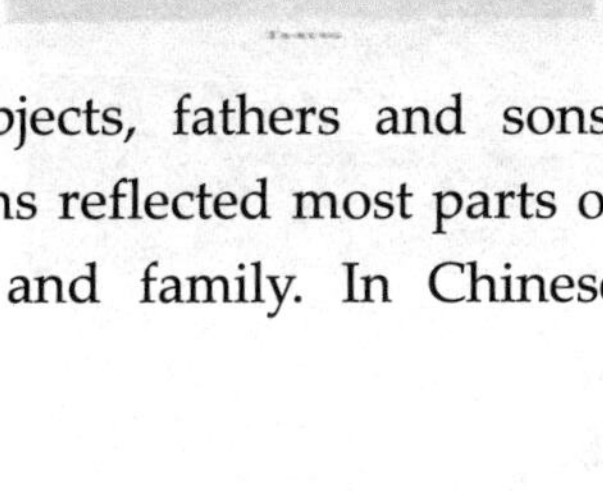

Chinese etiquette originated from the Zhou Dynasty. It was laid down in the Rites of Chou that social life should follow strict rituals and ceremonies, from sacrifices and deploying troops, to weddings and funerals. The rules of etiquette and folk customs were used to portray hierarchical ranks in the society. They showed the difference between superiority and inferiority, kings and subjects, fathers and sons, husbands and wives. Therefore, etiquette and customs reflected most parts of people’s life, such as politics, economy, religion, and family. In Chinese traditional society, etiquette existed all the time, and its contents were various. This unit introduces some traditional etiquette in our daily life.

Walking Etiquette: In ancient China, people who were in low positions had to bow when they passed someone in a higher position, running with short, quick steps to show respect for seniority. It is called "bowing etiquette". In traditional walking etiquette, people should walk along either side of the road but not in the middle of the road, and not stand in the middle of doors either.

Meeting Etiquette: In ancient China there were rules for how to meet people of different social ranks. Traditionally, "Gongshou etiquette" (also called scraping etiquette) was the most common one for general greeting. People made fist with the right hand and cupped it with the left, holding them to the chest, standing but stooping, to show respect as a greeting. When visiting someone at his or her house, hosts and guests would make profound gestures of courtesy and humility when coming into the house and being seated. This is also scraping etiquette. It is asked that people make fist with the right hand and cupped it with the left, then hold them to the chest and press down, bending their heads at the same time with the upper body leaning slightly forwards. In addition, people must scrape and bow to elders. Besides the above social occasions, the etiquette is also used to express your thanks, congratulations, apology, or ask someone to give you help. Gongshou etiquette came from the Western Zhou Dynasty and it is not only one of China's traditional etiquettes, but also reflects deep-rooted Chinese culture.

Furthermore, in traditional society, people must bow down upon their knees when meeting the king, kneeling and touching the head and hands to the ground rhythmically. This was called **"kowtow etiquette"** and originated from Eastern Han Dynasty. It was the oldest and the most prevalent social courtesy in Chinese history. Before Eastern Han Dynasty, people sat on the ground for dinner, business, and reading. Thus sitting posture in ancient times was almost the same as today's kneeling. When entertaining guests, the host or hostess would straighten his or her upper body and to show gratitude and respect for the guests (sitting with their backs straight), sitting then becoming kneeling, and bending downward. Gradually, it was called "kowtow etiquette". But nowadays it is only be practiced in remote villages for New Years Call. And people generally shake hands, which came from the West when meeting each other.

Seating Etiquette reflected the Traditional social order with seats differing in size and height according to seniority. People with higher status would sit at the front of the table, while the latter at the lower end of it. Different identities had different seating positions. Taking a seat improperly would make the host unhappy, a breach of etiquette was considered insulting and rude. Indoor seats to the east were for distinguished guests, with the host's company sitting in the east. The seniors would take northern seats facing to the south, while the accompanying descendants would take the southern seats facing to the north. When eating, people are to be as near the table as possible, but to sit back when not eating. Once distinguished guests came to visit, the host must stand up immediately in salutation.

Celebrating and Condoling Etiquette: Celebration etiquette, usually during festivals, was implemented by the inferiority to show reverence to those higher in status, and to their peers. People were expected to chant congratulations and bow in worship with a respectful attitude, and to give gifts. Condoling etiquette was mainly used during the most important events of life, such as birth, puberty rite, marriage, birthdays, and death, etc.

In a word, ancient Chinese etiquette once played an important role in Chinese history and culture. Now Chinese people have gradually simplified traditional etiquette with fresh breath and characteristics of the New Age. Facing the impact of diversification, those who inherit traditional Chinese etiquette and culture are asked to rationally maintain the traditions and to keep pace with the development of modern society.

段落译文

中国的“礼”文化源于周朝。周礼规定，社会生活的方方面面——从祭祀、用兵到婚嫁、丧葬，都要遵循严格的礼节仪式并成为传统民俗的礼仪规范。这些规则体现了君臣、父子、兄弟、夫妻的上下尊卑之别。礼仪风俗是人们在政治、经济、神会和家庭等各个方面的集中体现。“礼”在中国传统社会无时不在，内容极其丰富，下面就我们日常生活中的某些传统礼仪作择要介绍：

行走之礼：在中国古代，人们常行“趋礼”，即地位低的人从地位高的人面前走过时，一定要低头弯腰，以小步快走的方式表示对尊者的礼敬。在传统行走礼仪中，有“行不中道，立不中门”的原则，即走路应该靠边行走，不能在路中间走；站立时不能站在门中间。

见面之礼：在中国古代对与不同身份的人相见都有一定的规矩。比如一般性的打招呼，在传统上行拱手礼。拱手礼是最普通的见面礼仪，又叫作“揖礼”，即双手合抱(一般是右手握拳在内，左手加于右手之上)举至胸前，立而不俯，表示一般性的客套。如果到别人家做客，在进门与落座时，主客相互客气行礼谦让，这时行的是作揖之礼，即“揖让”。作揖同样是两手抱拳，拱起再按下去，上下加重摇动几下，同时低头，上身略向前屈。要是向长辈施大礼，还要作揖后再鞠躬。作揖礼在古代日常生活中为常见礼仪，除了上述社交场合外，向人致谢、祝贺、道歉及托人办事等也常行作揖礼。拱手礼始于西周，是我国传统的礼节之一，也是最具中国特色的完全可以体现我国悠久文化的一种礼节。

此外，在传统社会，人们对至尊者还有**跪拜礼**。跪拜礼要求双膝着地、头手有节奏触地叩拜，即“叩

首”。古人见面时行跪拜礼源于东汉，是历史最久远、使用最普遍的一种社交礼仪。在东汉以前，因为没有桌椅，人们吃饭、议事、看书都是席地而坐。所以古代的坐姿与现在的跪差不多。在接待宾客时，每当“坐”着向客人致谢时为了表示尊敬，总是伸直上半身，即“引身而起”，坐变成了跪，然后俯身向下，这样逐渐形成了跪拜礼。现今跪拜礼只在偏远乡村的拜年时能够见到，一般场合不再施跪拜礼。在现代中国人们见面时一般习惯用由西方传入的握手礼。

入座之礼：在传统中国，礼仪秩序井然，坐席亦有主次尊卑之分，尊者上坐，卑者末坐。身份不同决定了位置不同，如果盲目坐错席位，不仅主人不高兴，自己事后也会为失礼之事追悔莫及。室内座次以东向为尊，即贵客坐西席上，主人一般在东席上作陪。年长者可安排在南向的位置，即北席。陪酒的晚辈一般在北向的位置，即南席。入座的规矩是，饮食时人体尽量靠近食案，非饮食时，身体尽量靠后，所谓“虚坐尽后，食坐尽前”。有贵客光临，应该立刻起身致意。

拜贺庆吊之礼：拜贺礼一般用在节庆期间，是晚辈或地位低的人向尊长表示尊敬，同辈之间也有相互的拜贺。行拜贺礼时，需要态度恭敬，口诵贺词，俯首叩拜，同时得有贺礼奉上。庆吊礼主要行于人生大事中，如诞生、成年、婚嫁、寿庆、死亡等。

总之，中国古代传统礼仪礼俗在人类历史上曾起过十分重要的作用，它与中国历史、中国文化相伴而生、相伴而长。现今的中国社会已逐渐在简化传统礼仪礼俗，并注入新时代的气息，体现新时代的特征。在面对当下多元化的冲击时，传统礼仪文化的继承更需要我们理性辨析，立足传统，面向现代。

实用词汇

“三礼” Three Etiquettes（《仪礼 》Li Yi、《礼记 》The Book of Rites、《周礼》Rites of Chou）

礼仪 etiquette

孝顺 to show filial obedience

祭祀 to sacrifice

婚嫁 to marry

丧葬 funeral
礼节 ritual
尊卑 superiority and inferiority
叩头 to kowtow
仁 benevolence (humanity)
义 righteousness
理 propriety
智 wisdom
信 fidelity
礼器 sacrificial vessel
辞令 rhetoric
礼制 the rules of propriety
仪容 appearance
吉礼 Ji li
趋礼 bowing etiquette
拱手礼 Gongshou etiquette
作揖礼 scraping etiquette
跪拜礼 kowtow etiquette
俯身向下 to bend downward
贺词 congratulations
多元化 diversification

名言俗语

说"您先请"是一种礼貌。
"After you" is good manners.
年长者值得尊敬，年轻人高尚。
Age is honorable and youth is noble.
姜还是老的辣。
Aged ginger is more pungent.
有礼貌的拒绝，胜于无礼的应允。

A civil denial is better than a rude grant.

谦虚恭敬，不用分文。

Civility costs nothing.

谦恭有礼，即酬谢了大半。

A courtesy much entreated is half recompensed.

来而不往非礼也。

Courtesy on one side only lasts not long.

不懂得微笑待客就先别开店。

Don't open a shop unless you know how to smile.

讲礼貌的得友情，好心肠的得感情。

He who sows courtesy reaps friendship, and he who planks kindness gathers love.

衣食足而后礼仪兴。

Meat is much, but manner is more.

能言是银，沉默是金。

Speech is silver, silence is gold.

礼尚往来，往而不来，非礼也；来而不往，亦非礼也。

Propriety suggests reciprocity. It is not propriety not to give out but to receive, or vice versa.

君子在德不在衣。

It's not the gay coat that makes the gentleman.

要选择行动的一生，而不是炫耀的一生。（内波斯）

Choose a life of action, not one of ostentation.（C. Nepos）

真正的勇敢，都包含谦虚。（吉尔伯特）

Wherever valour true is found, true modesty will there abound.（W. S. Gilbert）

一言既出，驷马难追。

A word spoken is past recalling.

听宜敏捷，言宜缓行。

Be swift to hear, slow to speak.

入乡随俗。

Do as the Romans do.

己所不欲，勿施于人。

Do as you would be done by.

以德报德是常理，以德报怨大丈夫。

Good for good is natural, good for evil is manly.

俗语注解

肃拜：妇人之礼，又称手拜，妇人以肃拜，见举首下手，而不跪拜。

Su Bai (for the ladies): It is one of traditional Chinese etiquette, a solemn courtesy of women in ancient China. They did not bend down on knees when making a salute.

道万福：多福。祝祷之词。古代妇女相见行礼，多口称“万福”，后因以指妇女行的敬礼。行礼时，两手松松抱拳，重叠在胸前右下侧上下移动，同时略做鞠躬的姿势。

salutation of women: It belonged to some congratulation wishing someone live long. In ancient time, women would chant the congratulation when meeting and saluting. It was salutation of women with one clenched fist in the other hand moving about the chest.

折柳送别：起于西汉，当时官员商旅出入长安，必经灞桥，绿柳成荫，送行者正好折柳与行人尊别赠别。“柳”谐“留”音，赠柳表示留念，一为不忍分别，二恋恋不舍。另外柳树和其他树木相比，其特点是“随地可活”，这正可以拿来祝愿远别的人，到了异地后，随遇而安，能够很快地融入当地的人群中，一切顺遂。这一说法便有了深刻的哲理性和更高的文化品位。

Zhe Liu Song Bie (A willow as a gift to the departed)：It means a farewell with snapping off willows, originated from the Western Han Dynasty. Officials who went to Chang'an for business at that time had to cross Ba Bridge under the shade of willows which were snapped off to see somebody off. “柳(liu)” and “留(liu)” are agreeable sounds, which makes willows as a memento, showing that people could not bear parting and not tear himself or herself away. Furthermore, compared with other trees, that willows can live everywhere could be used to extend wishes to those who are far away from home, hoping they can engage the local people very soon as they wish and take things as they come, after coming to a strange land. It is full of profound philosophy and cultural literacy.

中西合璧

不同的历史条件、社会意识形态和文化背景造就了不同的礼仪礼节文化。在西方，也有鞠躬的礼节，鞠躬迎客，鞠躬送客，鞠躬向女士致意，鞠躬向他人致谢等，行礼时身体自然下倾，弯身不超过 15 度。然而，西方不像中国一样有下级向上级、晚辈向长辈、学生向老师鞠躬的礼俗。今天中西方通行的交际礼节应数握手礼，它已经远远超出了见面礼节的范畴而具有多重的社会功能。

Due to different historical conditions, social ideology and cultural background, etiquette culture is quite different between China and Western countries. The latter also has bowing etiquette which requires people to slope downward naturally within 15 degrees. The western people bow to welcome guests or see them out, to give greetings to ladies, to thank others, etc. However, different from China, their bowing etiquette does not show the relationship between superiority and inferiority, the old and the young, teachers and students, etc. Nowadays, the most common etiquette both in China and Western countries should be handshake etiquette when meeting each other. It has multiple social functions now but not just the meeting etiquette.

UNIT 5

Traditional Chinese Festivals

传统节日

题记

中国历史悠久，民族众多，因此产生了许多形式多样、内涵丰富的传统节日。而且每个节日都有着特定的风俗习惯、传说、禁忌和庆祝活动。比较重要的传统节日有春节、元宵节、端午节及中秋节等。而且在这些节日里，人们往往制作一些特殊的美食来庆祝。

China has many nations with a long history. Therefore, there are various traditional festivals, each of which has specific customs, legends, taboos, and celebration activities. The most important ones among them are the Spring Festival, Lantern Festival, Dragon Boat Festival, Mid-Autumn Festival, etc. And during these festivals, people often make some special foods to celebrate.

The Spring Festival, the traditional Chinese New Year's Day, is the most important traditional festival celebrated by the Hans and many of the ethnic groups. It falls on the first day of the first lunar month, commonly known as "Guonian". In fact, Chinese people celebrate the festival from the eighth day of the last month of the lunar year to the 15th day of the first month of the following lunar year. In ancient times, festival

festival activities were often related to farming. At the turn of a year, people would offer sacrifices from farming and hunting to their ancestors and gods, a token of their gratitude for their bounty as well as a manifestation of their wishes for a bumper grain harvest in the coming year. On New Year's Eve, the day before the Spring Festival, the people who work and study in other places have to hurry back so the family can have a reunion dinner.

As for the reunion dinner, there is a great difference between the north and the south. In Northern China, people usually eat Jiaozi or dumplings shaped like a crescent moon or the ancient ingot. Some people will put a piece of candy in one of the dumplings to pray for happy life in the coming year; more people like to wrap a coin in one dumpling, which means the eater will make a lot of money in the following new year. The southern people eat New Year Cakes and Tangyuan—a kind of round sweet dumplings. Both the cakes and sweet dumplings are made of glutinous rice flour. The New Year Cake is called Nian Gao in Chinese. It conveys the hope of improvement of life year after year. The round sweet dumpling is a symbol of reunion.

During the Spring Festival, many families decorate their houses in the traditional approach. They usually put up a pair of couplets designating good fortune on the front door, and stick the Chinese characters "Fu" up-side down in the middle of it. Recently on New Year's Eve most of Chinese people watch the CCTV Spring Festival Evening Show, they also set off fire crackers and some of them even stay up all night. On New Year's Day the whole family need to pay New Year call to the older generations and the children get lucky money in red paper packages from their parents and grandparents. People of different regions have their own celebration activities, such as the dragon dance, lion dance, Yangko, etc.

The Yuanxiao Festival is on the 15th day of the

first Chinese lunar month, is also called the Lantern Festival. In both north and south of China the family members reunite for a meal of Yuanxiao and enjoy the lantern shows. Most of the fillings inside Yuanxiao are sweet, made of white sugar, brown sugar, sweet-scented osmanthus, nuts, and sesame seeds. In recent years, a mixture of Chinese and Western style Yuanxiao with chocolate filling has been made. Eating Yuanxiao is a symbol of reunion of families in China.

Duanwu Festival falls on the fifth day of the fifth month of Chinese lunar calendar, which is also known as Dragon Boat Festival. The main customs are racing dragon boats and eating Zongzi. It is said that since the great patriotic poet Qu Yuan threw himself into the Miluo River for his native state, the people who loved him threw Zongzi into the river as food for the fish and shrimp to keep them from eating Qu Yuan's body. Zongzi have many flavors and they are different between the south and the north. In the southern China, people make Zongzi filled with a mixture filling of peanut and bacon. The northern people usually use dates or preserved fruit fillings.

The Mid-Autumn Festival falls on the 15th day of the 8th lunar month. It is said the moon is the fullest and brightest during the evening on that day. The ancients made sacrificial offerings of delicious foods to the moon, the main one of which was the mooncake that people like to eat today. Many kinds of cakes are with pine nut, walnut, melon seeds and sugar for fillings. Moon-cakes are not only delicious, but also have some beautiful patterns such as moon palace, the rabbit and Chang E flying up to the moon, bringing people into the wonderful myth and story of Chang E. Traditionally, it is also a day of family reunion.

The Double Ninth Festival is on the ninth day of the ninth lunar month. As the number nine was yang in ancient China, the ninth day of the ninth lunar month was called Double Yang

Festival. It is the Festival for the senior people. Hill climbing is the most popular activity on that day. It is a custom to drink chrysanthemum wine and Double Ninth cakes, also known as chrysanthemum cakes. The cake is made of flour with dates, chestnuts and meat, like a nine-storied pagoda. Eating Double Ninth Festival cakes also means "being promoted higher and higher every year".

China is a multinational country and each of them has its own traditional festivals, such as the Nadam Fair of the Mongolians, Water-splashing festival of the Dais, Torch Festival of Yi, Tibetan New Year's Eve and Third Month Fair of Bai.

段落译文

农历正月初一是中国传统新年——春节。春节是汉族和许多少数民族最隆重、最热闹的传统节日，俗称“过年”。实际上，人们把腊月初八到正月十五这段时间都视为春节。古时候春节的活动多和农事有关。人们每逢旧岁新年交替之际，都要以农猎所获祭祀祖先和上天，一是感谢恩赐，二来是祈求明年风调雨顺，五谷丰登。每到除夕——春节的前一天，在外地工作和学习的人都要尽量赶回家，全家要在一起吃团圆饭庆祝。

但是南方和北方的年夜饭有明显的差别，北方的人们在除夕夜一定要吃饺子(饺子是一种有馅的半圆形面食，样子很像中国古时候的元宝)，有人会在一些饺子里放糖，祈求来年生活更加甜美；更多的人家在个别饺子里包上硬币，谁吃到了就意味着此人在新的一年里财运亨通。初一早晨，很多人家还要吃饺子，这象征着新的一年招财进宝。南方除夕和大年初一都吃元宵和年糕，元宵又叫汤圆，汤圆里多包着糖，意味着全家团圆美满甜蜜；年糕是糯米做成，取其谐音，“年年高”，意思是希望人们的生活年年都有提高。

春节期间，很多人家常用传统的方式来布置房屋，如大门两旁贴上表达美好祝愿的“春联”，门中央倒贴着“福”字。除夕还要守夜，放爆竹。近年来，大多数中国人都要观看中央电视台的春节晚会节目。正月初一，全家要向长辈拜年，而小辈往往会从长辈那里得到“压岁钱”——红包。不同地区的人们还会有各自不同的庆祝活动，如舞龙、舞狮、扭秧歌等。

正月十五是元宵节也叫灯节，不论南方北方，都要合家团聚吃元宵、观花灯。大多数元宵是甜馅的，一般用白糖、红糖、桂花、果仁、芝麻等做成。近年来品种更多，甚至有人采用了中西结合的做法做元宵，比如用巧克力做元宵的馅。在中国，“吃元宵”象征着千家万户团圆幸福。

农历五月初五是端午节，也叫龙舟节。主要习俗有赛龙舟、吃粽子。传说古代爱国诗人屈原投江殉国后，爱戴他的人们把粽子投到江里，希望喂饱鱼虾，免得他们吃掉屈原的尸体。粽子有很多花样，也有南北之别。南方常用花生、咸肉等混在糯米里制成，北方多以枣、果脯等作粽子的馅心。

中秋节是在农历的八月十五日。据说中秋节夜晚的月亮最圆、最明亮。古人要在这天晚上祭月，其中主要的祭品之一就是人们今天喜欢吃的中秋美食“月饼”。很多月饼以松仁、核桃仁、瓜子仁或蛋黄为馅。月饼不但好吃，上面还往往会有月宫、蟾兔、嫦娥奔月等图案，常会把人们带到神话传说中的美妙世界里。这一天也是家庭团聚的日子。

九月初九是重阳节。因为农历九月初九的日和月都是“九”，而九在中国属于阳数，因此被称为“重阳节”。重阳节是老人节。登高是最受人们欢迎的活动之一。饮菊花酒、吃重阳糕也是重阳节的习俗。重阳糕是用面粉蒸制成，以枣、栗、肉为佐料。重阳糕一般有九层，做成塔状。吃重阳糕寓意是“步步高升”。

中国是个多民族的国家，各个民族都有自己传统节日。例如蒙古族的“那达慕大会”，傣族的泼水节，彝族的火把节，藏族的藏历节及白族的三月街等。

实用词汇

传统节日 Traditional Festivals
春节 the Spring Festival
除夕 New Year's Eve

大年初一 the first day of the lunar year
年夜饭 family reunion dinner on Lunar New year's Eve
团圆饭 the reunion meal
对联/春联 duilian; Chinese couplets
上联 the first line of a couplet
下联 the second line of a couplet
压岁钱/红包 lucky money / red paper packet
拜年 paying a New Year call
舞龙 performing the Dragon Dance
舞狮 performing the Lion Dance
扭秧歌 performing the Yanko Dance
爆竹、鞭炮 firecracker
元宵节/灯节 Yuanxiao Festival; Lantern Festival
元宵 Yuanxiao; sweet rice-flour dumplings eaten on the Lantern Festival
观灯 viewing the lanterns
灯谜 lantern riddles
端午节 Duanwu festival; Dragon Boat Festival
赛龙船 dragon boat race
粽子 Zongzi, a pyramid-shaped dumpling made of glutinous rice wrapped in bamboo or reed leaves
中秋节 Mid-Autumn Festival
月饼 moon cake
赏月 enjoying the full moon (in mid-autumn)
重阳节 Chongyang Festival; Double Ninth Festival
登高 hill climbing
菊花酒 chrysanthemum wine
傣族的泼水节 Water-splashing festival of the Dais
古尔邦节 the Corban Festival / animal-slaughtering day
那达慕盛会 the Nadam Fair / Nadam Meet
火把节 Torch Festival
藏历节 Tibetan New Year's Eve

名言俗语

每逢佳节倍思亲。

More than ever we think of the parents or children far away on a happy festival.

大吉大利!

Good luck and great prosperity!

恭喜发财!

Congratulations and may you prosper! / May you come into a good fortune!

恭贺新禧!

Happy New Year!

敬祝节日快乐，新年事事称心如意!

With many good wishes for the holidays and the coming year!

祝新年快乐幸福，大吉大利!

I hope you have a most happy and prosperous New Year!

祝愿你新年身体健康，事业昌盛!

Allow me to congratulate you on the arrival of the New Year and to extend to you all my good wishes for your perfect health and lasting prosperity!

词语注解

傣族的泼水节：中国傣族的传统节日，在公历四月中。节日期间，人们穿着盛装，互相泼水祝福，并进行拜佛、赛龙舟、文艺汇演、物资交流等活动。

Water-splashing festival of the Dais: Chinese traditional festival in April of Solar Calendar celebrated by the Dais during which folks are dressed in the holiday's best, exchange good will by sprinkling water on each other, worship Buddha, hold dragon boat races and variety shows, and buy and sell goods.

那达慕盛会：内蒙古地区蒙古族人民传统集会，活动内容有摔跤、赛马、射箭、舞蹈等。

the Nadam Fair: Traditional festival of the Mongolian in the Inner Mongolia, which is celebrated with such events as wrestling, horse races, archery, and dancing.

对联/春联：对联是中国一种独特的文学艺术形式。对联是律诗的对偶句发展而来的。对联的字数要相等，断句一致，内容相关，上下联的含义必须相互连接，横批起到画龙点睛的作用。

Duilian（Chinese couplets）is a unique literary genre in China, which developed from antitheses or antithetical parallelism of Lushi. The couplets must have an aqual number of characters, the same sense groups and the interconnection of the contents. The meaning of the first line must be interrelated to that of the other. A Heng Pi often adds the finishing touch to the couplet.

福字倒贴：其谐音意思是"福气"到了。

sticking/pasting the Chinese characters "Fu" up-side down: It means the happiness or good fortune has come according to the homophony.

中西合璧

中国农历五月初五的龙舟节要进行赛舟。意大利威尼斯的赛舟节是每年九月的第一个星期日。赛舟节活动分两部分，先是划船表演，后是划船比赛。据说赛舟节的起源是古代威尼斯附近的菜农每天清晨要用船把菜送到威尼斯出售。为了早去卖个好价钱，他们争分夺秒地尽快划船，争先到菜市场占据有利位置。因此逐渐形成了赛舟风俗。

The fifth day of the fifth lunar month is Dragon Boat Festival in China, which is celebrated by holding boat races. There is a Boat Festival in Venice, Italy too. It is on the first Sunday in September, which has two activities, performance of rowing and boat race. It is said that in the ancient Venice the vegetable growers near the city sent the vegetables to Venice by boat every morning. In order to arrive at the market early and sell the vegetables at a good price, they row their boats as quickly as possible. Therefore, the custom of boat race was formed.

UNIT 6

Chinese Gardens

中国园林

题记

园林，是中国建筑艺术的一朵奇葩，是中国传统建筑文化的集大成者，也是中国文化的精品之一。中国园林是以自然山水为主题思想，以花木、水石、建筑等为物质手段，在有限的空间里，创造出视觉无尽的，具有高度自然精神境界的环境。中国的园林艺术，是勤劳智慧的中国人民为世界创造的艺术杰作。

The Chinese Garden is a wonderful architectural art and one of the best in traditional Chinese culture. Chinese gardens, which are seen as masterpieces by the diligent and intelligent Chinese people create natural environments and landscapes with highly spiritual themes using flowers, trees, water and stone as tools.

Chinese gardens have a long history and great fame throughout the world. They are known as one of the world's three major garden systems, along with the West Asia and Europe. China's rich flora and long history of garden development has had a profound influence on the horticulture and garden design throughout the world. Chinese classical gardens represent a harmonious blending of man and nature.

Geographically, ancient Chinese gardens can be divided into two broad categories, namely, the Imperial Gardens in the north, and the Private Gardens in the south.

The term "Imperial Garden" generally refers to those in which emperors lived and entertained themselves. They are mainly located in Beijing and its surrounding areas. The design of an Imperial Garden gives expression to feudal autocracy and reflects the idea that the emperor was the richest man in the world. There is a liberal choice of locations, and the construction of an Imperial Garden is backed by abundant resources, so that not only mountains and lakes in their original forms could be incorporated, but lakes could be dug, and mountains constructed, as well, in imitation of natural scenes. All sorts of buildings could be constructed, too. The general layout of an imperial garden was magnificent, the buildings are beautiful, imposing and perform diverse functions, which a Private Garden can not be compared with.

The famous Imperial Gardens are The Forbidden City, Yuanmingyuan, Xiangshan Park, the Beihai Park in Beijing and The Mountain Summer Resort of Chengde, Hebei and so on. Yuanmingyuan, known as the "Garden of Gardens", has combined different styles of Chinese landscape art and integrated some of the Western architectural styles. The park was constructed with various intricate patterns of great interest. (The park is full of various intricate patterns and great fun.) Yuanmingyuan covers an area of 5000 acres, together with Changchun Park, Wanchun Park. In the garden, there are three major lakes, nine islands and nearly one hundred buildings, which are of a superb artistic level and the art has the essence of a large Imperial Garden. In Chengde Summer Resort with the total area of 8500 acres, there are 72 scenic spots and 11 temples, which is the largest Imperial Palace in the area, and the largest garden in China. The Private Gardens were built for the royal imperial wives'

families, the Princes and high officials, rich merchants. These gardens are mainly in Shanghai, Jiangsu and Zhejiang and so on, among which Suzhou's are the most famous and the most typical. Gardening in Suzhou reached its height during the Ming and Qing Dynasties. Suzhou became the center of a garden supply industry. It is for the reason that the gardens of Suzhou are considered classical standards of designs. Most of Suzhou's gardens are comparatively small in area by making good use of various forms and charming artistic features with flowers and birds in the limited space. Decorated by man-made rock, trees, arranged pavilions, ponds, and bridges, creating an artistic and poetic effect of the poetry during the Tang and Song Dynasties. The characteristics of these gardens are small-sized, so artificial rivers and man-made hills were created with small buildings in exquisite, elegant colors. There were over 280 Private Gardens then in Suzhou and landscaping became an art with established masters. 69 gardens in and around Suzhou are preserved as important national cultural heritage sites and some of them are on the World Heritage List.

Humble Administrator's Garden, Lingering Garden, Blue Wave Pavilion, and Lion Grove Garden, are referred as the four famous gardens in Suzhou. Humble Administrator's Garden in Suzhou City is one of the four famous ones in which there are 31 scenic spots with area of 60 acres. It is water-based, about three-fifths of the surface covered with lakes facing building complex. The whole garden is divided into east and west and the middle. The entrance of the east and the stretch of it were rebuilt after the founding of the country, and the rebuilt are Labxuetang, Hibiscus pavilion, Tianquan Pavilion, Fangyan kiosks, withal are wonderful scenery all in sight. In the middle, there is a pool, with rocks, trees, and buildings, gracefully and naturally surrounding it. Jinxiang Hall has doors or windows in all directions so that you can't miss any beautiful spots around. The rockery is slightly undulating, facing Shuiyue Platform in the north, trees such as willows are planted along the pond, and the north gallery has views of the Hill House with two storeys surrounded by water on three sides. On the west side is a pile of rocks, people can see winding around a mountain frame, Nanxuan faces Xiangzhou across the western compact. Another main building is Mandarin Kiosks, with rooms at each side. On the whole, Zhuozheng Garden owes greatness to its many pools distributed perfectly. The layout appears natural by making clever use of natural environment. It has the typical characteristics of southern gardens and is a national key cultural relics.

In short, picturesque Chinese gardens are integrated with painting, literature, gardening and other forms of art and traditional Chinese culture. It has not only omitted the artificial features of flower-beds, buildings and trees in the West garden, but also left out the blind indifference of the Japanese garden. They reflect an imitation of nature with artistic skill, to reaching implicit perfection. The Chinese garden is unique in its valuable historical and cultural heritage and its contribution to mankind.

段落译文

中国园林建筑历史悠久，在世界园林史上享有盛名。它同西亚、欧洲园林并称为世界三大园林系统。中国丰富的植物及园林的发展，对世界园林文化、园林设计影响深远，中国古典园林体现了人与自然的和谐关系。

中国古代园林，从地域和类型上可分为南北两大类，即北方的皇家园林和南方的私家园林。

皇家园林主要集中在北京及其周围地区，是专供帝王休息、享乐的园林。古人讲普天之下莫非王土，在统治阶级看来，国家的山河都是属于皇家所用的，所以其特点是规模宏大，真山真水较多，园中建筑色彩富丽堂皇，建筑体型高大，是私家园林无法比拟的。

著名皇家园林有北京的故宫、圆明园、香山公园、北海公园和河北承德的避暑山庄等。圆明园有“万园之园”之称，它集中国各地不同风格的园林艺术于一体，且借鉴了部分西方建筑风格，园内建筑巧夺天工，虽形态各异而趣味无穷。圆明园占地5000多亩，由长春园、万春园和圆明园组成；有三大湖泊，其中有九个小岛，近百座建筑，是一座具有高超艺术水平和艺术精华的大型皇家园林。承德的避暑山庄总面积8500亩，有72处景点11座庙宇，是我国帝王宫苑中占地最多、面积最大的园林。

私家园林是供皇家的宗室外戚、王公官吏、富商大贾等休闲的园林，集中于上海和江浙一带，其中以江苏苏州为最多、最有名，也最为典型。苏州园林在明清两代达到鼎盛时期。苏州成为园林中心，以经典的设计而闻名。苏州园林大都占地面积小，采用变换无穷、不拘一格的艺术手法，以中国山水花鸟的情趣，寓唐诗宋词的意境，在有限的空间内点缀假山、树木，安排亭台楼阁、池塘小桥，营造以小见大的艺术效果。其特点是规模较小，所以常用假山假水，建筑小巧玲珑，表现其淡雅素净的色彩。苏州有280多个私家园林，其中69个已是国家的重要文化遗址，还有一些已被认定为世界文化遗产。

苏州的拙政园、留园、沧浪亭、狮子林(狮园)并称为苏州四大名园。拙政园在苏州市娄门内。是全国四大名园之一。园内有31景，现园内面积60多亩。此园以水为主，水面约占五分之三，建筑群多临水。全园分中、东、西三部分。东部入园处是建国后扩建的，重建的有兰雪堂、芙蓉榭、天泉亭、放眼亭、景物空阔。中部正中为水池、山石、树木，建筑比较疏朗自然，其中进香堂是一座四面厅，四周景色呈现窗前。堂前假山，略有起伏，北面临水月台，池水林木葱翠，沿池植垂柳，长廊北面有见山楼，楼二层，三面环水，西侧假山一叠，登楼可至道盘山架阁，南轩与香洲隔水相望，西部紧凑，主要建筑物有鸳鸯亭、四面有耳室。此园水池面积很大，但有聚有分，山径水廊起伏曲折，古木蔽日，富有自然景色。布局采用分割空间，利用自然、对比借景的手法，吸收传统的绘画艺术，因地造景，景随步移，成为具有江南特色的典型园林。

简言之，中国园林如诗如画，是集建筑、书画、文学、园艺等艺术的精华为

一体的经典文化。它隐去了西方园林那种无论建筑还是花坛树木造型都留下的明显的人工印迹，也摒弃了日本园林那种一味淡然的“枯山水”，而体现出一种模仿自然，艺术手段又不外露的完美境界。中国园林在世界园林发展史上独树一帜，是全人类宝贵的历史文化遗产。

实用词汇

北海公园 Beihai Park

避暑山庄 Mountain Estate for Escaping the Heat

阿房宫 grand palace built by the first Emperor of the Qin Dynasty at E Pang, started in 212 BC and burnt down, when still uncompleted, in 206 BC

故都 former capital

故宫 imperial palace, the Forbidden City

黄鹤楼 Yellow Crane Tower

家兰若寺 Buddhist temple

祖庙 ancestral temple or shrine

玻璃塔 glazed pagoda

天坛 Temple of Heaven

圆明园 Yuanming Yuan, old Summer Palace; the Round Bright Garden or the Garden of Perfect Brightness; the old Summer Palace a few miles to northwest of Beijing, destroyed by British and French troops in 1860

长春园 the Garden of Eternal Spring

拙政园 Humble Administrator's Garden; Zhuozheng Garden in Suzhou Province

宗庙 ancient temple

沧浪亭 Blue Wave Pavilion

狮子林 Lion Grove Garden

留园 Lingering Garden

网师园 Master of the Nets Garden

环秀山庄 Mountain Villa with Embracing Beauty

名言俗语

近水楼台先得月。

"The waterfront tower gets the moonlight first." refers to the importance of being in a favored position.

花园里所长的植物总多于所种的作物。

More grows in the garden than the gardener knows he has sown.

别让脚下的草长得比脚高。

Not let the grass grow under one's feet.

忍耐是花朵，但并非人人的花园里都有这花朵。

Patience is a flower that grows not in everyone's garden.

俗语注解

城市绿化：栽种植物以改善城市环境的活动

urban greening, urban planting

盆景园：以盆景展示为主要内容的专类公园

penjing garden, miniature landscape

历史名园：历史悠久、知名度高，体现传统造园艺术的园林

historical garden and park

纪念公园：以纪念历史事件、缅怀名人为主题的公园

memorial park: in memory of the historical events and famous people

居住绿地：城市居住用地内除社区公园之外的绿地

green space attached to housing estate, residential green space

道路绿地：城市道路广场用地内的绿地

green space attached to urban road and square

屋顶花园：在建筑物屋顶上建造的花园

roof garden: the gardens on the roof of the buildings

中西合璧

中西园林的不同之处在于：西方园林讲求几何数学原则、以建筑为主；中国园林则以自然景观和观者的美好感受为主，更注重天人合一。如圆明园，在当时的中国是一座最出色的行宫别苑，通过传教士的信函、报告的介绍而蜚声欧洲，对18世纪欧洲自然风景园的发展曾产生一定的影响。中国园林的主要特点是因地制宜，掘池造山，结合环境布置房屋、花木，互为借景，构成具有自然情趣的园林。在风格上，含蓄蕴藉，既朴拙典雅又委屈细腻、巧夺天工，形成了中国园林独特完整的艺术体系，对西方国家，特别是英法德意的造园艺术产生了很大影响，至今仍在世界造园艺术上享有盛誉。

The difference between Chinese and Western gardens is: Western Garden emphasizes on mathematical principles of geometry to the main buildings, while Chinese gardens are based on natural beauty of the landscape and the viewers' experience of the scenery, focusing more on the harmony between Nature and Man. The Summer Palace was one of the most outstanding palaces at the time. Through letters and reports, the western missionaries introduced it and it became famous in Europe, which played a very important part in the development of the natural landscape gardens and the horticulture in the 18th century. The main characteristics of Chinese gardens are pools dug properly to the local conditions layout of houses designed with environment decorated with trees and flowers to construct the garden with natural taste. In style, subtle implication with elegant and simple, innocent and delicate, wonderful workmanship was imbedded to form a unique system of a complete art of Chinese gardens different from those of western countries, particularly Britain, France. Chinese gardens have a great impact on the horticulture, for which they have an important position.

UNIT 7

Chinese Residences

中国民居

题记

中国各地的居住建筑，又称民居。居住建筑是最基本的建筑类型，出现最早、分布最广、数量最多。由于中国各地区的自然环境和人文情况不同，各地民居也显现出多样化的面貌。中国民居是传统建筑宝库的瑰宝，是民族文化的重要载体之一。

The residential buildings throughout China, also known as homes, are the most basic types of buildings in China. They came into being at the earliest time and are the most widely distributed with the largest number. The environmental and cultural difference of the regions of China means the residences which are very diverse in design and construction. Chinese residences are treasures of Chinese traditional architectural history, and they have become an important carrier of our culture.

"The traditional houses" refer to those villages that are unofficial, folk like, and the private ones that have been inherited from generation to generation. These residences were not designed by architects or craftsmen which is why they are such an important part of Chinese architectural history. They have unique architectural forms and characterize the emergence and development socio-economically and culturally or their regions and environments. The most famous representatives are: Beijing's Siheyuan, Fujian Hakka group houses, cave dwellings in northern Shaanxi and Ganlan in Guangxi.

Beijing's Siheyuan are the most important example of Chinese traditional residential housing. Originated in Yuan Dynasty and popular in Beijing, they are great in number and wide in distribution. "Sihe" refers to the east, west, south, north, four sides surrounded with houses to form a mouth-shaped courtyard. Siheyuan can often be divided into two chambers. The centre of the main structure is where family rituals are held and distinguished guests are received, and all the houses face towards the central garden, and are connected by Verandas. In general, a formal courtyard House faces south, surrounded by houses which are known as the north or principal room, and the South or inverted seat Room. There are the East and West wing rooms, and the gate is located in south east corner. The open space in the middle known as the yard has flowers and trees planted in a way so that the people living in the courtyard house are very close to nature. This fits well with the traditional Chinese cultural concept of Heaven and Man. Siheyuan in Beijing reached its apogee during the Qing Dynasty and had a great impact on the residences of the time and those that would follow. These residences became the Han style of architecture.

Lingnan Hakka Group Houses or Hakka Kakoiya is a traditional dwelling for Hakkas in west Fujian, Guangdong, and Guangxi Province. They used rammed earth for load-bearing walls, hence the name Tulou. There are three to four floors on average, and the tallest can have up to six floors. The Group Houses are round or square with the kitchen or utility room on the ground floor, the storage house for grain, and people live on the above floors.

The Central Hall is built for the tribal events such as weddings, funerals, rituals and other activities. The Hakka people generally like to have a pond in front of their houses, which is an important symbol of the Hakka Kakoiya. Including the houses in the yard, Tulou can usually hold more than 50 families. Halls, storage houses, domestic animal houses, wells and other public houses are all located in the yard. The Hakkas created this special defensive layout to protect themselves, and it's still in use now. Among Chinese traditional residence, the Yongding Hakka Tulou are unique. There are square, circular, octagonal and oval shapes. With the total number of housing groups reaching 8,000 they constitute a wonderful residential world, their beautiful shapes, unique features, scientific and practical designs are truly unique throughout the world.

Ganlans are mainly distributed in the southwest provinces of China, such as Yunnan, Guizhou, Guangdong and Guangxi. These are the the residences for Dai, Jingpo, Zhuang and other minority groups. A Ganlan, is a wood or bamboo storeyed house, usually standing alone, which is separated from other Ganlan houses. Supported by poles, the living sector of a Ganlan is usually on the second floor high above the ground, while the first storey is retained for raising domestic animals and storage. The entire structure of Ganlan is very reasonable and practical. A Ganlan can ward off moisture, as well as the attacks from insects, snakes and other animals. They are suitable for people living in the damp and rainy mountains in southern China, often characterized by uneven terrain. Up to now, Ganlan can still be seen in parts of China. For example, in the northern part of Guangxi, layers of terraced fields are dotted by the relaxing and tranquil Ganlan villages.

Cave dwellings, a kind of traditional residence with a long history, are mainly distributed in central and west provinces like Shaanxi, Gansu and Qinghai, where the loess is of great depth and strong and solid enough for cave dwellings. Loess is a product of the accumulation of wind-blown silt and clay into geological formations. The loess has little seepage, and provides very good conditions for the development of cave dwellings. From the relationship between the cave and the ground, cave dwellings can be divided into three types: Cliff, ground, and hoop dwellings.

The cliff cave dwelling is an earth cave dug horizontally along the vertical earth cliff, with the top dug into a semicircle or circular arch shape to let sunshine go in. Ground or pit cave dwellings are those dug into square or rectangular pits from the flat ground with a courtyard bellow. From the inside walls of the pits, caves are dug. Ground cave dwellings appeared in the area where there isn't cliff to take advantage of. From the ground, one can only see treetops and the yard but not the caves such the ones in Luochuan. The hoop cave dwelling (or Indium) is not a real cave. It is a cave-shaped house which is built on the ground with stones, bricks or adobe construction. If the upper so-called cave is also a hoop, it is referred to as "a cave upon a cave", if the top is a wooden structure house, then "a house is upon a cave". The cave dwelling is cool in summer and warm in winter, and saves space. It is a harmonious combination of natural environment and human activities.

There are also many other special residential houses, such as the Jingsu residence, the Huizhou residence, Mongolian yurts, the Tibetan residence and even the boat house. The wide variety of forms and characteristics of Chinese residences reveal the complex interactions and factors that impacted the various ethnic traditional styles, customs, and traditional culture.

段落译文

“传统民居”是指那些乡村的、非官方的、民间的、一代又一代延续下来的、以居住类型为主的“没有建筑师的建筑”。它是我国建筑大家族中的重要组成部分，具有独特的建筑形式，其产生和发展是社会经济文化自然等因素影响的综合反映。中国民居多姿多彩，其中最有代表性的有：北京四合院、福建客家围屋、陕北窑洞和广西“干栏式”建筑等。

北京四合院是中国传统民居的最重要形式，数量、分布较广。它的格局大约始于元代，是北京人的传统民居。“四合”是指东、西、南、北四面的房屋合围在一起，形成一个“口”字形的院落。北京四合院分前后两院，居中的正房最为尊崇，是举行家庭礼仪、接见尊贵宾客的地方，各幢房屋朝向院内，以游廊相连接。一般来说，正规的四合院都是坐北朝南，四面的房屋分别称为北房(也叫正房)、南房(也叫倒座房)、东厢房和西厢房，大门开在宅院的东南角位置。四周房屋围着的中间空地称为院子。院子里栽花种树，使生活在四合院里的人们与大自然非常亲近，这正好符合中国人天人合一的观念。北京四合院在清朝达到极盛，对当时以及以后的民居都产生了极大的影响，成为汉族民居建筑。

客家围屋是两广、福建客家人聚族而居的群体住宅。多以夯土为承重墙，故名土楼。土楼平均三到四层，最高的达六层。其平面有圆有方，由中心部位的单层建筑厅堂和周围的四、五层楼房组成，底层做厨房、杂物间，二层储藏粮食，三层以上住人，中央建堂，供族人议事、婚丧行礼或其他活动。客家人一般都喜欢在围屋前面兴建一个风水塘，这是客家围屋的重要标志。一座土楼通常可以容纳超过50个家庭。大厅、仓库、家畜房、水井和其他公共用屋都在一个在院子里。

客家人创造了这个特殊的防御建筑保护自己，沿用至今。在中国的传统住宅中，永定的客家土楼独具特色，有方形、圆形、八角形和椭圆形等形状的土楼共有8000

余座，规模大、造型美，既科学实用，又有特色，构成了一个奇妙的民居世界。

干栏式住宅主要分布在中国西南部的云南、贵州、广东、广西等地区，为傣族、景颇族、壮族等的住宅形式。干栏式民居是用竹、木等构成的楼居。它是单栋独立的楼，这种房屋一般分为上、下两层。底层架空，用来饲养牲畜或存放东西，上层住人。整个房屋结构非常合理、实用。这种建筑隔潮，并能防止虫、蛇、野兽侵扰。“干栏式”建筑适合中国南方山区潮湿多雨、地势不平的特点，所以直到现在，仍然可以在中国的某些地方看到这种建筑。例如，在广西北部的层层的梯田间，点缀着由“干栏式”建筑构成的村落，显得悠闲而恬静。

窑洞是黄土高原的传统民居，历史悠久，主要分布在中国西部黄土层极深的省份如陕西、甘肃、青海等省，那里黄土层又深又厚、不渗漏的性质是挖掘窑洞很好的先决条件。从窑洞和地面的关系着眼，窑洞可分为三种型式：靠崖窑、地坑窑、锢窑(箍窑)。

靠崖窑：一般为土窑。在垂直崖面上开凿，窑顶掘成半圆或长圆的筒拱，阳光可以照进窑洞。

地坑窑：是在平地掘出方形或矩形地坑，形成地院，再在地坑各壁横向掘窑，多用在缺少天然崖壁的地段。人在平地，只能看见地院树梢，看不见窑洞。比如，洛川就有这样的窑洞。

锢窑(箍窑)：不是真正的窑洞，是在地面上用石头、砖或土坯建造的洞形房屋，可为单层，也可建成为两层。若上层也是箍窑即称“窑上窑”，若上层是木结构房屋则称“窑上房”。窑洞冬暖夏凉、节省空间，是自然环境和人类活动的和谐结合的产物。

除以上所提外，中国民居还有浙江民居、苏州民居、徽州民居、蒙古毡包、藏族民居、甚至还有船屋等等。中华民族的民居所表现的多种多样的形式和各异的特点，显示了许多因素之间复杂的相互作用和影响，强烈地表现出各民族的传统风格和风俗习惯，充满浓郁的文化气息。

实用词汇

民居 dwelling; private house; civilian residence

独门独院 Siheyuan occupied by a single family

故居 former fortress

坤宅 the wife's family

四合院 Siheyuan; traditional, residential compound with houses around a courtyard

凶宅 haunted house

祖居 ancestral home

靠崖窑 cliff dwelling

地坑窑 pit dwelling

客家围屋 Hakka Group Houses; Tulou

迁居，迁徙 the change of residence

校外住房 off-campus housing

公寓 apartments

合作公寓 cooperative residence halls (co-ops)

校外宿舍 off-campus dormitories

合伙租房 rooming houses

校园宿舍 on-campus housing

已婚学生住房 married student housing

宿舍楼 residence halls

大学公寓 university apartments

名言俗语

金窝银窝不如自己的狗窝。

Every bird likes its own nest.

住在玻璃房子的人不可向人丢石头。

Those who live in glass house should not throw stones.

尽管简陋，家仍是家。

Home is home, though never so homely, is a palace to a poor man.

穷人的寒舍就是他的宫殿。

A hut is a palace to a poor man.

一个人的家就是他的城堡。

A man's home is his castle.

单独一个人无法盖一栋房子。

A single man cannot build a house.

哪里有自由，哪里就是我们的家园。

Where liberty is, there is our country.

爱屋及乌。

Love for a person extends even to the crows on his roof; love me, love my dog.

安家立业。

Settle down and embark on a career.

私宅是个人的城堡。

The house of every man is to him as his castle.

金窝银窝，不如自己的狗窝。

East and west, home is the best.

英人私宅似城堡。

An Englishman's house is his castle.

俗语注解

百万买宅，千万买邻：近朱者赤，中国人特别重视邻居的选择。孟母三迁就是史例。

A good neighbour is more precious than a house worth a million, Chinese people think neighbors are important, so they choose them carefully as the story of Meng's mother.

独门独院：一家人独立住居，和邻居的房屋有一定的距离

Siheyuan occupied by a single family, away from the other houses.

故居：生前住过的地方

former fortress: the place people once lived before they died.

安家立业：建立家庭，置身事业，以事业为重

Settle down and embark on a career.

私宅是个人的城堡；家庭是人们的避风港

The house of every man is to him as his castle, which means that people can relax at home.

三顾茅庐：多次拜访某人，比喻求贤如渴

"making three calls at the thatched cottage", is used to a potentate who repeatedly request someone to take up a responsible post.

中西合璧

民居是历史上出现最早的建筑，也是建造量最大的建筑类型。民居建筑不仅紧紧地与自然环境及生活方式相辅相配，而且有着明显的地域性、民族性。中国传统民居庭院空间作为民居的重要组成元素，包含了华夏两千年的传统生活和文化，具有重要的文化和社会价值。中式住宅有着丰富的文化内涵。中式住宅与西式建筑体系最大的区别在于，西式建筑是以一个点往外发散的，而中式建筑是由外向内收缩的。例如，我们传统的中式住宅里边首先要有个院子，各个房间都是围绕这个内院来布置和展开的，生活的中心也是以这个内院来组织的，没有这个院子，感觉就好像不是一个完整的住宅。屋内变化万千，对外则以实墙居多，相对封闭和遮挡。而西式建筑的空间是紧凑的，组合在一起，向外充分展开，屋外才是花园，并且是开放式的。新式的中式住宅兼顾现代化生活方式的布局设计的国际化要素，在设计中参照了不少西式住宅的手法和风格。

Dwelling is the earliest architecture type, and is also the architecture type which has large amount of constructions. Dwellings are not only supplementing each other with environment and life style, but also have their obvious space shape and nationality. The courtyard in Chinese traditional dwellings contains the Chinese traditional cultural life style of 2000 years and it has the most important cultural and social value. Chinese residences have rich cultural connotations too. The great difference from western dwellings is that the western style is a divergence, while the Chinese-style is a contraction from outside to inside. For example, inside Chinese residence there must first be a courtyard and all rooms are arranged around it and it is the centre of the life traditionally. If there were not a yard, one would feel it was not like a house to live in. There is an external wall which is mostly solid, relatively closed. On the contrary, the Western-style houses are built with a garden outside and usually open. Modern Chinese residence is designed to take the western designs into account to follow internationalization.

UNIT 8

Famous Temples in China

中国名刹

题记

中国宗教文化源远流长，其中佛教是我国历史上影响最大的一种。它不仅对中国传统思想产生了重大影响，而且留下了丰富的建筑和艺术遗产。无论是在人口密集的城市，还是在风景秀丽的名山胜地，都可以看到具有宗教色彩的建筑——寺庙。

Chinese religious culture has a long history, and Buddhism is the one which has had the most influence. It had not only a major impact on the traditional Chinese thinking, but also left behind rich architectural and artistic heritage. The religious temples can be seen both in the densely populated cities and the scenic mountain landscapes.

Many Chinese temples were built in the mountains, most of which were courtyard-style buildings. The main buildings of them are temple door, Heavenly King Hall, the great Buddha's hall, the hall for preaching Buddhist doctrines and the depositary of Buddhist texts. Mitufo is enshrined in the Heavenly King Hall. Four heavenly kings are at side halls and each of them protects one direction respectively. They are also representing the timely wind and rain. The main hall worships Sakyamuni, the founder of Buddhism. The east side hall is Garan, and the west worships the first ancestor of Zen, Damo.

The hall where the monks perform the theory of Buddha lesson is behind the main hall. The Depositary of Buddhist texts, the library of temple is often built in the inside courtyard. Arhat hall is purely Chinese, and there are usually 500 different and lifelike statuaries of arhats in it.

White Horse Temple in Luoyang is the first temple built by Chinese government. Originally, it was only the dwelling place of foreign monks. However, Baima Temple is looked upon as Buddhism headstream in China.

Many temples are located in the Chinese famous mountains. Shaolin Temple is known as the most famous temple in China and is located in Songshan mountain, Henan province. During the Tang Dynasty Shaolin monks had rescued the king, Li Shi Min and won award since then the temple has become world famous. In the biggest hall, Qianfodian, there are a lot of shallow pits on the floor, which are said they are the traces left by the monks from kung fu training. Many martial arts enthusiasts home and abroad visit Shaolin Temple every year.

Foguang Temple known as the gem of ancient Chinese architecture is in Wutai county, Shanxi Province. The temple stands high at the mountainside with green pines and quiet environment. Many visitors visit the charming scenery every year.

Located in the west of the west lake, Lingyin Temple is the largest and the oldest one in Hangzhou, with over 1,600 years of history. Lingyinsi temple is famous for the beautiful Feilai peak, dignified pavilions, clear cold spring, and the inscriptions of the Tang and Song Dynasties. It is a museum of nature, history, culture, and architecture.

The largest Lama Temple in China is Potala Palace which is located in the northwest of Abdallah hill, Lhasa. It is composed of five different style palaces covered with golden glazed tile roof and magnificent walls that were built with red and white stones. In order to marry Princess Wen Cheng of the Tang Dynasty, the king of Tibet Songtsan Gampo built the Potala Palace in the seventh century AD. Inside it, there are more than 200,000 statues of Buddha and many fine murals. On the top of it, there are a row of tall Nepal-style tomb towers. One of them is Dalai Lama XIII's, which is up to 14 meters and covered with gold. According to statistics, it used 18.8 thousand ounces of gold (590 kg), 200,000 pearls, and thousands of other kinds of precious stones, thus the Temple is known as the most beautiful tomb tower.

It is well known that there are many other famous temples in China, such as Yong He Gong, Kaiyuansi Temple, Pujisi Temple and so on.

段落译文

很多中国的寺院建在山林之中，多为院落式建筑。寺内的主要建筑是：山门、天王殿、大雄宝殿、法堂和藏经阁等。

天王殿中供奉着弥勒佛。东西两侧供奉四大天王，他们各护一方，并代表着风调雨顺。大雄宝殿是正殿，也称为“大殿”，供奉着佛教缔造者——释迦牟尼佛像。大雄宝殿两旁常有配殿，东边是迦蓝殿，西边是祖师殿，供奉着禅宗初祖达摩，他是禅宗理论的输入者。

“法堂”在正殿之后，是僧人演论佛法的地方。藏经阁是存放经书的地方，

是寺院的图书馆。常常建在寺院的最里面。罗汉堂是纯粹中国化的殿堂。殿中有五百罗汉的雕像，神态各异，栩栩如生。

洛阳白马寺是中国官方建造的第一座寺庙。最初的白马寺，只是个安置外国僧人的住所。现在白马寺被视为中国佛教的发源地。

中国的很多名山都建有寺庙。被誉为“天下第一名刹”的少林寺，位于河南省嵩山。由于在唐朝初期，少林武僧营救唐王李世民有功，受到了奖赏。从此少林寺成了中外驰名的大寺院。其中千佛殿规模最大，保存最完整，殿内地面砖上有许多脚踏的浅凹坑，据说是寺僧们演练少林拳时留下的痕迹。如今每年都有很多国内外的武术爱好者到少林寺参拜访问。

佛光寺被誉为“中国古建筑之瑰宝”，位于山西省五台山县。寺院高踞山腰，寺区苍松翠柏，环境清幽，景色迷人，吸引了很多游客。

位于西子湖的灵隐寺是杭州最古老、规模最大的名刹，已有1600多年的历史。它与周围秀美的“飞来峰”、典雅端庄的亭阁、晶莹澄澈的冷泉及唐宋时代的碑刻，形成一个自然、历史、文化和建筑的博物馆。

中国最大的喇嘛寺院——布达拉宫，坐落在拉萨西北的布达拉山上。整个建筑用红白相间的石条依山垒砌，由五座覆盖着琉璃金瓦各具风格的宫殿组成。布达拉宫始建于公元七世纪，是藏王松赞干布为迎娶唐朝文成公主而建。寺庙中大小佛像多达20多万尊，寺内还有许多的精美壁画。布达拉宫的最高层是一排高大的尼泊尔式坟塔，其中达赖十三世的灵塔，高达14米，外部用金皮包裹。据统计，用在墓塔建筑上的纯金达18800盎司(590公斤)，珍珠20万粒，各种宝石10万多颗，是中国最精美，最华丽的灵塔。

中国还有很多具有独特的建筑风格著名寺庙，诸如雍和宫、开元寺、普济禅寺等等。

实用词汇

白马寺 White Horse Temple
观音菩萨 Buddha

喇嘛教寺庙 lamasery
喇嘛 lama
舍利子塔 dagoba
少林寺 Shaolin Temple; Shaolin Monastery
山门 Temple door
大殿 vihara; main hall of a Buddhist temple; main hall
大雄宝殿 the great Buddha's hall
藏经阁 depositary of Buddhist texts
后殿 rear hall
内殿 penetralia
经堂 lectorium
佛经 Buddhist scripture
琉璃宝塔 glazed pagoda
六和塔 Liuhe Pagoda
布达拉宫 Potala Palace
佛光寺 Foguang Temple（in Wutai county, Shanxi Province）
灵隐寺 Lingyinsi Temple（in Hangzhou, Zhejiang Province）
舍利塔 sarira stupa（a pagoda for Buddhist relics）
钟楼 bell tower
鼓楼 drum tower
十八罗汉 the Eighteen Disciples of Buddha / Luohan
四大天王 four heavenly kings; heavenly guardians
韦驮 Weito; the temple guardian
弥勒 Maitrya
观音菩萨 Bodhisattva; Godesss of Mercy; Guanyin
禅宗 Chan Sect; Zen Sect
朝山进香 pilgrimage
普济禅寺 Temple of Universal Relief, in Puto county, Zhejiang Province

名言俗语

佛要金装，人要衣装。

As Buddha needs a gilt statue, man needs fine clothes.

佛争一炷香，人争一口气。

As Buddha needs incense, so man needs self-respect.

普度众生。

Deliver all living creatures from torment.

不看僧面看佛面。

Doing sth. not for the monk's sake, but for the Buddha's.

当一天和尚撞一天钟。

To go on tolling the bell as long as one is a monk.

放下屠刀，立地成佛。

One drops his cleaver and becomes a Buddha.

词语注解

山门：一般佛教寺庙的大门被称为"山门"。

The gate of a temple is called the door of the mountain.

跑了和尚跑不了庙：意思是虽然人逃跑了，但是他的住地或工作地点会给出线索。

The monk may run away, but not the temple. It means a fugitive must belong to some place that can provide clues.

平时不烧香，急来抱佛脚：指事到临头才着急。

Never burn incense when all is well but clasp Buddha's feet when in distress.

丈二和尚，摸不着头脑：弄不懂什么事情。

You can't touch the head of the ten-foot monk, which means that you can't make head or tail of something or you can't make something clear.

当一天和尚撞一天钟：指人应付做事。

To go on tolling the bell as long as one is a monk, which is often used to describe the person who does the least that is expected of him.

放下屠刀，立地成佛：意思是只要停止做坏事，心灵就会得到解脱。

One drops his cleaver and becomes a Buddha, which means that someone can achieve salvation as soon as he gives up evil.

中西合璧

教堂是与中国寺庙相对应的西方的宗教建筑。很多西方著名教堂都是哥特式建筑，如英国的威斯敏斯特教堂，法国的巴黎圣母院，德国的科隆大教堂等。很多教堂的设计为十字形，如意大利的圣彼得大教堂，英国的圣保罗大教堂等。尽管教堂的外形各有不同，但是大多数教堂有着高高的大穹隆，众多的与宗教有关的著名雕刻和绘画，精美的彩色玻璃，巨大的钟楼等。其中圣彼得教堂的钟最大，有 24 吨重。罗马式教堂也有很多著名的钟楼，意大利的比萨斜塔就是其中之一。

Western religious buildings are known as churches. Many famous Western churches are the Gothic-style buildings, such as Westminster Abbey in UK, Notre Dame in France, Germany's Cologne Cathedral and so on. Many churches like St. Paul's Cathedral in London and St. Peter Cathedral of Italy are cross-shape designs. Despite the different shapes of the churches, but most of the big churches have a high dome, many well-known sculptures and paintings, exquisite stained glass and huge clock towers. Among them the bell of St. Peter is the biggest which weighs 24 tons. There are also many famous clock towers in Roman-style churches and the Italian Leaning Tower of Pisa is one of them.

UNIT 9

The Lunar Calendar and the 24 Solar Terms

中国历法和二十四节气

题记

历法和节气的产生是和人类生活需要分不开的。随着农业的发展，人们掌握天时节气就变得越来越重要了。中国古人从观察天象及气候开始，先后制定了历法和节气。

The creation of the calendar and the solar terms has a close relationship with human life. With the development of agriculture, it is more important to make use of weather and the solar terms. The ancient Chinese people created the Chinese lunar calendar and the 24 solar terms, from observing astronomical phenomena and the climate.

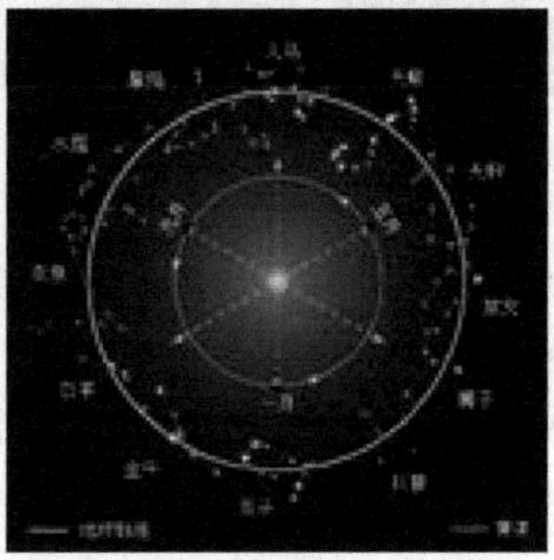

There have been more than 100 kinds of calendars in Chinese history. At present, only the lunar calendar and solar calendar are commonly used. The solar calendar is based on the rotation of the sun and the four seasons. There are 12 months a year, a total of 365 days, and there is a leap year every four years. The leap year has 366 days in total and an extra day is added at the end of February.

Chinese lunar calendar was created according to agricultural production.

The lunar calendar is based on the rotation circle of the moon. There are 12 months a year, a total of 354 days; there are 13 months in a leap year, and the extra month is called the leap month. About seven leap months are in every 19 lunar years, among which the leap months are based on the 24 solar terms of the year. The 24 solar terms can be divided into 12 minor solar terms and 12 major solar terms. Generally, the month without a major solar term in more than every two years is called "leap month".

The minor solar terms and major solar terms are collectively called solar terms. From "Moderate Cold", there is a minor solar term at about 30-day intervals, such as Spring Commencement, Insects Waken, Bright and Clear, and so on. From "Winter Solstice", there is a major solar term at about 30-day intervals, such as Severe Cold, Spring Showers, Vernal Equinox, and so on. Every solar term is about 15.22 days on average.

A Chinese lunar year is divided into four seasons, spring, summer, autumn and winter and there are spring, summer, autumn, and winter

commencements in the 24 solar terms. Since the days of a solar term are fixed and are not related to the certain months, the collocation of the solar terms and the lunar calendar months are not completely consistent every year. However the 24 solar terms have laid the foundation for farming on time.

In fact, every solar term has a clear meaning, for example; "Great Heat" refers to the period where hot weather has reached a peak; "Severe Cold" means the coldest days of the year have come; "Insects Waken" indicates that the spring thunders have wakened the hibernating animals; "Corn Rain" suggests the rainfall has increased, which is

beneficial to the corn's growth; "Corn on Ear" is the harvest time of the wheat, then the summer planting will begin.

The Chinese farmers have created many farming proverbs according to the 24 solar terms. For example, "Three days after the term of Spring Commencement, all the plants sprout"; "Spring plough should not stop, after Insects Waken term"; "It is not time to plant the grains after the term of Corn on Ear" and "It is a busy time during the terms of the Autumn Commencement and the end of heat, and people have to gather in the early rice and plant the coarse cereals then", and so on. The 24 Solar Terms are unique cultural heritage of the Chinese working people, and not only guide the people's farming activities, but also reflect the changes in season. They have been applied by the Chinese farmers for thousands of years.

段落译文

中国曾有过一百多种历法。目前最常用的是阴历和阳历两种。阳历是以太阳的旋转制定的四季，一年有十二个月，一共 365 天，四年一闰，闰年共 366 天，往往在二月末加上一天。

中国的阴历是古人根据农业生产所创造的，因此也叫做农历。阴历是以月亮自转一圈为一个月，并有平年和闰年之分。平年有十二个月，一年共有 354 天；闰年有十三个月，共 384 天为一年，多出的一个月叫闰月。大概 19 年中有 7 个闰月。但具体闰哪个月，要取决于那一年中的二十四个节气。中国的农历将二十四节气分为十二个节气和十二个中气。一般每两年多就有一个没有中气的月份被称为闰月。

二十四节气是节气和中气的统称。从小寒起，每隔大约三十日有一个节气，如立春、惊蛰、清明等十二个节气。从冬至开始，每隔大约三十日就有一个中气，如大寒、雨水、春分等十二个中气。每个节气平均为 15. 22 日。

一年分为春夏秋冬四个季节，二十四节气中有立春、立夏、立秋、立冬。“立”是开始的意思，表示每个季节的开始。但是由于节气的日期是固定的，与每月时间没关系，因此节气和阴历月份的搭配不是每年都绝对一致的。排定节气，是为掌握天时季节，按时农耕奠定基础。

其实每一个节气的名称都有十分明确的含义，如“大”是极端的表示，“大暑”是指气候酷热达到最高峰；“大寒”表示到了一年最冷的日子；“惊蛰”表示春雷响起来了，惊醒了蛰伏在地下冬眠的动物；“谷雨”顾名思义，指雨水增多，有利于谷物的生长；“芒种”时，麦类等有芒的农作物成熟了收割了，夏种开始了。

中国的劳动人民还根据二十四节气创造了很多与农业生产有关的谚语。例如，“立春三日，百草发芽”，“过了惊蛰节，春耕不停歇”，“过了芒种，不可强种”，“立秋处暑地越忙，收了早稻种杂粮”，等等。二十四节气是中国劳动人民独创的文化遗产，它既能反映出一年四季的变化，还能指导人们的农事活动，因此，几千年来，一直被广大中国农民所应用。

实用词汇

日历 calendar
阳历 the Gregorian calendar; solar calendar
农历，阴历，夏历 the lunar calendar; also yinli or xiali
皇历，黄历，历书 almanac, also huangli or lishu
大月 great month（a solar month of 31 days or a lunar month of 30 days）
小月 lesser month（a solar month of 30 days or a lunar month of 29 days）
上旬 the first ten-day period of a month
中旬 the middle ten-day period of a month
下旬 the last ten-day period of a month
二十四节气 the twenty-four solar terms
中气 major solar terms
节气 minor solar terms

立春 Spring Commencement
雨水 Spring Showers; Rain Water
惊蛰 Insects Waken; Waking of Insects
春分 Vernal Equinox
清明 Bright and Clear
谷雨 Corn Rain
立夏 Summer Commencement
小满 Corn Forms
芒种 Corn on Ear
夏至 Summer Solstice
小暑 Moderate Heat; Slight Heat
大暑 Great Heat
立秋 Autumn Commencement
处暑 End of Heat
白露 White Dew
秋分 Autumnal Equinox
寒露 Cold Dew
霜降 Frost
立冬 Winter commencement
小雪 Light Snow
大雪 Heavy Snow
冬至 Winter Solstice
小寒 Moderate Cold
大寒 Severe Cold
闰月 leap month
闰年 leap year
回归年 tropical year
朔望月 synodic month

名言俗语

未过惊蛰先打雷，四十八天云不开。

Freezing cold in spring promises water-logging in summer. / Cold in spring, the weather is wet.

立春雨淋淋，阴阴湿湿到清明。

If it drizzles on the Beginning of Spring Day, the rainy period will last until Pure Brightness Day.

小暑热得透，大暑凉飕飕。

If it is extremely hot on Slight Heat Day (or Mid-Heat Day), it will be very cool on Great Heat Day (Scorching-Heat Day).

晚霞晴千里，早霞别出门。

If there is sunset glow, it will be sunny tomorrow; if there is morning glow, you'd better stay at home.

雪兆丰年

Timely snow foretells a bumper harvest. / Auspicious snow promises good harvests. / A snow year, a rich year.

一年之计在于春，一日之计在于晨，一生之计在于勤。

The whole year's work depends on a good start in spring; the whole day's work depends on a good start in the morning; the success of one's lifework depends on one's industriousness.

四月凉，谷满仓。

A cold April the barn will fill.

五月刮风天气冷，五谷丰登装满囤。

A cold May and a windy makes a full barn and findy.

二月天气好，全年气候糟。

All the months in the year curse a fair Februeer. (Februeer, 古语：二月)

去年的皇历，今年看不得。

Last year's almanac is useless for this year.

词语注解

老皇历：比喻陈旧过时的规矩。

Last year's calendar, which means ancient history or outdated ways of doing things.

闰年：阳历有闰日的一年叫闰年，一年有 366 天。农历有闰月的一年也叫闰年，这年有 13 个月，即 383 天或 384 天。农历中，每三年有一个闰年。

leap year, intercalary year: intercalary year which contains 366 days in the Gregorian calendar; leap year, which contains 383 or 384 days in 13 months, occurs in every third year in the Chinese lunar calendar.

闰月：农历三年一闰，五年两闰，十九年七闰，每逢闰年所加的一个月叫闰月。

leap month, intercalary month: In Chinese lunar calendar, an intercalary month or a leap month occurs once every three years, twice every five years, and seven times in every 19 years.

闰日：阳历四年一闰，在二月末加一天， 这一天叫做闰日。

Leap day, intercalary day: extra day that occurs in February once every four years in the Gregorian calendar.

回归年：太阳中心连续两次经过春分点所需要的时间。一个回归年等于 365 天 5 小时 48 分 46 秒。

tropical year, solar year: time between one vernal equinox and the next. One tropical year equals about 365days, 5 hours, 48 minutes and 46 seconds.

朔望月：月亮连续两次呈现同样的月相所经历的时间。一个朔望月等于 29 天 12 小时 44 分 2.8 秒。

synodic month, lunar month: period of time , averaging 29 days, 12 hours, 44 minutes, and 2. 8 seconds, spanning two successive moons of the same phase passing.

中西合璧

有些西方国家习惯用黄道十二宫来计算年份。同中国人根据农历和节气进行耕种一样，美国中南部的欧扎克人也习惯利用天文年历和黄道十二宫来决定农作物的耕种时间。他们也有很多相关的谚语，如："种洋白菜和包心菜最好选在白羊宫的月份"、"7 月 25 日种萝卜，旱涝保收"、"在狮子宫、室女宫或双子宫的月份割杂草和伐枯木"等等。

The signs of the Zodiac are commonly used to measure the year in western countries. As the Chinese people use solar terms for farming, the Ozark people in South America are also accustomed to using the almanac and the signs of the zodiac to determine when the best time is to proceed with the farming schedule. There are many relevant proverbs, too. For example, "Cabbage and head lettuce are best planted in Aries.", "Sow your turnips on the 25th of July." and "Cut weeds and dead timber during Leo, Virgo, or Gemini."

UNIT 10

Great Chinese Inventions

中国四大发明

题记

美国学者坦普尔在《中国——发明创造的国度》中统计，现代世界文明赖以建立的基本发明创造，有一半以上来源于中国。特别是造纸术、火药、印刷术、指南针的发明曾经改变了世界。直到15世纪以前，中国的科学技术在世界上保持了数千年的领先地位！

An American scholar, Temple, declared in his book *China—The Land of Invention and Creation* that more then half the basic inventions were from China. Particularly, the inventions of paper making, gunpowder, printing and the compass have changed the world. The science and technology in China maintained a leading position in the world for a millennium until 15 centuries!

The Four Great Inventions of ancient China have been revolutionary inventions for the world's development, namely papermaking, gunpowder, printing and the compass. They propelled our political, economic and cultural development forward and created enormous impetus to the development of world civilization as well.

Paper: The writing materials during early China were turtle shell, animal bones, bamboos, wood slips, stone and so on. Writing on these was sometimes inconvenient, they were not easy to carry, more expensive and not suitable for wide use. In 105 AD, Cai Lun improved papermaking, based on the former paper-making technology. The principles of the ancient paper craft had been developed over 2000 years, but there was still no substantive change in the process of paper making: to collect the main raw material (hemp plants)—mashed, steamed—whiten—natural fermentation, pulp—copied into the paper (with bamboos and the like)—dried in the sun. Owing to the widespread use of paper, the record of information, dissemination and inheritance had a revolutionary progress.

Gunpowder: As early as the Shang and Zhou dynasties, people used charcoal widely in metallurgical practice, furthermore the raw materials of gunpowder—sulfur, saltpeter were also well known to others, thus paved the road for the invention of gunpowder. In Tang Dynasty, the alchemists absorbed various experiences in production and life from working people. Then they gradually found a mixture of sulfur charcoal and some material, flammable and explosive. The earliest record was found in Sun Simiao'book *The Method of Using Sulfur*. So it could be concluded that in the early Tang Dynasty gunpowder was invented in China. In 904 AD of the Tang Dynasty, Zheng Pan made gunpowder to attack Yuzhang. This was the beginning of gunpowder for military use. During Northern Song Dynasty, gunpowder was widely used in the military and then spread to the Arab countries. In the late half of the 13th century, Europeans gradually learned how to manufacture and use gunpowder.

Typography has been recognized as one of the greatest inventions in the world. Before the invention of printing, people used to copy by hand, which was both time-consuming and labor-intensive, moreover it was prone to errors. In Sui and Tang Dynasties, people got inspiration from seal and rock carving, so they carved characters in wood to make them bulge on the opposite side. They brushed on the ink, covered with paper, finally the printing came out. Nevertheless, it was a forward leap to invent woodblock printing in early Tang Dynasty. It was still a time-consuming and laborious job until the year 1041~1048, when Bi Sheng in Northern Song Dynasty produced a kind of movable type for printing books. Soon after this it was spread to the countries around the world, which made it a great contribution to promote cultural exchange and developing human civilization.

A Compass is a directional instrument based on the principle of magnets and it is another great invention of Chinese people. During the Warring States period, they made use of the magnetic feature which is always pointing to the North to make a directional instrument, Sinan, before the invention of the Guide car and the Guide fish came into being. Till Northern Song Dynasty, people built compass from artificial magnets, which could be used in navigation. Sinan is a natural magnet grinded by artificial means of striking jade, it was used to create "Sinan's Spoon," "Guide to the handle." The Guide fish was made by cutting a thin iron into magnetized fish-shaped leaves, which was able to tell directions, and it was of a great help when marching. The compass was more practical and convenient than Sinan or the Guide fish. The invention of the Compass and its application provided the conditions for Navigator Zheng in Ming Dynasty to complete his voyage to the East Africa and other places; and for Columbus' discovery of America, Magellan's global navigation and modern sailing.

段落译文

四大发明是指中国古代对世界的发展和格局具有革命性意义的四种发明——**造纸术、火药、印刷术、指南针**。四大发明对中国古代的政治、经济、文化的发展产生了巨大的推动作用，对世界文明的发展也产生了非常大的影响。

纸：中国早期书写材料是龟甲、兽骨竹简、木牍、金石等，或书写比较麻烦、不易携带，或价格也比较昂贵，不适合广泛使用。东汉元兴元年 105，蔡伦在前人造纸术的基础上，改革和推广了造纸技术。古代造纸工艺机原理，发明至今 2000 多年来，并无实质性变化：收集主要原料(麻类植物)—捣碎，蒸煮—自然变白—发酵，制浆—抄成纸张(用竹帘之类)—晒干。纸的广泛使用，使得信息的记录、传播和继承，都有了革命性的进步。

火药：早在商周时期，人们在冶金实践中已经广泛使用木炭，之后制作火药的原料硫黄、硝石又为人们所熟知，为火药发明准备了条件。唐代炼丹士们在炼丹实践中吸取了劳动人民生产和生活的丰富经验，逐渐发现硫黄、木炭和其他材料的混合物有燃烧和爆炸能力。最早称作"硫黄火法"。由此可知，我国火药最迟在唐代初年就已经发明了。公元 904 年，唐朝人郑潘制成"发机飞火"，进攻豫章。这是火药用于军事的开始。火药在北宋年间大规模地用于军事，在南宋末年传到了阿拉伯各国。13 世纪下半叶，欧洲人逐渐学会了制造和运用火药。

活字印刷：被公认为世界最伟大的发明之一。在印刷术发明前，人们用手抄书，既费时耗力，又易出错。到隋唐，人们从印章和拓石中受启发，把字雕刻在木板上，使它成为反的凸字。然后刷上墨，铺上纸，一张一张地就印成了，到唐代初年发明了雕版印刷术，这是一个飞跃，但依然费时费力。直到公元 1041~1048 年，北宋毕昇用制作活字来印书发明了活字印刷。活字印刷术问世不久，便传到世界各国，对促进人类文化交流和文明进步作出了巨大贡献。

指南针：是利用磁铁中的南北指极性而制成的一种指示方向的仪器，是中国人民的又一项伟大发明。

战国时期，中国就利用磁石指南的特性发明了指南仪器——司南，此后又出现了指南车、指南鱼等。北宋时，进而发明了使用人工磁体的指南针，应用于航海。司南是用天然磁石经人工用琢玉的办法磨成，并用天然磁石制造"司南之勺"，"其柄指南"。指南鱼是用薄铁叶裁成鱼形，然后使它带有磁性，在行军需要时将它浮在水面，铁叶鱼就能指南。指南针是以天然磁石摩擦钢针制得，比司南和指南鱼更为简便更有实用价值。指南针的发明和应用为明代航海家郑和远航东非等地提供了条件；为哥伦布发现美洲的航行和麦哲伦的环球航行，提供了技术保障。

实用词汇

地动仪 mobile celestial globe invented by the Chinese scientist Zhang Heng in 132 AD for observing of earthquake

候风地动仪 ancient seismograph (invented by Zhang Heng in the Han Dynasty)

浑天仪 ①armillary sphere, ②celestial globe

活版印刷 typographic printing

火器 firearm

刻版 cut blocks for printing

刻版印刷 block printing

刻本 block-printed edition

刻花 engraved designs

司南 southward-pointing instrument—prototype of the compass

四大发明 ancient China's four great inventions, namely, the compass, gunpowder, paper-making and printing

印刷术 art of printing

印台 ink pad

指南车 compass vehicle, an ancient Chinese vehicle with a wooden figure, always pointing to the south

名言俗语

我们不是历史的创造者，而是由历史创造出来的。

We are not makers of history. We are made by history.

探索者有收获。——海伍德

He that seeks finds. —Haywood

有耐心的人才能达其目的。——本杰明·富兰克林

He that can have patience, can have what he will. —Benjamin Franklin

人不是环境的奴隶，环境是人所创造的。

Man is not the creature of circumstances, circumstances are the creatures of men.

爱情会激发人的创造力。

Love makes people inventive.

有时奇迹也会出现，但必须努力工作去创造。

Miracles sometimes occur, but one has to work terribly hard for them.

成功的秘诀在于坚持不懈地奔向目标。

The secret of success is constancy to purpose.

卓越的天才不走旁人走过的路。他寻找迄今未开拓的地区。 ——林肯

Towering genius disdains a beaten path. It seeks regions hitherto unexplored. —Lincoln

生活没有目标就像航海没有指南针。

Living without an aim is like sailing without a compass.

人有耐心，无事不成。

He that has patience may compass anything.

需要是发明的动力。

Necessity is the mother of invention.

工作没有打算，犹如航海没有罗盘。

Working without a plan is sailing without a compass.

光是科技进步不足以推动社会改变。至少要有一些人愿意拥抱改变，否则那不会发生。——比尔·盖茨

Progress in science and technology is not powerful enough to push the society to change. At least some people are willing to embrace change, or it will not happen. —Bill Gates

科学和艺术是源于世界的，他们没有国界。——歌德

Science and art are originated from the world; they are borderless. —Goethe

科学是社会进步的标志。——徐特立

Science is a sign of social development. —Xu Teli

艺术家和科学家的价值在于没有私欲的服务，在于为万人的利益服务。——富兰克林·罗斯福

The value of artists and science lies in their selfless service for all people's interests. —Franklin Roosevelt

没有大胆的猜测就做不出伟大的发现。——牛顿

No bold conjectures, no great findings. —Issac Newton

思想就是力量。——雨果

The thought is the power. —Victor Hugo

科学根本精神，全在养成观察力。——梁启超

The basic spirit of science is forming insights. —Liang Qichao

没有想象力的灵魂，就像没有望远镜的天文台。——爱因斯坦

A soul without imagination is like an observatory without the telescope. —Einstein

对搞科学的人来说，勤奋就是成功之母。——茅以升

To the scientific researcher, diligence is the mother of success. —Mao Yisheng

在科学上没有平坦的大道，只有不畏劳苦沿着陡峭山路攀登的人，才有希望达到光辉的顶点。——卡尔·马克思

There is no royal road to science, and only those who do not dread the fatiguing climb of its steep paths have a chance of reaching its luminous peak. —Karl Marx

词语注解

四大发明：中国古代四大发明——造纸术、火药、印刷术、指南针

ancient China's four great inventions, namely, the compass, gunpowder, paper-making and printing

候风地动仪：汉代张衡发明的地动仪

ancient seismograph invented by Zhang Heng in the Han Dynasty

指南车：中国古代用来指南的木制交通工具

compass vehicle, an ancient Chinese vehicle with a wooden figure, always pointing to the south

黄道婆：元代纺车发明者

Huang Daopo, woman innovator of textile technique of the Yuan Dynasty

中西合璧

四大发明中的火药除了可制作烟花和炮仗等，亦是一种炸药，中国在实用性火器的使用上早于欧洲五个世纪左右。而欧洲人约在 13 世纪时才懂得黑火药的作用。活字印刷术促进了文化的传播和发展，是我国对世界文明的卓越贡献。活字印刷术由我国传到朝鲜、日本、埃及和欧洲。欧洲到 15 世纪才有活字版，比毕昇的发明晚了 400 年。造纸术于公元 8 世纪传到阿拉伯，改变了中世纪欧洲文化落后的状况，加速了文化知识的传播。

The gunpowder of the four great inventions is also a kind of explosives, as well as a material to produce fireworks and firecrackers. The use of firearms in China was about five centuries earlier than that in Europe. However, the Europeans didn't know of the effect of black powder until the 13th century. Typography has promoted the spread the development of culture and become an outstanding contribution to world civilization as well as our country. Typography was later spread to North Korea, Japan, Egypt and Europe. Not until the 15th century did typography appear in Europe, which was 400 years later than Bi Sheng's invention.

Papermaking was spread to Arab in the 8th century AD, which helped change the situation in the medieval European culture and to speed up the dissemination of cultural knowledge.

UNIT 11

Chinese Characters

方块字

题记

汉字距今已有 3000 多年的历史。因为它字形成方块状，又称为“方块字”。汉字以它悠久的发展史，神奇的造字方式、形音意三位一体的表示功能，被称为世界独特的文字体系。

Chinese characters have a history of 3000 years. It is also known as square-shaped characters and a unique writing system because of its magical method of word-formation and the expressive functions of shape, tone, and meaning.

Chinese characters are one of the oldest and the most widely used characters in the word. How did it come into being? A very widely spread legend said that in the period of Yellow Emperor more than 4500 years ago, a mysterious man named Cang Jie created the Chinese characters. It was told that he was born with four eyes and could write and observe everything in the world immediately. In fact, it was Chinese ancestors who created the character through hard work and civil life.

In China, people have found rock paintings of hunting that are more than

10,000 years old. The shapes of "deer", "dogs", and "shot" were found to be similar to the related Chinese characters now. Rock paintings played an

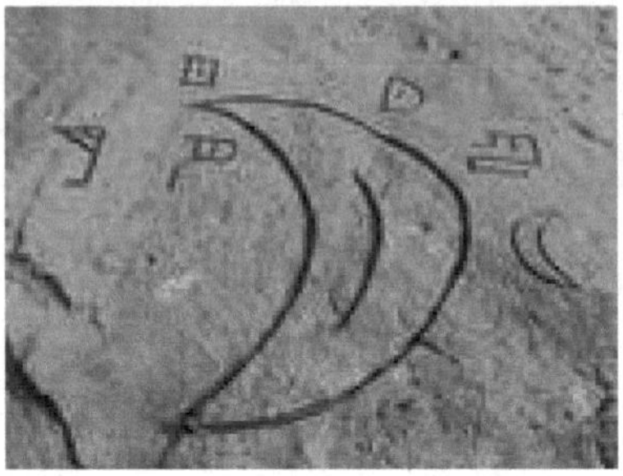

introductory role in the formation of Chinese characters. The symbols on ancient pottery 4000~5000 years ago were some of the origins of Chinese characters and the oracle-bone inscriptions should be the earliest mature Chinese characters. There are about 500000~600000 Chinese characters in all, so it is impossible to create all of them by drawing. Four methods for forming Chinese characters were used by Chinese people, they are pictographic characters, self-explanatory characters, associative compound characters, and pictographic characters.

Pictographic characters or pictographs represent an object in pictorial form, such as "日" (the sun) and "月" (the moon). Some experts and scholars believe that Chinese Characters were developed from pictographs. But some words that could not be represented by pictographs were pointed out a certain place on the other word, such as "刃" (edge) which has a dot added to the side of the word "刀" (knife). This kind of word-formation is called self-explanatory characters.

The composition of two or more words belongs to associative compound characters. For example, the character "林" which means "forest" is composed of two trees, and "灾" shows us a house that is on fire, which means disaster. Since there are some limitations to this type of word-formation, Chinese people tried to create new characters by combining the meanings of a character with the pronunciation of another. For instance, "loyalty" (忠), is a mixture of heart (心) and the pronunciation of "中". This is known as a pictophonetic method for the formation of Chinese characters. These characters account for over 80 percent of the total number of Chinese characters.

A unique part of Chinese characters is that almost every Chinese character reflects the thinking of the ancient culture. For example, the character “安” (peace) shows that the peace can be found when there is a woman in a house according to the components, which means a house and the character under it is a woman. The ancient Han people believed that a quiet and comfortable family life mainly depended on women. The character, “鲜”means delicious. It was that the ancient Chinese had regarded fish (鱼) and mutton (羊) as the most delicious food.

Chinese characters can also reflect customs of ancient Chinese society. For example, the character “婚” means marriage, because in ancient time women (女) always got married at dusk (黄昏). It was a traditional wedding custom for a man to marry a woman by force and dusk was a convenient time for him to do so. Marriage customs like this can still be seen in some ethnic minorities now.

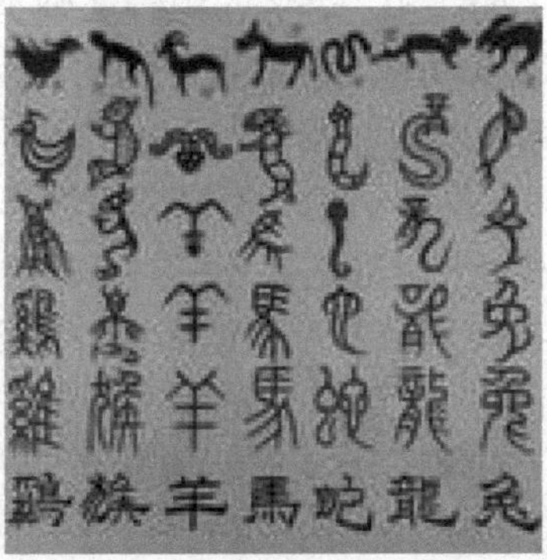

There are some Chinese characters that have the same component and couple it with another to create characters with similar meanings. For example, most fish have the component “鱼” (fish), such as cod(鳕鱼), plaice (鲽鱼), mackerel (鲭鱼), herring (鲱鱼); nearly all liquids have “氵” (water) as a component, such as river (江), sea(海), juice(汁), soup(汤) and so on.

During the 3000 years from Shang Dynasty to the present, The writing forms of Chinese characters have experienced many changes from the oracle-bone and Bronze Inscriptions, the big and small seal scripts, to the official script, and the regular script. However, the simplification has been the mainstream of the development of Chinese characters.

段落译文

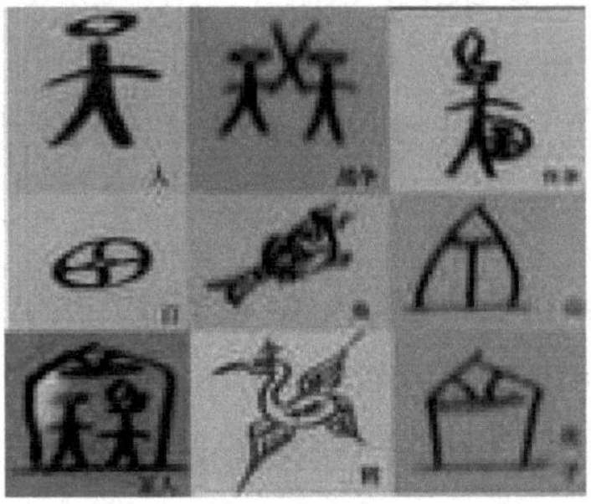

汉字是世界上历史最悠久、使用人数最多的文字之一。汉字是如何产生的呢？中国有个流传很广的传说：在 4500 多年前的黄帝时代，有一个神奇的人叫仓颉，他生来就会写字，长着四只眼睛，善于观察世界万物，据说汉字是他创造的。实际上，汉字是中国祖先在长期的劳动和社会生活中集体创造出来的。

在中国，人们发现了 10000 年前的围猎岩画，岩画中的一些图像和汉字“鹿”、“犬”、“射”的样子非常相近。可以说岩画对后来汉字的形成具有某种启发作用。五六千年前的远古陶器上刻画的符号应该是汉字的起源。著名的甲骨文则是中国最早成熟的文字。但是汉字总数有五、六万个，这么多的汉字都用画画的方法造出来是不可能的。因此中国人很早就用象形、指事、会意、形声等四种方法来创造新汉字了。

象形字是一种描画事物形状的字。如“日”和“月”都是象形字。有些研究汉字的专家和学者认为，汉字是由图画文字发展起来的。然而还有些字，无法用这种象形的方法画出来，就采用了在某一个字形上指出意义所在的部位来表示，例如，在刀的一侧加一点，表示“刃”字。这就是“指事字”。

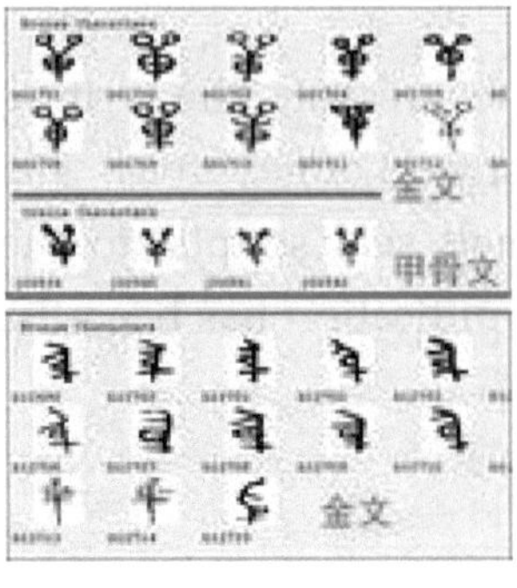

会意字是指由两个或两个以上的字组成的一个合体字。如“林”就是由两个“木”组成的。从“灾”字可以看出屋子里着火了，就意味着是大灾难了。由于用表意方法造字，数量有限，后来产生了一种用表示意义类型的符号与表示读音的符号合起来造新字的方法。例如，“忠”，其中“心” 表示此字与心理活动有关，“中”表示读音，这种字叫“形声字”。汉字中大约有 80%的字是用这种方法创造出来的。

汉字的独特之处表现在几乎每个方块字的形体都能反映出古代汉民族的思维文化。如“安”字，从字形上分析，部首是家或屋子的意思，屋里有女人则安，说明古人认为，家庭的安稳舒适主要在女人。再如“鲜”字，那时的人们认为鱼和羊肉是最鲜美的食品。

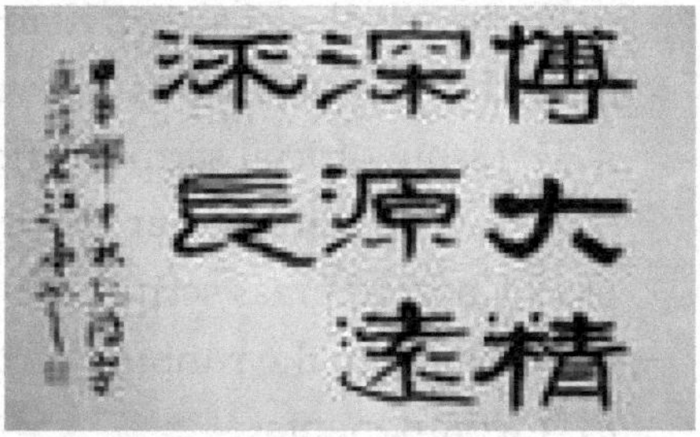

汉字还反映了中国古代社会的一些文化风俗。如“婚”字，这是一个表意兼形声字，表示古代女子在黄昏时出嫁。这是源于古代的“抢婚”习俗，黄昏时天色不明，便于抢婚。这种婚俗在现代的一些少数民族的婚礼上还能看到。

中国文字的另一个特点是：同类的字常加一个相同的偏旁部首。例如，大多数的鱼类，都加鱼字偏旁，如鳕鱼(cod)、鲽鱼(plaice)、鲭鱼(mackerel)、鲱鱼 (herring)等；几乎所有的液体类都加了三点水，如江、海、汁、汤等等。

从商代到至今的三千多年中，汉字的书写主要经过了甲骨文、金文、小篆、大篆、 隶书、楷书等演变过程。而简化一直是汉字发展的主流。

实用词汇

汉字 Chinese character
汉语拼音 hanyupinyin; phonetic transcriptions of Chinese character
简化汉字 simplified Chinese
简化偏旁 simplified character components
繁体字 traditional Chinese character; unsimplified Chinese character
方块字 (Chinese) character
表意文字 ideograms
岩画 rock painting
象形 pictographic characters
指事 self-explanatory characters
会意 associative compound characters
形声 pictophonetic characters

甲骨文 tortoise shells and animal bones; the scrip on shell-and-bone; oracle-bone inscriptions

钟鼎文，金文 the bronze inscriptions; the script on bronze vessels; Jin Characters;

小篆 the small seal script; Xiaozhuan; lesser seal script; small seal style

大篆 the big seal script; large seal style

隶书 Lishu; official script ; official style

楷书 Kaishu; the regular script;

草书 Caoshu; grass script ; the cursive script

行书 Xingshu; the running script ; running hand

部首 components

笔画 strokes

点儿 dot

横儿 horizontal bar

竖儿 vertical bar

撇儿 left-falling stroke

捺儿 right-falling stroke

提 upward-hook stroke

折 turning stroke

钩儿 hook stroke

笔顺 stroke order

字义 literal meaning

毛笔字 Chinese brush writing

美术字 artistic calligraphy

拼音化 alphabetization

平声 level tone

阳平 rising tone

阴平 high-level tone

文字改革 reform of a writing system

名言俗语

读书需用意，一字值千金。

Read critically, and you will find each word worth a thousand ounces of gold.

开卷有益。

Reading enriches the mind.

沉默是从未被文字记下的言词。

Silence was never written down.

与君一席话，胜读十年书。

A single conversation with a wise man is better than ten years of study.

美言不能当饭吃。

Soft words butter no parsnips.

要说就索性说得清清楚楚，说出前字字句句都要斟酌。

Speak clearly if you speak at all. Carve every word before you let it fall.

中文的“危机”分为两个字，一个意味着危险，另外一个意味着机会。

The Chinese word for crisis is divided into two characters, one meaning danger and the other meaning opportunity.

词语注解

一字千金：用来称赞文章诗词的精妙。

One word worth a thousand pieces of gold which is often used to describe the excellent literary work or calligraphy.

一字一板：形容说话从容清楚。

Speak unhurriedly and clearly.

字斟句酌：对每个字，每句话都仔细推敲，形容说话或写作的态度慎重。

Choose one's words with care or weigh every word.

字正腔圆：说或唱时，字音准确，强调圆润。

Pronounce every word correctly and in a sweet, mellow voice.

字帖：供学习书法的人临摹的范本，多为名家墨迹的石刻拓本，木刻印本或影印本。

Book for calligraphy; book containing models of handwriting for others to copy, mostly books of stone inscription rubbings, woodcut printing or photoprinting.

中西合璧

尽管英语和汉语是两种截然不同的文字，但是在造字方面，两者都使用了大量的词缀。例如中国人几乎把所有用电的东西前都加上个“电”字，如电视、电冰箱、电扇等；英语中很多电动的器物也都加上“electric”（电），如，electric clock（电钟），electric fire（电炉），electric blanket（电热毯），等等。

Although English and Chinese are two completely different writing styles, in word- formation, a large number of affixes are used in both of them. For example, Chinese people add “电”（electric）to most of the objects run by electricity, such as 电视（television），电冰箱（refrigerator），and 电扇（electric fan）. In English, many objects that run on electricity use “electric-“, such as electric clock, electric fire, electric blanket, and so on.

UNIT 12

The Four Treasures of the Study

文房四宝

题记

中国的“文房四宝”其实是笔(毛笔)、墨、纸、砚四种文具的雅称，是中国书法和绘画不可缺少的工具。这四种文具在中国有悠久的制作历史，品种繁多。其中最著名的是浙江湖州的“湖笔”、安徽歙县“徽墨”、安徽宣城的“宣纸”和广东端州的“端砚”等。

"The four treasures of Chinese study" are the formal names for writing brush, ink stick, paper and ink slab, which are the essential tools of Chinese calligraphy and paintings. With a long history, the Four Treasures are varied. The most famous ones are the Hu Bi (Hu brush) made in Huzhou of Zhejiang, the Hui Mo (Hui ink stick) produced in She county of Anhui, the Xuan Zhi (rice paper) made in Xuan city of Anhui, and the Duan Yan (Duan ink slab) produced in Duan Zhou, Guangdong.

The writing brush was the first to be invented of the four treasures of Chinese study. The earliest brush was unearthed from the grave of Chu, Warring States Period, in Xin Yang, Henan province in 1957. The penholder was made of bamboo and the brush was tied to the holder with string. At the beginning, the people made writing brushes with the hair of deer and sheep, which was called "Jian Hao". The Tang Dynasty saw the peak of Chinese calligraphy and art, so the better materials were selected to make writing brushes. After the Yuan Dynasty, the brushes were mainly made of wool. People also used other materials to make brushes, such as the hair of deer, raccoons, dogs, and tigers, sheep mains, wolf tails, and the feathers of geese and chickens. Some penholders were even considered artworks themselves for they are made of ivory, keratin-fiber horn, bolder, colored glaze, porcelain, enamel, and rosewood.

Hu Bi (Hu brush) was produced in Huzhou, Zhejiang province. They are famous for the selected materials and exquisite craftsmanship, which are excellent for painting and calligraphy. It was said that the general of the Qin Dynasty whose name was Meng Tian once made writing brush with sheep's hair in Shanlian village, Huzhou, so he has been given the title as the inventor of the writing brush and the local people built a temple in his name to commemorate him.

Chinese ink can be traced back to very early time, too. There is no doubt that the black color of ancient pottery, and the inscriptions on the bones of tortoise from the Yin and Shang dynasties were painted or written by the crude ink. The early ink stick couldn't be ground into ink, without the help of a grind. With the popularization of the painting and calligraphy in the Tang Dynasty, the ink manufacturing industry underwent further development. Some masters of painting and calligraphy made ink-sticks themselves and became master-hands. Many scholars loved to collect and enjoy good ink sticks. Now a lot of famous ink sticks that were handed down from ancient times have become works of art.

The best ink stick, Hui Mo, was made in Huizhou, Anhui province. They are famous for their light weight, pleasant smell, clear and deep black when grinding. The emperor, Li Yu, at the time appreciated Hui Mo very much and granted his own family name "Li" to the producer, which was a great honor.

Since then "Li ink stick" had become very famous. So there was an old saying then: "It is easy to get a thousand pieces of gold, but it is difficult to buy a bar of Li ink stick".

Paper is one of greatest inventions in China. Before the invention, Chinese characters were engraved on bones and tortoise shell, later, on bronze ware and stone, then on bamboo slips and thin silk. In the middle period of the Eastern Han Dynasty, a person whose name was Chai Lun invented a type of paper successfully, and was praised by the emperor at that time, who ordered the spread the paper to the whole country. Later, Chinese people made different kinds of paper according to the different requirements. The four most common ones are as follows:

Hard yellow paper—it can be kept very long, so in the past, it was used to copy Buddhist Scriptures, which have been kept perfectly well till now. Jin Hua paper (golden flower paper)—the one was mainly used to decorate. In the process of making such paper, gold was smashed into powder, which was sprinkled on colored paper or sticky paper. Mao Bian paper was made from bamboo, which was most appropriate for book printing in large quantity. Rice Paper is the one with more Chinese characteristics. It was offered as an article of tribute to emperors or courts in many dynasties. Rice paper is mainly used for traditional Chinese painting and calligraphy, which is soft but tensile and resistant to insect bites, absorbing ink evenly, and good for long term preservation. The style of Chinese painting and calligraphy is closely related to the properties of rice paper.

The Ink slab is a uniquely Chinese writing tool, which is used to grind ink stick for writing. Ink slabs have many kinds of shapes and materials. After the Han Dynasty, most ink slabs were round and pottery ink slabs were very popular. During the Sui and Tang dynasties, triangle shaped and tortoise shaped ink slabs were mainly used. The most popular ones were dustpan shaped ink slabs. Since the Song Dynasty, most ink slabs were made of stone. The great four famous ink slabs in China are Duan yan (Duan ink slab), She Yan (She ink slab), Taohe Yan (Taohe ink slab), and Dengni Yan (Dengni ink slab). Duan Yan is considered to be the best as it has many traits, such as moistness, durability, colourful materials and does no damage to the brush.

段落译文

毛笔在文房四宝中起源最早。1957年在河南信阳战国早期楚墓中发现了中国最早的毛笔。笔杆为竹质，笔毫用绳系在笔上。开始人们用鹿毛和羊毛制笔，称之为“兼毫”。唐代的书法艺术达到了一个高峰，笔的选材制作也更精良。元代以后，笔毫以羊毛为主，也有用鹿毛、狸毛、虎毛、羊须、狼尾、鹅毛、鸡毛等做笔毫。笔杆则用象牙、犀角、玉石、琉璃、瓷、珐琅、紫檀等珍贵材料制作。这些笔往往作为艺术品。

著名的“湖笔”产于浙江湖州。历来以选料精细、工艺精致考究、书画得心应手而闻名天下。相传秦国大将蒙恬曾在湖州善琏村用羊毫制笔，故被当地人奉为“笔祖”，并修建了蒙公祠以示纪念。

墨的制作也很早。新石器时代彩陶上的黑色，殷商甲骨、龟板上的墨书文字都无疑是天然的墨写成。最早的墨块是不能直接研墨的，而是要借助于研石。唐代书画艺术的大普及，促使制墨业有了进一步的发展。一些书画家也亲自制墨并成为高手。不少文人还收藏鉴赏好墨。至今还有很多名墨传世，成为文房中的艺术珍品。

墨中精品“徽墨”产于安徽省徽州地区。徽墨有“拈来轻、嗅来馨、磨来清”之妙，深得当时皇帝李煜赏识，并赐制造者“国姓”李。从此徽州“李墨”誉满天下，曾有“千金易得，李墨难求”的说法。

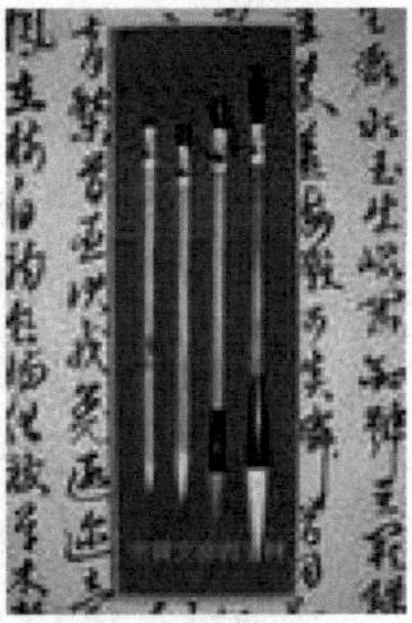

纸是我国最伟大的发明之一。在发明纸以前，文字主要契刻在龟板和甲骨上，后来有人把文字写在缣帛、竹筒、或木牍上。东汉中期，蔡伦制造出质地较好的纸张，得到了当时皇帝的称赞，并下令在全国推广。人们还为了各种不同的需要制造出了不同的纸张。其中最常用的有以下四种：

硬黄纸是能保持很久的纸。在中国古代有很多佛经都是用硬黄纸抄写的，至今保持完好。金花纸是将金子砸成粉末，洒在涂有胶料或有颜色的纸上制成，主要用来装饰。毛边纸是以竹子做原料制作而成，最宜于大量印书的纸张。宣纸是最具有中国特色的一种纸张。历代都作为贡品奉献朝廷， 用于写毛笔字和画国画。宣纸质地绵软坚韧，不容易破裂被虫蛀，吸墨均匀，适于长期保存。中国书画的独特表现方法及风格与宣纸的性能有着密切的关系。

砚是我国特有的文书工具，是用来研墨的。砚的形状和质地多样。汉代以后的砚多是圆形，并盛行陶砚。隋唐时期的大多数砚是三角形或龟形，但是最流行要数箕形砚。宋代以后主要以石砚为主。著名的四大名砚是端砚、歙砚、洮河砚及澄泥砚。端砚具有滋润、结实、色泽五彩缤纷、调墨不损笔豪等特点，为名砚之冠。

实用词汇

宣纸 rice paper
镇纸 paper weight
毛笔 writing brush
笔架 rest; pen rack; pen holder
笔筒 pen container; brush barrel
笔毫 writing brush
兼毫 fine long hair
墨 ink stick
墨汁 Chinese ink
研石 grind, pestle,

笔祖 writing brush founder
圆形 round
三角形 triangle
箕形 dustpan
铅笔 pencil
自动铅笔 propelling pencil; mechanical pencil
铅笔芯儿 black lead
卷笔刀 pencil sharpener
钢笔 pen
自来水笔 fountain pen
钢笔尖儿 nib
钢笔帽儿 pen cap
蘸水钢笔 pen with a nib fixed into a penholder
墨水瓶 ink bottle
圆珠笔 ball-pen; ball-point pen
石笔 slate pencil
蜡笔 crayons
粉笔 chalk

名言俗语

笔之强大胜过刀剑；笔胜于剑；文力胜过武力。
The pen is mightier than the sword.
笔乃心灵的喉舌；笔是手中之舌。
The pen is the tongue of the mind.
白纸和青春，最易留印痕。
Youth and white paper take any impression.
生活是一张白纸，每个人都在上面写上自己的一两句话。
Life ia a leaf of paper white, thereon each of us may write his word or two.
笔墨是才智之犁。
Pen and ink is wit's plough.

近墨者黑。

Bad company may corrupt a good boy.

好记性不如烂笔头。

The palest ink is better tan the best memory.

思想能跑，笔墨能言。

The thought has good leg, and the quill a good tongue.

世界上只有两种力量：刀和笔；而其结果后者总是战胜前者。

There are only two powers in the world, the sword and the pen; and in the end the former is always conquered by the latter.

俗语注解

洛阳纸贵：赞扬其著作广泛流行，风行一时。

Paper price soars means the price of paper soars in Luoyang. In fact it is a way to praise an exceptionally good piece of writing.

罄竹难书：比喻罪行很多，难以说完。

Too numerous to inscribe on all bamboo strips: Before the paper was invented the ancient Chinese people had used bamboo for writing. Today people use this idiom to describe a multitude of crimes committed by someone.

打笔墨官司：指书面上的争议。

To engage in written polemics; battle of words.

投笔从戎：指文人从军。

Throw aside the writing brush and join the army; throw away the writing brush and take up the sword.

笔走龙蛇：形容书法笔势雄健活泼。

Make vigorous and graceful strokes in calligraphy.

纸包不住火：指事实是隐瞒不了的。

Paper can't wrap up a fire; You can't wrap fire in paper which means that there is no way concealing the truth.

中西合璧

尽管西方的笔和墨水与中国笔墨的制作方式有所不同，但是用法却有相同之处，例如，西方人最早使用的鹅毛笔，也是要蘸墨汁才能使用的。据说我们现在使用钢笔是一百多年前一位叫华特曼外国商人发明的。因为那时的鹅毛笔存不住墨水，经常弄脏纸张，使他丢掉很多生意。因此，他对笔进行了改革，首先他给笔增添了皮囊储灌墨水，他又为笔设计了特殊的钢笔尖。从此，钢笔代替了欧洲人长期使用的鹅毛笔。

Although the production of the Chinese brush and ink is quite different from that of the west, the usages are similar. For example, the goose quills that the westerners used long time ago must be dipped in ink before they were used as Chinese brushes did. It is said that the fountain pens we use now were invented by a foreign businessman named Waterman more than one hundred years ago. Because the quill couldn't deposit the ink cleanly and often dirty paper, he failed to do a lot of business. So he decided to improve it. First, he added a reservoir to store ink and then designed a special writing point. Since then, the pens took the place of the goose quills which were used by Europeans for many years.

UNIT 13

Lute, Chess, Calligraphy and Painting

琴棋书画

题记

“琴棋书画”被誉为中国的四大古典艺术，而这四者作为艺术，在本质上确有相通之处，在手法上都表现为对虚实、均衡、张弛的把握，在意境上表现对深邃、灵动、高远的追求等。琴棋书画是中国文化的精髓，是风雅文化的象征，古往今来深得文人名士的推崇喜好。

“Lute, chess, calligraphy, and painting” are described as four major classical artistic forms or four arts in China. Among them, there are similarities in the way of the performance of authenticity, equilibrium and relaxation and the pursuit of the depth, smartness, and loftiness. They are the soul of Chinese culture, the symbol of elegance, which always wins the literary esteem of scholars and celebrities.

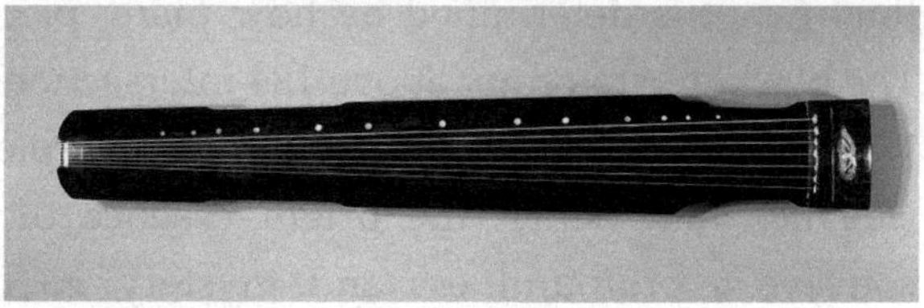

Lute, chess, calligraphy, and painting, are known as the “four arts”. They are Guqin, chess, calligraphy and painting, all of which the ancient Chinese literati admired, respected, and mastered. More than 2000 years ago, Confucius advocated that people should master six arts and here are two among them. In fact, the four mentioned here are the refinements of the six artistic forms, so in ancient China, all the literati loved them, and they became a symbol of the literate and educated.

Lute（**Qin**）, commonly known as "Guqin", is the oldest musical instrument in ancient China and was one of the earliest stringed instruments, and it is said to be the "father of Chinese music". According to the literary record, Qin has more than three thousand years of history. It is 130 cm long, 20 cm wide, about 5 cm thick. In total there are seven strings and on the panel there are 13 small round emblems used to mark the location of sound. Qin has a wide range, up to four octaves, meaning one can play many variations of the rich sound. Qin was the representative of the ancient scholars.

Chess（**Qi**）, in ancient China, mainly refers to Xiangqi and Weiqi. However, unlike literature, "Chess" means the elegant Weiqi. Weiqi originated from China, it has more than 2000 years' history up to now. Playing weiqi is called "duiyi", or "yi", both sides are always attacking and surrounding each other, thus, we call it weiqi. The chess-men（pieces）are divided into Black and White, symbolizing the Yin and Yang. There are 181 black and 180 white, with a total number of 361, exactly the same points on the chess board. When playing chess, we need to put the pieces on the checkerboard's intersections; they cannot be changed after being set down. Black has the first turn and then White, both sides do alternately in turn; we can also only put one piece down at a time. The final result is determined by how many pieces they hold on the intersection. The black must occupy above 184 intersections, while the white just needs over 178. The rules of Chinese chess are simple, but wit is the simplicity and elegance that depict the bright essence of Chinese culture. Chinese chess conveys a profoundness and mystery, so many rulers and even common people absorbed themselves in playing it, and it has also inspired plenty of legendary and charming stories, poetries, and even books on military strategies. Governing policies have also often been influenced by Chinese chess. It has been a gorgeous hallmark of Chinese civilization and history.

Calligraphy (**Shu**), namely Chinese calligraphy, is a unique Chinese artistic skill. It is sometimes accompanied with drawing, which is known as "calligraphy and painting". It is a kind of art that takes the Chinese character as the object, and a brush pen as a tool. After years of development, Chinese calligraphy has become a marvelous art form, with its unique style that changes constantly.

The history of calligraphy may be roughly divided into five categories: namely the seal script (big seal, small seal script), the official script, the regular script, the running script, and the cursive script.

Seal script: Big seal went previously to the small seal script. The big seal appeared in Western Zhou Dynasty, the strokes are powerful and dignified, the structure is shaped square and this formed its classic style. After Chin Shihuang unified China, the typeface had been simplified and unified, people called it Xiaozhuan ("small seal script"), the typeface was long and had the neat stroke circle as well as elegant form.

Official script appeared as early as in the Eastern Han Dynasty, and it is the basis of today's writing. Nevertheless, it was a revolution that changed the circle to the square, the joined-up writing to the session writing, from the line to the stroke, and all these are convenient for writing. This kind of style was popular among the lower officials in the court. Therefore, it was called the official script. The appearance of official script was a turning point in the evolution of Chinese calligraphy and laid a solid foundation for regular script.

Regular script is a type of calligraphy, which has gradually evolved from official script. It streamlined its shape from the flat size; because this typeface became tidy and formal, it eventually got the name of "kaishu"; therefore, this calligraphy can be used as a "sample" type to press a book. So far, it is still in use. Regular script was prevalent in Six Dynasties, and until Tang Dynasty, it became widely used, reaching its peak. This kind of calligraphy is still the most important for the beginners.

Running script is used to write the regular script swiftly. If it is similar to the regular script, we called it "Xingkai"; and if it is similar to the cursive script, we call it "Xingcao".

Cursive: Cursive can not be regarded as arbitrary scribble for it is based on its own principle. The greatest feature is that its art appreciation value which is superior to its practical value. Generally, it can be classified into two types: Zhang Cao and Jin Cao. Zhang Cao is a kind of official sketch, every character is independent but not written continuously; while Jin Cao is a fast regular script writing, up and down strokes between the characters are often found.

Chinese calligraphy takes the advantages of various lines to demonstrate various styles and elegance. The Chinese character, the brush pen and the cultural thought have created a unique artistic world.

Painting (**Hua**), namely, Chinese painting, "national" or "native painting" has distinctive ethnic features and a long traditional history. It is a valuable cultural legacy for the world. As early as the Warring States Period, more than two thousand years ago, the two paintings on silk of Chu Dynasty rested on their vivid pattern, simple style of drawing and smooth lines to express the perfect wonderland, which finally established the art of Chinese painting with lines to form the shape of the national style.

Traditional painting was done with a brush dipped in black or colored ink on fine rice paper or silk. According to the content, it can be divided into kinds: figure painting, landscape painting, flowers and birds painting. Figure painting was more mature in the Warring States period and reached its peak in the Tang Dynasty. Landscape painting was based on the theme of showing the natural beauty. Flowers and birds paintings focused on the flowers, birds, bamboo, fish and insects as its imagery. There are mainly two techniques in Chinese painting, which are meticulous—Gong-bi often is referred to as "court-style" painting and freehand—Shui-mo, loosely termed water colour or brush painting. The Chinese character "mo" means ink and "shui" means water. This style is also referred to as "xie yi" or freehand style. The characteristics of court-style painting original looks and strokes with great detail, focusing on detail depiction; freehand is a kind of exaggerated painting, the works are simple but vivid, with strong performance. Chinese painting focuses a lot on harmoniousness as well as poetic situations and has become one of the eastern great representatives against Western art styles.

段落译文

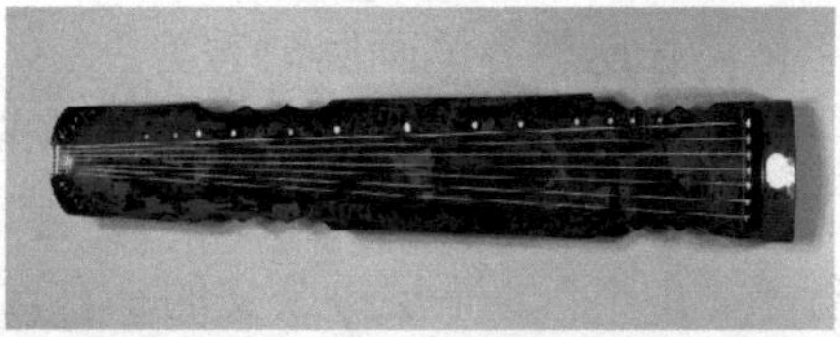

琴棋书画，又称“四艺”，指古琴、围棋、书法、绘画，是中国古代文人所推崇和要掌握的四门艺术。两千多年前孔子所倡导的为儒家所尊奉的便有两项在琴棋书画之中。琴棋书画其实是古人对六艺的精简和提炼，于是在漫长的中国古代，琴棋书画便成了士大夫们的钟爱，也成为文人雅士的标志。

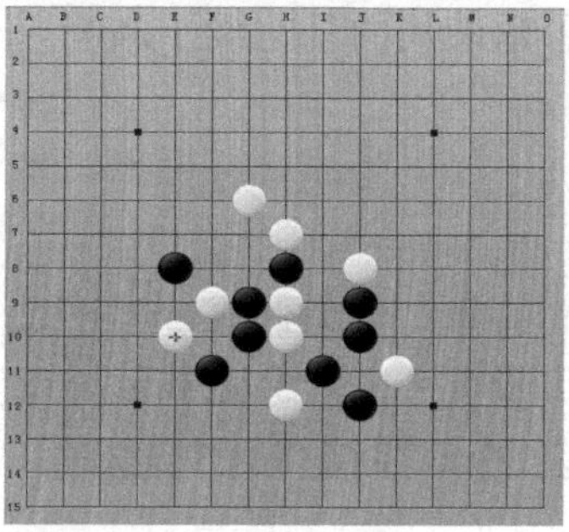

琴，也称“七弦琴”，俗称“古琴”，是中国古代最古老的乐器之一，是中国最早的弹弦乐器，称为“国乐之父”。据文献考证，琴有三千年以上的历史。琴全长 130 厘米，宽 20 厘米，厚大约 5 厘米，共有七根弦，面板上有 13 个小圆徽，用来标记音的位置。琴的音域宽广，达四个八度，可以奏出丰富的音色变化。琴被古时文人视为高雅的代表。

棋，在中国古代主要指围棋和象棋。不过，与琴棋书画合称的“棋”是指被古人看做高雅的围棋。围棋起源于中国，它迄今已有

2000 多年的历史。下围棋称为“对弈”、“弈”，有人根据下棋时双方互相攻击，互相包围的特点，称“下棋”是“围棋”。围棋的棋子分为黑白两色，象征着阴阳，其中黑子 181 枚，白子 180 枚，共 361 枚，恰好和棋盘的点数相同。下棋时棋子要下在棋盘的交叉点上，棋子下到棋盘上之后就不能再移动位置了。黑方先下子，随后白方落子，双方交互轮流下子，一步棋只能下一子；终局时以黑白方占据盘上交叉点的多少决定胜负。黑胜要占 184 个交叉点以上，白胜需占 178 个交叉点以上。围棋规则简单而变化无穷，体现出鲜明的中国文化思想精髓；千古以来，多少帝王将相、文人雅士，市井布衣乐此不疲，也演绎出多少传奇佳话、美文诗赋、乃至兵书演算法、治国方略，成为中华文明史上一朵绚丽的奇葩。

书，即书法，是中国特有的汉字书写艺术。历来与绘画并列，合称“书画”。它以汉字为表现对象，以毛笔为主要表现工具的一种线条造型艺术。经过千百年的创作和发展，中国书法已成为一门风格独特、奇妙无穷的艺术。

中国书法大体可分为篆书(大篆、小篆)、隶书、楷书、行书、草书(章、今草)等五种。

篆书：先有大篆后有小篆。大篆出现于西周，笔画雄强而凝重，结体略呈方形，风格典丽峻奇。秦始皇统一中国后，简化统一字体，后人称之为“小篆”，字体略长而整齐笔画圆匀秀美。

隶书：最早见于东汉，是今体的开端，是书界的一场革命字形变圆为方，笔画改曲为直，改“连笔”为“断笔”，从线条向笔画，更便于书写，这种书体流行于“隶卒”（下层办公文的小官)之中。故称为隶书。隶书的出现是汉字演变史上的一个转折点，奠定了楷书的基础。

楷书又称“正书”、“真书”。从隶书逐渐演变而来，更趋简化，字形由扁改方，特点在于规矩整齐所以称为楷法，是因为此书法可以作为“楷模”通行的书体，一直沿用至今。楷书盛行于六朝，至唐代出现了繁荣局面，达到了高峰。这种字体至今还是初学书法的关键。

行书：行书是楷书的快写。行书中带有楷书或接近于楷书的叫“行楷”，带有草书或接近于草书的叫“行草”。

草书：草书是按一定规律将字的点划连字，结构简、省，偏旁假借，并不是随心所欲地乱写。草书的特点是艺术欣赏价值大于实用价值。一般分章草和今草二种：章草是隶书简易快写书的书体，字字独立不连写；今草是楷书的快速写法，点画飞动，上下之间笔画痕迹往往牵连。

中国书法靠线条的变化表现不同的风采和神韵，由中国文字、书写工具和文化思想共同构成了一个独特的艺术世界。

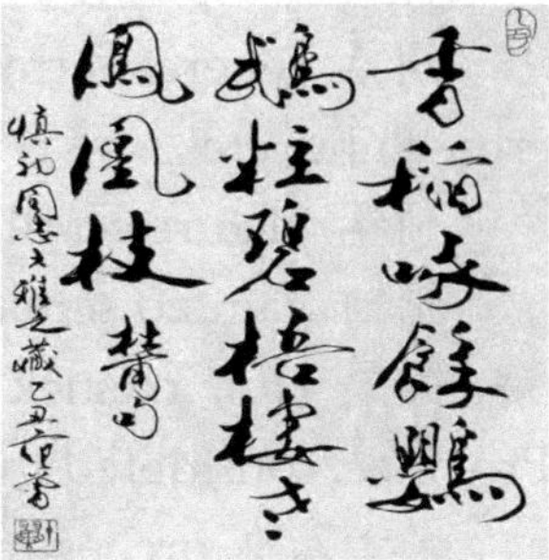

画，即中国画，又称国画，具有鲜明的民族特色和悠久的传统，是举世瞩目的珍贵文化遗产。早在两千多年前战国时期楚国的两幅帛画，就以其生动的气韵，简洁的笔墨，流畅的线条，表达出完美的意境，确立了中国绘画艺术以线条造型的民族风格形式。

中国画是用毛笔、墨和颜料在宣纸或绢上作画，按内容可分为人物画、山水画、花鸟画三种。人物画在战国时就比较成熟，唐朝达到顶峰。山水画以表现山川自然景色为主题的画种。花鸟画以自然中的花卉、竹石、鸟兽、鱼虫为描绘对象。按画法分工笔和写意。工笔画的特点是按照事物原来的样子，一笔一画非常细致，注重细节的描绘；写意画是一种概括、夸张的画法，笔墨简单但意趣生动，表现力强。中国画注重整体和谐并具有独特的诗性意境，在世界美术领域中自成体系，成为与西方艺术风格迥异的东方代表之一。

实用词汇

板胡 a Chinese two-stringed fiddle

编钟 chimes

帛画 painting on silk

帛书 book copied on silk

草隶 (of Chinese calligraphy) cursive executed characters in an ancient Han style, precursor to the cursive hand; cursive script and official script

草书 (of Chinese calligraphy) cursive script

草字 (of Chinese calligraphy) grass character—character written in the cursive hand

吹拉弹唱 blow, pull, pluck and sing—perform various kinds of instrumental as well as vocal

高胡 high pitched two-stringed musical instrument

高山流水 high mountains and flowing water—a bosom friend music

古琴 even-stringed plucked instrument

管风琴 pipe organ

胡琴 general term for certain two-stringed bowed instruments, such as erhu, jinhu, etc

画卷 picture scroll; magnificent scenery or stirring battle scene

画轴 painted scroll

徽墨 Hui, inkstick (originally produced in Huizhou, a prefecture in Anhui Province, considered the best of its kind)

急管繁弦 orchestral music with quick rhythm and rich melody

记谱法 musical notation

简化汉字 simplified Chinese characters

简谱 numbered musical notation

简体字 simplified Chinese characters

简写 write a Chinese character in a simplified form

交响诗 symphonic poem

交响乐 symphony

楷书 (in Chinese calligraphy) regular script

楷体 block letter

狂草 wild cursive hand (Chinese calligraphy with unbroken and winding strokes)

练笔 practise calligraphy

岭南画派 Lingnan School of Painting, one of the modern schools of Chinese brush painting

柳琴 a plucked stringed instrument

龙飞凤舞 like dragons flying and phoenixes dancing—lively and vigorous flourishes in calligraphy

芦笙 a reed-pipe wind instrument, used by the Miao, Yao and Dong nationalities

墨宝 your beautiful handwriting; treasured calligraphy or painting

琴棋书画 lute, chess, calligraphy, and painting—accomplishments of a scholar of the old school

琴瑟和谐 the qin and se are in harmony—a happy marriage

琴师 stringed instrumentalist, especially a jinghu player

琴书 story-telling, mainly in song with dulcimer accompaniment

琴心剑胆 the sentiments of lute and the spirit of sword—a cultivated mind animated with a chivalrous spirit

清明上河图 The River of Pure Brightness on the River

苏黄米蔡 Sushi, Huang Tingjian, Mi Fu and Cai Xiang, four noted calligraphers of the Song Dynasty

文房四宝 four treasures of the study—writing brush, ink stick, ink slab and paper

文翰 article; official documents and correspondence

跳棋 Chinese chequers

小篆 an ancient style of calligraphy, adapted in the Qin Dynasty for the purpose standardizing the Chinese script

书翰 Chinese calligraphy; letter writing

行书（of Chinese calligraphy）running script

宣纸 Xuan paper, a high quality rice paper made in Xuancheng or Jingxian of Anhui Province

颜体 the Yan style（a calligraphic style created by Yan Zhenqing of the Tang Dynasty）

瑶琴 fiddle inlaid with jade

玉版宣 strong white Xuan paper

月琴 a four-stringed plucked instrument with a full-moon-shaped sound box

运笔 wield the pen

赵体 Zhao style, a style of Chinese calligraphy created by Zhao Mengfu during Yuan Dynasty

正楷 regular script

名言俗语

一笔一画，循规蹈矩。

Dot the i's and cross the t's.

举棋不定。

"holding a piece and hesitating". People use it to describe anyone who is in tow mine.

文如其人。

Like author, like book.

画家和诗人有权撒谎。

Painters and Poets may have leave to lie.

勤思，寡言，少写。

Think much, speak little, and write less.

白字黑字。

Written in black and white.

词语注解

"扬州八怪"（金农、汪士慎、黄慎、李鲜、郑燮、李方膺、高翔、罗聘）是中国清代中期活动于扬州地区一批风格相近的书画家总称，或称扬州画派：画得怪、文章怪、性情怪、行为怪。他们开创了一代新画风，为中国绘画的发展立下了不朽的功业。

Eight Eccentrics of Yangzhou (the eight being Jin Nong, Wang Shishen, Huang Shen, Li Xian, Zheng Xie, Li Fangying, Gao Xiang and Luo Pin): They were all living and working in Yangzhou during the reign of Emperor Qian-long of the Qing Dynasty, they could be described as "eccentric" for their eccentric painting, eccentric articles, eccentric temper and eccentric behavior, and created new styles of painting and made a great contribution to Chinese Painting.

欧体：以唐代欧阳询为代表的书法

the Ouyang style, style of calligraphy represented by Ouyang Xun of the Tang Dynasty

破体字：不标准的汉字形式

a non-standard or corrupted form of a Chinese character

柳体：唐代柳公权创造的书法称柳体

the Liu style (a calligraphic style created by Liu Gongquan of the Tang Dynasty)

中西合璧

琴、棋、书、画，是中国文人雅士所推崇和要掌握的四门艺术。在世界艺术之林中，中国的四艺正如中国的书法，独具风格。自从有了文字就有了书法，中国书法是汉字的书写艺术。因为中国书法是在中国文化里产生、发展起来的，而汉字是中国文化的基本要素之一。以汉字为依托，艺术家们用毛笔而不是用羽毛创造、表达他们的思想和感情的书法，是中国书法区别于其他种类书法的主要标志；琴、棋、书、画，是我国传统文化中的瑰宝，也是陶冶情操，使人心情舒畅，促进心理健康的手段。

Qin, qi, shu , and *hua* , known as *siyi* (*four arts*), is a term used to describe four main accomplishments required of Chinese scholars. They are unique among the arts of the world. Chinese calligraphy is based on Chinese characters, which dates back to the origins of recorded Chinese history, in essence ever since writing has existed. Chinese calligraphy is said to be an expression of a practitioners poetic nature. Chinese calligraphy has evolved for thousands of years and differs from western calligraphic script in the sense that it was done with a brush instead of metal implements or a quill. Calligraphy, as well as the other three arts, was the art by which a scholar could compose his thoughts to be immortalized. It was the scholar's means of creating expressive poetry and sharing his or her own learnedness. The four arts are of treasures of traditional Chinese culture, a way to cultivate people's minds and to promote our mental health.

UNIT 14

Chinese Medicine

中 医

题记

中国是世界上医药发展最早的国家之一。中国的古典医书数量之大，名医人数之多，在当时的世界各国都是很少见的。几千年来，中医为人民解除了无数的疾病和痛苦，为中华民族的繁衍和昌盛做出了巨大的贡献。

China is one of the earliest countries in the world to develop medicine, and the number of classical Chinese medical books, written by famous doctors, was so large that it was a rarity at that time. For thousands of years, Chinese traditional medicine has relieved a lot of diseases and suffering from the Chinese people and has made a tremendous contribution to the reproduction and prosperity of China.

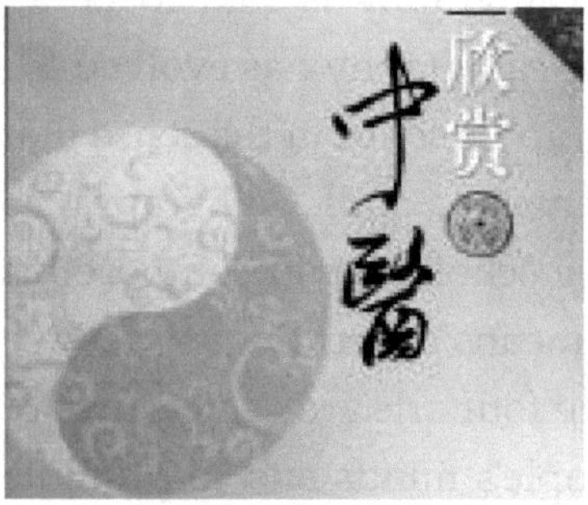

The formation of Chinese medicine can be traced back to the primitive period. We can see that Shen Nong tasted hundreds of herbs in ancient literature. The ancient people gradually invented some medical treatments, implements, methods and medicines, such as stone needle, moxibustion therapy, and herb soup. They used sharpened sides of stones as acupuncture needle to cut carbuncle, or to stimulate certain parts of the body to eliminate pain. Moxibustion means that the people alleviate pain or suffering with heated stones and sand, they also developed baking herbs to treat diseases. Herb soup is a common remedy, which was boiled in water or liquor. It is the earliest and widely used method of treatment in China.

There are four diagnosis methods in Chinese medicine. They are observation, auscultation and smelling, interrogation, pulse feeling and palpation. Observation mainly means to observe the patient's face, figure, tongue, urine; auscultation is to listen to the patient's speaking, breathing, moaning, breathing, and coughing sounds; smelling refers to sniffing the patient's breath and urine; asking about the background, such as the duration of the disease, symptoms, and living habits; pulse feeling and palpation means to read the pulse, check skin exposure, chest and abdomen. According to the theories of Chinese medicine, the four methods of diagnosis should be employed together for the correct diagnosis and the proper treatments.

The earliest Chinese medical book is "The Yellow Emperor's Canon of Interior Medicine", which has been one of the must-read books in Chinese medicine for thousands of years. The book discusses the details of the theoretical knowledge of the yin yang and five element principles of Chinese medicine, zang-fu, jinglou, causes of disease, diagnosis, treatments, and so on. The first book of pharmacology was published in the later Han Dynasty. It summarized the early medical experience and documented 365 kinds of herbs and their places of production, character, collection and the major functions of every medicine in great detail. The book had far-reaching influence and offered the great guidance to the development of Chinese medicine.

Four great Chinese medicine works are "The

Yellow Emperor's Canon of Interior Medicine", "Shen Nong's Canon of Herbs", "Shang Han Lun" and "Jin Gui Yao Lue". The last two of them were rearranged from "Shang Han Za Zheng Lun" which was written by a famous medical scientist Zhang Zhongjing. The book analyzed the medical cases using four methods of diagnosis from traditional Chinese medicine, observation, auscultation and smelling, interrogation, pulse feeling and palpation and selected more than 300 prescriptions. These prescriptions were the ancestor of current prescriptions and carried very high value.

There were many famous doctors in Chinese history, such as Bian Que, Hua Tuo, Sun Si Miao, Li Shi Zhen and so on. Bian Que was born during Warring States period. He could cure various diseases. He was good at pulse feeling and observation and was the founder of them. There are many stories about how he cured the sickness and saved patients. Once, as he was passing the state, Bian Que heard the prince of Guo had died. Bian Que entered the palace and observed the dead body of the prince carefully. He believed that the prince had not died so he used acupuncture to treat him. The prince regained consciousness at last. From then on, people spoke of him as a highly skillful doctor.

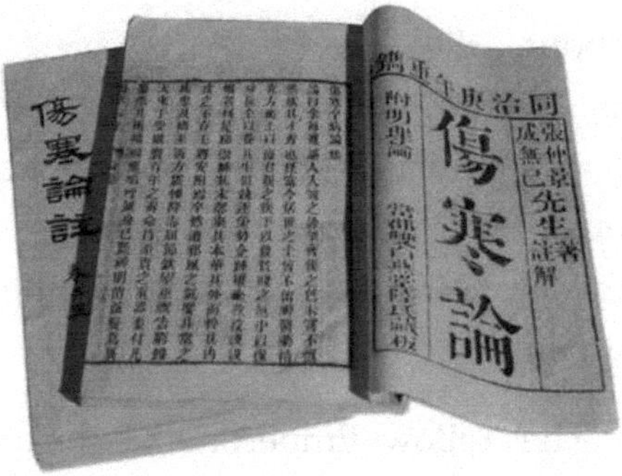

Hua Tuo was a famous doctor in the Eastern Han Dynasty. He was good at surgery and was the first to invent anesthetics. The patient who took his "Ma Fo San" could not feel any pain during the operation.

Sun Simiao was a famous medical expert of the Tang Dynasty. He specialized in the treatment of various diseases and cured many dying patients. On one occasion, he saved a pregnant woman who had already been placed in the coffin and helped the woman to give birth successfully. He also finished writing two medical books, "Qian Jin Prescriptions" and "Qian Jin Yi Fang", which included more than 6000 prescriptions. So he was called the king of medicine.

Li Shi Zhen was a well-known scientist of Chinese medicine during the Ming Dynasty. In order to write "the Compendium of Materia Medica", a Chinese medicine masterpiece with millions of words, he had hard work for 30 years, walking around the mountains and rivers of China and risking his life to collect and taste a variety of herbs. The book recorded 1892 kinds herbs and more than 1000 prescriptions. It was important work for the development of medicine and pharmacology throughout the world and has been translated into many languages.

More and more people have paid close attention to the mysterious medical effect of TCM. The Chinese medicine has made the great contribution to the progress and development of world medicine.

段落译文

中医的形成可以追溯到原始社会时期。从古代文献上我们就可看到"神农尝百草，始有医药"的传说。通过生产和生活实践人们逐渐发明一些医疗工具、方法和药物，如砭石、灸法、及汤药等。砭石是一种石器，古人用其尖锐的锋面切开痈肿，排脓放血，或刺激身体的某些部位以消除病痛；灸法是指人们用加热的石块或沙土来温暖人体的某些部位以缓解或解除病痛的方法，后来用点燃某种草药烘烤来治疗疾病。汤剂是将草药加水或酒浸泡后再煮一定的时间，去渣取汁，主要用于内服。汤剂是中医学使用最早、应用最广泛的治疗方法。

传统中医有四种诊断方法，即望、闻、问、切。"望"主要是观察病人的神色、形态、舌苔、大小便等；“闻”是指听病人的语言、呼吸、呻吟、喘息和咳嗽等声音，嗅病人的口气、大小便的气味等；“问”是询问病史、发病经过、现在的症状、生活习惯等；“切”是按病人的脉象和接触肌肤、胸腹等身体某些部位来查看有无异常情况。根据中医的理论，四种诊断方法必须综合运用，互相参证，才能弄清病情，正确治疗。

中国最早的医学著作是《黄帝内经》。此书详细地论述了中医学的阴阳五行、脏象、经络、病因、诊法和治疗等方面的理论知识。几千年来，此书成为中医学必读书籍之一。汉朝末期出现了我国第一部药物学专著《神农本草经》。书中总结了汉代之前劳动人民在实践过程中所创造的医药经验，记载了 365 种药物，并详细地记载了每一味药的产地、性质、采集和主治的病症等。此书对后世中医学的发展具有深远的影响和极大的指导价值。

著名医学家张仲景的《伤寒杂病论》被后人整理成《伤寒论》和《金匮要略》，两本书与《黄帝内经》 和《神农本草经》一起被称为中医四大名典。《伤寒杂病论》中运用望、闻、问、切四种诊疗方法分析病情，并收选了 300 多个精炼的药方，被后人称为众方之祖，有很高的使用价值。

中国古代有很多名医，其中最著名的有扁鹊、华佗、孙思邈、李时珍等。扁鹊是战国时期的人，他的医术高明，能治疗各种疾病。扁鹊精通望诊和脉诊，是中医诊脉法的创始人。史记中记载了很多扁鹊治病救人的故事。有一次，扁鹊路过虢国，听说虢国的太子死了，扁鹊进宫仔细观察太子的尸体，认为太子没死，他用针灸给太子治疗，太子果然苏醒了过来。从此人们称他为起死回生的神医。

华佗是东汉时期的医学家。他擅长外科手术，是世界上第一个发明麻醉剂的医生。病人服下他发明的“麻沸散”做手术就不会感到疼痛了。

孙思邈是唐朝著名的医药学家，他能治疗各种疑难杂症，救活过很多垂危的病人。有一次，他用针灸救活了一个已被放在棺材里的孕妇，并使该孕妇顺利产子。他还写了《千金药方》、《千金翼方》两本医书，共记载 6000 多个药方，被后人称为“药王”。

李时珍是明朝著名医药学家。他为了编写《本草纲目》这部上百万字的中国医药学巨著，历经 30 年辛劳，走遍了中国的山山水水，并冒着生命危险亲自采集和品尝各种草药。《本草纲目》共记载了 1892 种药物，10000 多个药方，是李时珍一生心血的结晶。后来这本著作被译成很多种文字，堪称是世界医药学的一部重要著作。

中医神奇的医疗效果得到了世界上越来越多人关注和认可。中医为世界的医学进步和发展做出了应有的贡献。

实用词汇

传统中医 Traditional Chinese Medicine ; TCM
《黄帝内经》The Yellow Emperor's Canon of Interior Medicine
《神农本草经》Shen Nong's Canon of Herbs
《本草纲目》the Compendium of Materia Medica; Bencaogangmu
《备急千金药方》Prescriptions Worth A Formulas for Thousand Gold and Precious for Emergency
《伤寒论》 Shang Han Lun
《金匮要略》Jin Gui Yao Lue
中药店 traditional Chinese medicine store; Chinese pharmacy
药柜 medicine drawer
中草药 medicinal herb; herbal medicine
砭石 stone acupuncture needle or piece
汤药 herb soup; decoction of medicinal ingredients
药丸儿 pills of Chinese medicine
膏药 medicated plasters
糖浆 medicinal syrup; syrup
药面 medicinal powder
清凉油 mentholated slave
望诊 observation; ask
闻诊 auscultation and smelling; hear
嗅诊 interrogation; questioning; ask
切诊 pulse feeling and palpation; touch
把脉 pulse feeling
叩诊 percussion

按诊 pressing
舌诊 tongue diagnosis
推拿疗法 naprapathy; anmo
针灸 acupunctur
灸术 moxibustion
拔火罐 cupping
推拿 massage
刮痧 gua sha
麻沸散 mafeisan / anesthetic
人工正骨法 manual bone-setting
补药 tonic
良药 good medicine
偏方 folk prescription
刀创药 drugs for incised wound
中成药 Chinese patent medicine

名言俗语

防病胜于治病。
Prevention is better than cure.
良药苦口利于病。
Bitter pills may have sweet effects. / Good medicine tastes bitter.
一分预防比得上十分治疗。/ 三分医，七分防。
An ounce of prevention is worth a pound of cure.
最好的医生是：饮食得当，清心静养，达观豪放。
The best physicians are Dr. Diet, Dr. Quiet and Dr. Merryman.
确诊病症，一半治愈。/ 对症下药，药到病除。
To know the disease is half the cure.
能给自己看病的才是好医生。
He is a good physician who cures himself.
宿疾难医。

A chronic disease is difficult to treat.

病来如山倒，病去如抽丝。

Agues come on horseback, but go away on foot. / Sickness comes like an avalanche but goes like reeling silk.

重病需下猛药。

Desperate diseases need desperate cures.

外科医生怎样好？眼明、胆大、手灵巧。

A good surgeon must have an eagle's eye, a lion's heart and a lady's hand.

时间是最佳药物。

Time is generally the best medicine.

欲劳于形，百病不能成。

Move your body, so hundreds of diseases will not infect you.

旧门久用，病夫命长。

A creaking door hangs long.

有病方知无病乐。

Health is not valued till sickness comes.

切莫讳疾忌医。

Hide nothing from your physician.

幸运的人才能遇到好医生。

It is the fortunate person that the physician undertakes to help.

词语注解

望闻问切：是指中医四种诊断疾病的方法

Observation, auscultation and smelling interrogation, pulse feeling and palpation are four methods of diagnosis on traditional Chinese medicine.

针灸：是针法和灸法的合称。针法是把毫针按进一定穴位刺进患者体内，用捻、提等手法来治病。灸法是把燃烧的艾绒按一定的穴位靠近皮肤或放在皮肤上，利用热来治疗疾病。

It means acupuncture and moxibustion. Acupuncture means to put filiform needles into the patient's body according to certain acupoints, treating ailments by twisting and pulling the needles, while moxibustion is to put burning moxa close to or on the skin according to certain acupoints, using stimulation of the heat to treat ailments.

麻沸散：是名医华佗发明的一种麻醉剂

An anesthetic which was invented by Hua Tuo, a famous doctor

扶正祛邪：增加抵抗疾病的能力，驱除疾病的影响

To foster resistance to disease and dispel pathogenic influence

灵丹妙药：灵验有效的奇药，比喻能解决一切的方法

A magic / wonder medicine. It also means the remedy for all problems.

同病相怜：患同样疾病的人互相同情

Those who have the same illness sympathize with each other

中西合璧

中医和西医在诊疗方面有很多不同之处。中医主要通过望、闻、问、切来诊病；西医则注重体温和化验等结果。中医往往从宏观的角度看问题，强调整体和辨证地治疗，西医则通常从微观入手进行诊疗。中医多用天然药物或针灸等疗法，西医则用化学合成药物或手术。目前比较受欢迎的是中西结合的医疗法——治疗阶段采用西医，恢复阶段选择中医。

Traditional Chinese medicine and Western medicine are very different in examination and treatment. The doctors of TCM give the diagnoses by observation, auscultation, smelling and pulse feeling and palpation. They often look at the illness from the macroscopic angle and stress the overall and dialectic treatment. The doctors in Western medicine focus on body temperature and laboratory results and treat the patients from a microcosmic point of view. Natural medicine and acupuncture are used in Chinese medicine while Western medicine practitioners prefer to use chemical synthetic drugs and surgery. At present, it is popular that during the treatment stage the patients turn to Western medicine and choose Chinese medicine in the recovery phase.

UNIT 15

The Chinese Way to Stay Healthy

养生文化

题记

中国有着五千多年的文明史，并保存着很多的灿烂文化，养生术就是其中之一。“养生术”是中国人民在生活中逐渐形成的。“养生术”的宗旨是让人们通过某些途径或方法保养和护理自己的身体，从而达到健康长寿。

China has a 5000 years civilization and a lot of splendid culture, one of which is staying healthy. It was developed through the experiences of Chinese people. The main purpose of it is to keep people fit and living longer by means of some methods.

The earliest experts at staying healthy were Confucius and Chuang Tzu. Confucius put forword some methods of healthy diet and also stressed the need to foster morals. “Xiao Yao You“ written by Chuang Tzu played a great role in the fostering of moral values and staying the health of Qigong. The best works of caring for life are “The Yellow Emperor's Canon of Interior Medicine”, “Lv Spring and Autumn”, and “Xing Qi Yu Pei Ming”. The first one emphasized the principles between the human and nature. The second suggested that people should keep in good health by adhering to principles of the four seasons. "Xing Qi Yu Pei Ming" expounded that Qigong exercises and medical Qigong should be used to stay healthy. These books have had a significant effect on the development of keeping in good health in China.

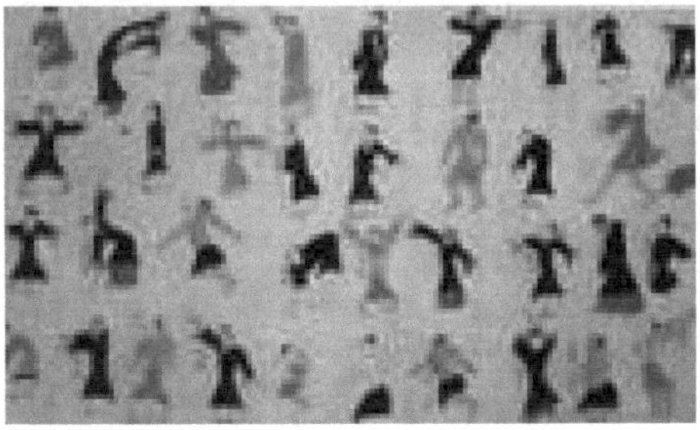

According to the ancient Chinese health experts, the Chinese ways to stay healthy could be divided into two aspects. One is the maintenance of the body configuration, known as "the way to maintain a good figure". The other is the maintenance of the spirit, which is called "repose".

In order to keep a good figure, people must do some exercises. An ancient and renowned doctor, Hua Tuo created the "the five-animal exercises", with which people physically exercise, to prevent diseases and extend life. The "five-animal exercises" is a set of exercises imitating five kinds of animals such as tiger, deer, bear, ape, and bird. Although the regular exercises can help people keep fit, it must be moderate. The appropriate amount of exercise is the key to keeping in good health because excessive exercise may be harmful.

Another key part to keep in good health in China is repose. There are many ways to rest to attain tranquility. Lao Zi believed that the key is to keep "quiet", and the most important part of it is being tranquil, thinking less, and having fewer desires.

Chinese medicine also places emphasis on a "diet regimen". Most Chinese people are firmly convinced that "kitchen physic is the best physic" and if the balance of food is not reasonable, it will be harmful to health. Chinese diet regimen requires a light diet and no rich food, eating both refined and coarse grains, more beans and vegetables with a regular quality at fixed times. There are many old sayings about diet and health, for example, "Eating radishes can keep a doctor away"; "If we want to keep fit, please don't eat too much"; "Many dishes make many diseases", and so on.

The Chinese diet regimen has a close relationship with the five flavors (sour, bitter, sweet, hot, and salted), the five internal organs (liver, heart, spleen, lung and kidney), and the four seasons (spring, summer, autumn and winter). In spring, more sour and sweet tasting food should be eaten because sour tasting food is good for the liver and sweet food can nourish the spleen. In summer, bitter is the main flavor to eat because most of the bitter tasting vegetables can relieve internal heat and eliminate fatigue. It is said that hot is a good flavor in autumn and salted food is suitable for winter. So in the dry autumn, people ought to eat more fruit and vegetables, such as pears, grapes, Chinese dates, lilies, and white fungus, which can nourish the lungs.

The old ways to stay healthy in China are extensive, profound and enigmatic. If people study them carefully, and practice, they can preserve their health, get rid of diseases and even prolong life.

段落译文

中国最早的养生家应该是孔子和庄子。孔子曾提出过一些关于饮食养生的方法，而且还强调养生须养德。庄子的"逍遥游"，对后来的精神修养和气功养生术有着很大的贡献。最著名的养生文献是《黄帝内经》、《吕氏春秋》和《行气玉佩铭》等。《黄帝内经》强调了人与天地自然相应的养生原则。《吕氏春秋》则重点提出了人们要顺应四时气候来养生的问题。《行气玉佩铭》简要地阐明了气功养生术。这些著作对中国后来的养生学的发展产生了重大的影响。

中国古代的养生家认为，养生可分为两个方面：一是对人们体形的保养，称为“养形术”；二是对人们精神上的养护，称为“养神术”。

人们若要养好“形”，首先要经常进行合理的运动。古代名医华佗创造了“五禽戏”来锻炼身体，预防疾病，以达延年益寿的目的。“五禽戏”实际上是一套模仿虎、鹿、熊、猿和鸟等五种动物的姿态和动作的体操。尽管中国养生术提倡人要经常运动来保养身体，但是要求“动”得适度，强调过量的运动反而对身体有害。因此，适量的运动，是养生之道的关键。

中华养生的另一个关键在于“养神”。如何“养神”的说法有很多。老子认为，养神的关键在“静”，而“静”的关键则在恬淡无为、少思寡欲。

中医学也很重视“饮食养生法”。大多数中国人都坚信“药补不如食补”，并认为如果食物搭配不合理，则有损身体健康。中国饮食养生要求清淡的饮食，多吃五谷杂粮，豆类和蔬菜。而且要定时定量，不可暴饮暴食。民间还有很多关于饮食养生的俗语和歌谣，例如，“萝卜入了口，大夫抄了手”；“要想身体好，吃饭不过饱”，“暴饮暴食疾病多”，等等。

中国的饮食养生还与五味(酸、苦、甘、辛、咸)、五脏(肝、心、脾、肺、肾)、四季(春夏秋冬)有着密切的关系。例如春季养生宜多吃些酸味和甘味食物来养肝补脾。因为中医认为酸味食物有增强消化功能和保护肝脏的作用。夏季养生要以苦味为主因为苦味的蔬菜大多具有清热的功能，因此夏季经常吃些苦味食物，能起到解热去暑，消除疲劳等作用。秋季气候干燥，饮食要以滋阴润肺为主，要多吃些梨、葡萄、大枣、百合、银耳等果蔬。古人还有秋宜辛，冬宜咸等养生的说法。

中国古老的养生术博大精深，奥妙无穷。人们若能认真学习和研究，并身体力行，则能达到强身健体，去疾去病的效果，更能延年益寿。

实用词汇

养生术，养生之道 way to stay healthy; way to care for life; regimen
健康长寿 have a good health and a long life; keep fit and live to a ripe old age
养神 rest to attain tranquility; repose; quietude
闭目养神 sit in repose with one's eyes closed
保养身体 care for life; preserve one's health; keep in good health; take good care of one's health
饮食养生法 diet regimen
定时定量 fix the time and fix the quantity
暴饮暴食 engorgement; immoderate drinking and eating
延年益寿 prolong life; promise longevity
五禽戏 the five-animal exercises
食疗 diet therapy; food therapy
开胃健脾 improving the appetite and invigorating the spleen
补血益气 enriching the blood and replenishing qi
保健气功 Qigong exercises and medical Qigong
运动健身疗法 exercise therapy

名言俗语

笑一笑，十年少；愁一愁，白了头。/ 心宽体胖。

Laugh and be fat.

饭后百步走，活到九十九。

After supper walk a mile.

宁愿健康清贫，不愿富裕多病。

Better is a poor man healthy in body than a rich man stricken in his flesh.

药补不如食补。/ 请医师不如请厨师。

Better wait on the cook than on the doctor. / Better bid the cooks than the mediciners.

病从口入。

Diseases enter by the mouth.

节食是良药。

Fasting is the best medicine.

健康与强身，价值超万金。/ 身安抵万金。

Health and strength is above all gold.

一闲生百病。

Lack of work brings a thousand diseases.

静养是生活的皇冠。/ 清静为生活之冠。

Quietude is the crown of life.

欢乐就是健康，忧郁就是病痛。

Cheerfulness is health; its opposite, melancholy, is disease.

人到四十，如果不是傻子，就该知道保养身体。

Every man at forty is a fool or a physician.

心胸坦荡寿命长。

A light heart lives long.

健康是人生第一财富。

The first wealth is health.

保持健康，是对自己的义务，甚至也是对社会的义务。

Keeping fit is an obligation not only to oneself but also to the society.

善养身者，使之能逸而能劳。

A person who is good at keeping fit makes his body adaptable to leisure and hard work.

保持健康的秘密就是适当的节制食物、饮料、睡眠和爱情。

The secrete to keep fit is a proper control of food, beverage, sleep, and love.

俗语注解

三月吃葱，五月吃蒜。医生没事全年傻玩。/ 葱蒜是个宝，常吃身体好。

Eat leeks in Lide and ramsin in May, and all the year after physicians may play.

（Lide :（古）三月。Ramsin = ramson: 大蒜）

食疗是最好的治疗。

Kitchen physic is the best physic.（physic（古）医学，医术）; Better bid the cooks than the mediciners.

健康者费鞋子，久病者费床单。寓意为多锻炼身体才能保持健康。

Sound men wear out shoes, sick men sheets. It also means it is better to do more physical exercises than go to the doctor.

一日一苹果，医生不找我。多吃水果有益于健康。

An apple a day keeps the doctor away. Fruit is good for us to keep fit.

中西合璧

在中西方各国，人们对养生有很多相似的观点。例如，中国俗语说："要想身体健，七分饱三分寒"，英语也有相似的谚语："饮食有节，医生失业"。苏格兰谚语是："暴饮暴食身体糟"，法国谚语"贪吃者自掘坟墓"，拉丁谚语"死于暴食者多于死于剑下者"。由此看来，中西方的养生方法在饮食适当、多吃蔬菜、少吃肉食等方面有很多共同之处。

There are many similar sayings in China and in western countries about how to stay healthy. For example, an old Chinese saying goes: "If you want to keep fit, leave with an appetite and dress less." There is a similar saying in English: "Feed by measure and defy the physician." "Many dishes make many diseases" is a Scottish proverb. A French proverb says: "Greedy eaters dig their graves with their teeth." And the Latin saying is "More are killed by gluttony than by the sword." Therefore, in order to keep fit, it is common for the people from the west and east to diet properly, eat more vegetables, and eat less meat.

UNIT 16

Chinese Wushu

中国武术

题记

中国武术博大精深，门派众多。它是人类文明的一大奇迹，也是中华民族传统的体育项目。在古代，人们练习武艺，主要是为了打斗时更好地克敌制胜。而现在，人们练习武术主要是为了强身健体。

Chinese Wushu is extensive and profound and it has a lot of schools. It has thousands of years of history and is an amazing symbol of traditional Chinese physical philosophy. In the ancient times, the main purpose of Wushu was to defend against the enemy in military affairs, but nowadays people practice it just to keep in good health.

Chinese Wushu can be traced back to primitive society. In the harsh struggle for survival, some attacking and defending skills were needed. In an effort to improve physical strength and advance their wisdom of hunting, the original Wushu was developed. After entering into a slavery and feudal society, fighting skills developed quickly as wars burst out very frequently. The turbulent society was another reason to promote people to practice Wushu.

Actually, Wushu or martial arts is a defensive and offensive combat system that includes many set patterns such as kicking, hitting, throwing, catching, hacking, and sticking.

During the long history of China, Wushu has been developed and perfected. There are many kinds of martial arts and different factions or groups. Two main boxing skills were formed in the Ming and Qing Dynasties, namely Shaolin and Wudang. Shaolin boxing is famous for its outside skills and Wudang has gained the good reputation for the inside skills. Long boxing, Short boxing, and Ditang boxing, belong to the Shaolin style and are mainly used for fighting. Only Taichi boxing and Eight Diagram belong to Wudang boxing, which are mainly used for defending and keeping in good health.

In addition to boxing, another important aspect of Chinese Wushu is the weapon skills, such as broad swords, swords, spears, cudgels, axes, hammers, and forks hooks, and halberds.

The most prosperous time of Chinese Wushu appeared in the Sui and Tang dynasties. From then on, it was a popular way to choose outstanding talents as military commanders from the martial arts competition. Many ancient heroes like Yue Fei were chosen from these competitions. It also improved the practice of martial arts in the whole country. At that time, soldiers practiced martial arts, so did scholars. It was said the most famous poets in China Li Bai and Du Fu also learned how to use swords when they were young.

Shaolin temple rising to prominence was one of the most important things in Chinese Wushu history. The temple is located on Mt. Songshan in Dengfeng county, Henan Province.

It is said that during the Tang Dynasty, the monks helped Li-shimin, a would-be emperor, making a great contribution to unite the states, thus the temple was given a handsome reward. Since then, the Kung Fu of Shaolin has been developed and became famous all over the world.

After the Southern Song and Northern Song dynasties, Wushu was popular among the ordinary people and became an important skill to keep good health and defend the homeland. As time went by, the military function of Chinese Wushu gradually weakened, but it became a popular way to keep fit. There has been a close relationship between martial arts and the ways to keep in good health, especially after the Qin and Han dynasties. It is these functions that have made Chinese wushu continue to flourish.

Chinese Wushu pays great attention to harmony from inside and outside and combining people's actions with their environment. People usually use something natural as conduct object when they practice it. The forms are often described as looking like a monkey, standing like a tree, sitting like a clock, as light as a leaf, and as quick as wind.

Nowadays, many physical education colleges and universities have set up Wushu specialities. There are a lot of Wushu enthusiasts in China and abroad now. Chinese wushu has been officially listed as a sports competition project, and has obtained a greater promotion and popularization.

段落译文

中国武术的源头，可以追溯到原始社会。在严酷的生存斗争中，人们自然产生一些拳打脚踢的初级攻防手段。在狩猎活动中，人们不断改善体力、提高智慧，于是就出现了原始形态的武术。进入奴隶社会和封建社会后，民族、国家之间经常爆发战争，武术的格斗技能在军队中得到重视和发展。社会动荡不安也大大促进了民间习武之风。

所谓武术，就是以踢、打、摔、拿、劈、刺等技击动作为主要内容，组成进攻和防守套路的对抗形式。

在漫漫的历史长河中，武术得到了极大的发展和完善，形成了许多武术套路，以及不同的流派。例如，明清时期，中国拳术已初步形成两大派别，即“北派少林”和“南派武当”。少林以外家拳著称于世，而武当则以内家拳名闻天下。外家拳的种类很多，包括长拳、短拳、地躺拳等，主要用于格斗。内家拳的种类主要有“太极”和“八卦”两种，其特点是“以静制动”，“主在御敌”，更侧重于健身。

除了拳术外，中国武术的另一个重要方面是运用武器和器械形成的武术套路，如刀术、剑术、棒法和枪法等。中国武术的主要器械有刀、剑、枪、棒、斧、锤、叉、钩、戟等多种。

隋唐时期，中国武术出现了空前繁盛的局面。后来各代朝廷都采用武术考试的方法来选拔武艺出众的人才担任军事统帅，如民族英雄岳飞等。此项举措大大促进了官方和民间的练武活动。当时不但武人练武，文人也以配剑，舞剑为荣。著名诗人李白、杜甫年轻的时候都学过剑术。

少林寺的崛起是中国武术史上的一件大事。少林寺位于河南省登封县的嵩山上。据说唐朝时期，少林寺的武僧帮助秦王李世民作战，为唐朝统一天下立下汗马功劳，少林寺因此受到了皇帝的封赏。从此，少林寺武功日益发展，并扬名天下。

自两宋以后，武术运动开始向民间发展。武术成为中国劳动人民强健身体、保家卫国的重要手段。随着时间的推移，中国武术在军事战斗中的作用逐渐减弱，强身健体的作用日益突出。特别是秦汉以后，养生术与武术更是密不可分。可以说，武术之所以能发展至今，并日益兴旺发达，是与它具有健身和防身双重作用分不开的。

中国武术讲究“内外合一，形神兼备”。常把大自然的景物作为练武的参照对象，如把武术动作形容成“动如猿”、“站如松”、“坐如钟”、“轻如叶”、“快如风”等。

目前，中国的很多体育院校都设立了武术专业。国内外有很多的武术爱好者。武术已被正式列为体育竞赛项目，得到了更好的推广和普及。

实用词汇

武术 Wushu
功夫 Kung-fu; martial arts
中国拳术 Chinese boxing
外家拳；少林拳 Shaolin Boxing; Shaolinquan
长拳 Changquan; Long Boxing
短拳 Duanquan
地躺拳 lying boxing
南拳 Nanquan; South Boxing
猴拳 monkey-style boxing
蛇拳 snake-style boxing
太极拳 Taichi Quan
八卦掌 eight-diagram boxing
武术器械 Chinese traditional weapons
枪术 spearplay
棍术 cudgel play
剑术 sword play
刀术 broadsword play
武僧 military monk
武艺高强 adept in wushu skills
治病防身 to cure illness as well as for self-defense
健身 promote health
套路 forms
武林高手 martial arts masters
武林新秀 new martial arts specialist
武侠 knight; swordsman
武侠小说 swordsman fiction

名言俗语

最有效的防御是进攻。/ 进攻是最好的防卫。

The most effective defense is offense. / Offense is the best defence.

稳扎稳打，无往不胜。

Slow and steady wins the race.

知彼知己，百战不殆。

Know the enemy and know yourself, and you can fight a hundred battles with no danger of defeat.

会战斗会退却的人，才有可能保存自己，他日再战。

He that fights and runs way may live to fight another day.

化敌为友。/ 化干戈为玉帛。

Make your enemy your friend.

强中自有强中手。

Diamond cut diamond.

以其人之道还治其人之身。

Do unto him as he does unto others.

自我保护，天经地义。

Self-preservation is the first law of nature.

害人之心不可有，防人之心不可无。

Never harbor the intent to victimize others; but never let guard down against being victimized.

文武难双全。

One who has literary tastes is rarely expert in military exercises.

俗语注解

文武双全：人具有一定的文才并且武艺高强。

Be well versed in both polite letters and martial arts; adept with both pen and sword.

路见不平，拔刀相助：看到不公平的事，出手帮助。

See injustice on the road and draw one's sword to help the victim , which really means to take up the cudgels for injured party.

拳不离手，曲不离口：指无论是是武术还是唱歌都要经常练习。

A boxer never spends a day without practising boxing, and a singer never passes a day without practising singing; practice makes perfect.

十八般武艺：指使用十八种古式兵器的武艺，一般用来比喻各种技能。

Skills in wielding the 18 kinds of ancient Chinese weapons, and also means the skills in various fields of work.

中西合璧

众所周知，中西技击术正在互相逐渐融合。例如，美国一项新的搏击运动——踢拳术(Kick-boxing)悄然兴起。它是与东方武技的相互交流和切磋的基础上形成的，是具有现代风格的美国搏击运动。另外，李小龙的截拳道也是中西武术融合的典型范例。

As we all know, Chinese and Western arts of attack and defense techniques are mixing together gradually. For example, a new combat sport, kick boxing has become popular in the United States. It is a modern style of American Combat, which is formed on the basis of the mutual exchange and interflow of both western and oriental martial arts. Jeet Kune Do created by Bruce Lee is another typical example of integration of Chinese and Western martial arts.

UNIT 17

Traditional Chinese Weapons

中国古代兵器

题记

中国兵器是指从原始社会晚期到清朝晚期军队和民间所使用的进攻性兵器和防护装具的总称。古时候，人们为了争取生存空间，氏族或部落之间不断发生争斗，于是带锋刃的生产工具被用于人们互相残杀。到了新石器时代晚期人们已熟练地掌握磨制石器的技能，开始制造进攻性兵器了。中国主要包括远射兵器、格斗兵器和卫体兵器等。

Traditional Chinese weapons refer to offensive weapons and protective equipment, used by the Chinese military and civilians from the late primitive society to the late Qing Dynasty. During ancient times, in order to survive there were a lot of fights among clans and tribes, so tools with sharp points or cutting edges were used as weapons. By the late Neolithic period people had mastered the skills of polished stone tools and started to make offensive weapons, many of which were long-range weapons, combat weapons, body-protection, and so on.

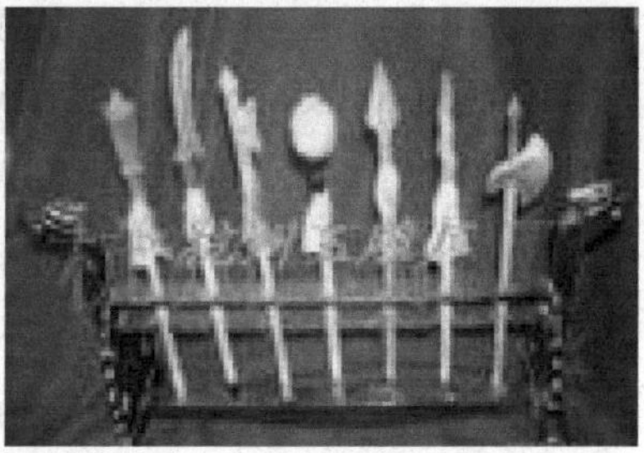

With the constant changes and the development of the materials and processes, hundreds of kinds of ancient Chinese weapons have been invented. They were divided into short weapons, long weapons, and hidden weapons.

Generally speaking, the length of the short weapon was not taller than an ordinary person's eyebrow and was light enough to be used with one hand. Knives and swords are the most common short weapons. There are two kinds of swords in China known as the Wen Sword, which has a tassel at the handle, and the Wu Sword , the one without a tassel. The mace, hook, and ax belong to short weapons, too.

The most common long weapons are spears, machetes and staffs. The spear is the king of them. In Chinese history, there were a lot of heroes who used spears, such as the famous generals Yue Fei and Yang Zaixing in the Song Dynasty. The Broadsword is a long-handled blade, which was usually 3 meters long and 7.5 kilograms in weight in Tang Dynasty. The weapon used by the famous general Guan Yu in "Three Kingdoms" was a type of broadsword known as the crescent moon shaped sword.

There are many types of sticks such as long sticks, Qimei sticks, three-section cudgel. Many monks of world-famous ShaolinTemple used the stickss as weapons. It is said that once a group of bandits rushed into the Shaolin Temple and defeated many monks. A monk with fire stick jumped out of the kitchen and trounced the bandits, since then the monks in Shaolin Temple have used sticks as weapons. Halberds, forks and shovels and palladiums which were farm tools also belong to long weapons.

Hidden weapons are easy to carry out an attack in secret. They are small, portable, quick and very powerful, when used at close range. They are divided into four types: hand-throwing, cable hitting, machine firing and spraying.

Hand-throwing hidden weapons are most extensively used, among which are javelins, darts, money darts, flying knives, stones, needles, flying rings, etc. The ancient people who were good at kung-fu often used the pocket coins as hidden weapons. The flying ring was made of iron and had a diameter of 15 cm and hit the enemy by flying. People adept in Wushu could throw two of them at once. In *Journey to the West*, the classic Chinese fairy tale, Nezha, the third prince, took a flying ring as a weapon and often defeated his enemies with it.

The cable hitting hidden weapon which has a long rope and can be thrown and taken back at will. The most common ones are meteor hammer, rope barbell, soft whip. The machine firing hidden weapon is the arrow in the sleeve. People tie the arrows tin to the arms, covering it with their sleeves. When the spring button is pushed the arrow can be fired forward and some of them can fire continuously.

In China, most of the people who practice martial arts can use a variety of weapons. Some people who are adept in martial arts are often known as being adept in the 18 kinds of martial arts, which means that they have skills in wielding the 18 kinds of ancient Chinese weapons. However, different dynasties had different views about the 18 kinds of weapons, but they were the most commonly used weapons in actual combat at that time. Therefore, they generally refer to all ancient Chinese weapons.

段落译文

随着材料和工艺不断地变化和发展，中国的古代兵器总数多达数百种，分为短兵器、长兵器和暗器等三种。

短兵器的长度一般不超过常人的眉际，重量较轻，常指能单手使用的兵器。其中刀和剑是最常用的。中国的剑有文剑和武剑之分，在剑柄配有剑穗的剑为“文剑”。没有剑穗的剑称为“武剑”。短兵器还包括锏、钩、斧等。

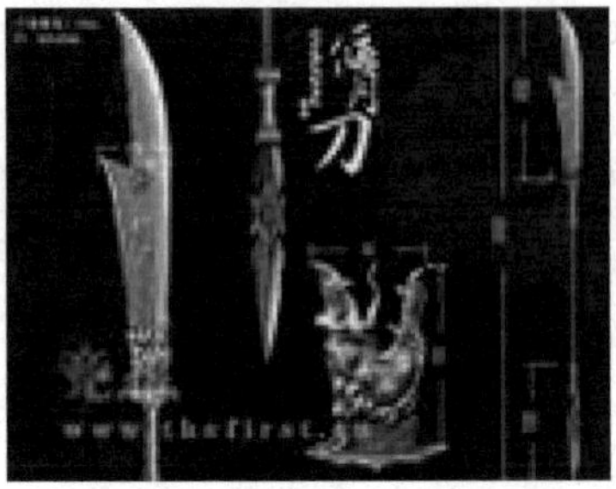

长兵器中人们最常使用的是枪、大刀和棍。在中国众多兵器中，枪被称为“百器之王”。中国历史上出现过很多使枪的英雄，如宋代名将岳飞、杨再兴等。大刀是刀上安装长柄。唐代的大刀长为 3 米，重 7.5 公斤。中国名著《三国演义》中的名将关羽所使用的兵器就是大刀的一种——偃月刀。

棍的种类也比较多，通常有长棍、齐眉棍、三节棍等。世界闻名的少林寺武僧多以棍为武器，因此少林棍法闻名于天下。传说少林棍是来自烧火棍。有一次一群流寇闯进少林寺，僧人们被打得节节后退，这时从厨房跳出一个拿烧火棍的僧人，把流寇打得落花流水。从此少林寺的僧人就开始把烧火棍当兵器练习了。长兵器中还有戟、叉，及由农具演变成兵器的铲和钯等。

暗器是指便于在暗中进行袭击的兵器。暗器体积小，携带方便，且速度快，威力大，是中国武林人士近距离对打的常用兵器。暗器分为手掷、索击、机射、药喷四大种类。

手掷类暗器是所有暗器中应用的最广泛的一种，有标枪、飞镖、金钱镖、飞刀、鹅卵石、梅花针、乾坤圈等。其中金钱镖是古时练武之人常当暗器使用的随身携带的铜钱。乾坤圈是铁制的圆圈，一般直径 15 厘米，抛出后以旋飞击敌。武艺高强的人可一手抛出两个铁圈。中国经典神话故事《西游记》中的哪吒三太子的兵器之一就是乾坤圈，并多次以此反败为胜。

索击类暗器是指本身带有长索，发出后又可立即收回的兵器。主要有流星锤、绳镖和软鞭等。机射暗器是以袖箭为主。使用之人将箭筒绑在小臂处，用衣袖遮盖住，筒上有弹簧机关，一按机关，袖箭即可向前射出，有的可连续发射。

在中国，一般的习武之人都会使用多种兵器。因此人们经常把武艺高强的人称为精通十八门武艺。这里的十八门武艺是指会使用十八种兵器。但是十八种兵器究竟是指哪些兵器，各个朝代和派别都有各自不同的说法。但都是指在各时期实战中最常用的兵器，因此常用来代替中国兵器的统称。

实用词汇

短兵器 short ancient weapons

长兵器 long ancient weapons
暗器 hidden weapons
戈 dagger-axe
矛 lances; spears
戟 halberd
枪 spears
刀 knife; sabre
大刀 broadsword; machetes
偃月刀 crescent-moon-shaped sword
剑 swords
长穗单剑 long-tassel sword
短穗单剑 short-tassel sword
斧 axes; hatchets
钩 hooks
锤 hammers
流星锤 meteor hammer
绳镖 rope barbell
叉 forks; trident
抓(飞钩) clawlike weapon; flying hooks
挝(双飞挝) twin flying hooks
弓 bow
矢(箭) arrow
盾 shield
匕首 dagger
铲 spade
月牙铲 crescent spade
鞭 whips
三节鞭 three-section whip
锏 mace
钺 battle-axe; tomahawk
棍 stick; cudgel; staff

三节棍 three-segmented cudgel

乾坤圈（qiankun）flying ring

名言俗语

明枪易躲，暗箭难防。

Better the devil you know than the devil you don't know. Better an open enemy than a false friend.

一箭双雕。

Catch two pigeons with one bean.

箭未上弦休拉弓。/ 不打无准备的仗。

Draw not your bow till your arrow is fixed.

杀鸡用牛刀。/ 用矛刺杀苍蝇。

He takes a spear to kill a fly.

远射难杀鸟。/ 强弩之末，势不能穿鲁缟。

Far shooting never killed bird.

人舌利如剑。

Men's tongues are a sharper weapon than the sword.

获胜靠勇气，不是靠兵器。

Courage wins the victory, not the sword.

刻舟求剑。

A lost sword means finding a lost sword by marking the gunwale of a moving boat.

手中只有一支箭的猎人会更谨慎地射击。

A hunter who has only one arrow does not shoot with careless aim.

笑里藏刀。

A dagger can be concealed in a smile.

手握武器才会有和平。

Weapons bode peace.

俗语注解

百步穿杨：指人能在一百步以外射中柳树的叶子。现在用来形容箭法或枪法非常高明。

shooting a willow leaf; to shoot an arrow through a willow leaf hundred paces away. Now it is widely used to describe an expert marksman regardless wether he uses an arrow, a stone, a knife, or a gun.

班门弄斧：在有名的木匠——鲁班门前摆弄斧子。比喻在行家面前卖弄本领。

A carpenter shows his proficiency with axe before Lu Ban—a master carpenter. Today, it is cited either to ridicule someone who displays his slight skill before an expert or to express one's modesty when demonstrating a skill in front of colleagues.

鸟尽弓藏：比喻事情成功以后，把曾经出过力的人一脚踢开。

"When birds are gone" means to put away the bow after the birds are gone, which also refers to the practice of kicking out the assistants when their services are no longer needed.

自相矛盾：经常用来形容不能自圆其说的人。

Spear and shield; attacking one's shield with his own spear. It is often used when people contradict themselves or their behaviour contradicts their position.

中西合璧

东西方兵器发展的相同之处是很多兵器是由日常生活或耕种的工具演变而来。例如欧洲的十字弓和中国作战使用的弓箭是由用于狩猎的传统弓箭发展而来。农民起义，最容易获得的武器当然是身边的农具。镰戟就是由欧洲人收割小麦所用的长柄镰刀演变的。短斧原是欧洲人常用的工具，也成为一种兵器。古时步兵经常选择斧来当做肉搏时的近身武器。

There were many similarities in the weapons development of East and

West countries. A lot of weapons evolved from the tools for daily life and cultivation. For instance, both the European cross bow and the bow from China evolved from the bow and arrow that were used for hunting. When peasants revolted, the most available weapons were the farm tools around them. Scyberd evolved from the long-handled sickle that was used by the Europeans during the wheat harvest. The Hand axe was originally a common tool in Europe, it was used as a melee weapon by ancient foot soldiers.

UNIT 18

Chinese Personal Names

中国姓名

题记

中国人的姓氏，从其开端、发展、演变的漫长历史看，曾是中华民族物质生活和精神生活的主要环扣之一。在政治、文化及社会活动诸领域中，都发挥着极其重要的作用，从而形成了举世无双、特色独备的中国传统姓名文化。

Chinese naming used to be the key point in Chinese material and spiritual life. From the very beginning it has played a big role in the process of development and in various fields such as politics, culture and social activities. As a result, Chinese traditional naming culture remains of exceptional global importance.

The naming culture is an important component of Chinese traditional culture. In the development of our society, it has various functions, and has played different roles in different periods of time. The occurrence and development process of Chinese names not only reflects the vicissitudes of five thousand years of Chinese history, but also reflect the origins of Chinese culture.

In ancient China, naming was very complicated

and involved process including the naming of a person, a tribe, or a place where a person lived. Surnames represented a common blood relationship on behalf of the ethnics, while names were derived from surnames. The purpose of adopting Xing, was appropriate for one person to marry another. If a boy and a girl had the same Xing(姓)but their Shi(氏)was different, they could marry each other. However, if the opposite was true, they were not allowed to get married. It shows that Chinese people knew that marriage between close relatives might breed unhealthy and less intelligent offsprings. Xing and Ming became integrated as Xing, a family name, since Han Dynasty. Our surnames nowadays are mostly passed down from generation to generation, and have been there for thousands of years.

Primarily, we have 13 kinds of surnames according to the study. First, Xing and Shi were the same in matriarchal society, people took their surnames from their mothers' names, so many of the old names have a character "女", as left part of the names as Jiang (姜), Yao (姚), Ji (姬), etc., even the character Xing (姓) is formed with nv (女) and sheng (生). Another kind of surnames was from the names of the ancient states as Song, Qi, Lu and Zheng, etc., titles as Sima, Sikong; the landforms and physiognomy of residence, natural phenomena as Dongge, Ximen, Chi, Liu. The names of professions as Tao (a person who made pottery); the names of their ancestors as the name of Huangdi, XuanYuan turned to be a family name. The names of totem as dragons, oxen, horses, poplars and plums, so on and so forth.

Chinese people generally have one family name and two or more names. One-word name is a single surname, while names with two or more words are double-barreled surnames. Two words or more than two words are combined surnames. We have had no exact number as for the surnames up to now. Baijia Xing—One Hundred Surnames, a book complied in North Song Dynasty, listed 472 surnames, beginning with Zhao, Qian, Sun and Li and 60 double-barreled surname. The statistics shows, that we have 6362 surnames in literature. The most common family names are Zhang, Wang, Li, Zhao and Liu. While Zhuge, Ouyang, Sitou and Sima, the most common double-barreled surnames.

Our Chinese names carry our traditions and features with family names first followed by the given names. In ancient China names were more complicated than the ones now, people had Zi and Hao in addition to Xing and Ming. Ancient Chinese people's Ming and Zi were often related and they complemented each other, Quyuan was named Ping with Zi as Yuan, for instance. As given names, all Chinese traditionally received a "milk name" at birth, and a "formal name" when entering school. In ancient China, when boys were 20 and girls were 15, they would have formal names. Besides, the literates or people with titles had Hao. Hao was a person's complimentary address or honorific title, which is similar to today's pseudonym. The ancient Chinese scholars took the names of the places, in which they lived or their interests as their Hao. For example, Li Bai, a poet in Tang Dynasty, lived in a village called Qinglian in childhood, so he named himself Qinglian Jushi as his Hao. People called themselves by their given names, while the others by their Zi or Hao to show their respect.

Chinese names have special meanings and show their parents' wishes and expectations. Girls' names reveal that their parents want them to be nice, while boys' to be strong and brave. Some of the names represent a time, place, or natural phenomena from the time when they are born such as Jing（京，Beijing）, Chen（晨，morning）, Dong（冬，winter）, or Xue（雪，Snow）, etc. Others wish for virtues such as Zhong（忠，loyal）, and Li（礼，polite）, etc. Some names represent health, longevity and happiness, Jian（健，healthy）, Shou（寿，long life）, Song（松，pine tree）and Fu（福，happiness）. Masculine persona in names often show braveness such as Tiger（虎）, Dragon（龙）,

Strong and Great (刚强), etc., while feminine persona in names are often seen as Wind (风), Flower (花), Jade (玉), and Color (彩). Modern names sometimes are influenced by foreigners so parents name their babies Mary (玛丽), Yangzi (洋子) or Henry (亨利).

Chinese names are not only symbols of social status and etiquette, but also signify Chinese culture, social development and change.

段落译文

姓氏文化是中华民族古老文化的一个重要组成部分。随着社会的发展，姓氏在不同的历史阶段具有不同的职能，起着不同的作用。我国姓氏的产生、发展过程既体现了中国历史五千年的沧桑，也反映出中国文化的渊源传承。

在古代中国，姓名非常复杂，而且包含了很多内容，诸如部族的名称、居住的名称等。姓代表有共同血缘关系的种族标记，氏是姓的衍生分支。采用姓氏的目的是为了区分种族以及男女双方婚配是否合适。氏同，姓不同者，可通婚；姓同，氏不同则不可以通婚，这表明古时人们就已清楚近亲结婚所生的后代会不健康或智力低下。从汉代开始，姓氏合一，统称姓。现代中国人的姓，大部分是从几千年前代代相传下来的。

考其来历，大致可分为 13 种，主要有：以姓为氏。母系氏族社会，以母亲的名为姓，所以，很多古姓都有“女”字旁，如姜、姚、姬等，就连“姓”字本身也是由“女”、“生”二字合成的；以国名为氏；如宋、齐、鲁、郑等；以邑(皇帝的封地)为氏。以官职为姓；如司马、司空等；以住地的方位和景物为姓；如东郭、西门、池、柳等。以职业为姓；如做陶器的人姓陶。以祖先的名号为姓，如中国人的祖先黄帝名叫轩辕，后来，轩辕就成了一个姓。以图腾为姓；如龙、牛、马、杨、梅等。

中国人的姓有一个字的，也有两个字和两个字以上的。一个字的是单姓，两个字或两个字以上的是复姓。中国到底有多少个姓，到现在也没有准确的统计数字。宋朝时，有个读书人写了一本《百家姓》，里面收有以赵、钱、孙、李开头的 472 个单姓，60 个复姓。有人统计，见于文献资料的姓氏有 6362 个。张、王、李、赵、刘等是中国最常见的单姓，诸葛、欧阳、司徒、司马等是中国最常见的复姓。

中国人的名字具有自己的传统和特点。我们的姓名都是姓在前、名在后。古代中国人的姓名比现代人的更复杂， 除了姓、名以外，还有字、号。名和字既有区别又有意义上的联系。字是对名的解释和补充：如屈原，名平、字原。在起名时，中国人一般在刚出生时取一个“乳名”，入学后会有一个“大名”。古时男子到了 20 岁，女子到了 15 岁时，要取一个正式的名称。有地位、有文化的人还要有号，号是除一个人名字以外的称谓，是一种美称或是对某人的尊称，和现在的笔名差不多。古代文人往往以自己的住地或志趣为自己取号，如唐代诗人李白幼年居住在四川的青莲乡，他就给自己取号青莲居士。自称用名，称他人用字或号，以示礼敬。

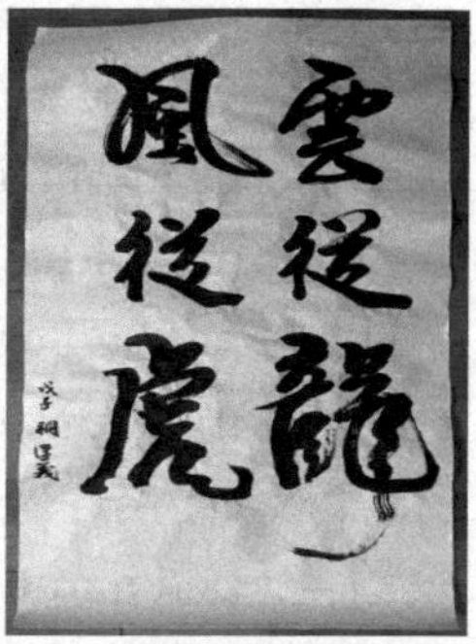

中国人的名字特别讲究、要有特别的涵义、有特点并表示父母对后代的的愿望。女孩的名字寄托父母祝福，有祝她们美丽贤良的意思；男孩的名字一般有强壮、勇敢之意。有的名字还体现着孩子出生时的地点、时间或自然现象，如“京、晨、冬、雪”等。有的名字表示父母希望孩子具有某种美德，如“忠、义、礼、信”等。有的名字则表示健康、长寿、幸福，如“健、寿、松、福”等。男人的名字和女人的名字也不一样。男人的名字多用表示威武、勇猛的字样，如“虎”、“龙”、“雄”、“伟”、“刚”、“强”等。女人的名字常用表示温柔美丽的之意，如“风”、“花”、“玉”、“彩”、“娟”、“静”等。现当代有些名字也带上洋色彩，如玛丽、洋子、亨利等。

纵观中国人的名字，它不仅是身份地位的象征，是礼仪的表示，也是中国文化的再现、是中国社会发展变化的见证。

实用词汇

传宗接代 have a son to carry on one’s family name
姬 complimentary term for women used in ancient China

籍贯 place of one's birth or origin

家谱 family pedigree

家书 home letter

客姓 a surname different from that of most of the families in a village（e.g. the surname Zhang or Li in Wang Family Village）

六亲 the six relations（father, mother, elder brothers, younger brothers, wife, children）

龙的传人 descendant of the dragon—the Chinese nation

五族 five nationalities（Hans, Manchus, Mongolians, Huis and Tibetans）

宗谱 family tree

宗亲 members of the same clan

宗社 the state; the country

宗室 imperial clan

宗族 ①patriarchal clan, ②clansman

族长 head of a clan

族尊 clan elder

祖传 handed down from one's ancestors

祖师 the founder of a school of learning, a craft, etc.

爱称、小名：pet name

笔名 pen name

绰号 nickname

单用名 former name

骂名 ad name

化名 assumed name

男性名字 masculine personal name

女性名字 feminine personal name

父姓 paternal surname

母姓 maternal surname

娘家姓 maiden name

艺名 stage name

通俗的名字 popular name

同名人 namesake

拗口的名字 jaw-breaking name

名言俗语

姓名来自祖先，荣誉来自美德。

From our ancestors come our names, from our virtues our honours.

有其父必有子。

Like father, like son.

血浓于水。

Blood is thicker than water.

有名有姓。

identifiable by both name and surname—of established identity.

在背后说某人的坏话。

Take someone's name in vain.

词语注解

乳名：婴儿时的名字，昵称

milk name, infant name or pet name

假名：写文章用的名字

Pseudonym: false name used when writing

艺名：演戏用的名字

stage name: a name used in playing a role

宗谱：家族的分支情况记录

family tree :the record of the branches of the family

宗师：有学问的、正直的长者

master of great learning and integrity

中西合璧

作为一个特殊的社会和语言现象，人名广泛而深刻地涉及各民族文化。中英文名字有许多相似、相异之处。古人对自然力量、自然现象又惧怕又尊重，因此，中英文人名很多采用地名，动物名和植物名。例如，中国的炎帝——中华民族的祖先住在姜水附近(河流名)，所以他的部落姓姜。在英国人们将自然现象如“濡，雨，雪作为自己的名字，有些名字从动物名如鸟、牛、狮子、狐狸、狼等；有些来自植物的名称，例如，花卉，苹果，百合，玫瑰。这种现象反映了人名的文化内涵与原始的图腾崇拜关系。中国人的名字和西方人名不同的是姓名都是姓在前，名在后。相反，西方人的姓在后，名在前。如篮球明星姚明，应该称为“姚先生”而不是“明先生”。

As a special social and linguistic phenomenon, names relate to cultures extensively and profoundly. There are many similarities and differences in Chinese and English names. “In ancient times, the human beings were not only afraid of natural power, but also respect it. Therefore, both in Chinese and English personal names, we can find lots of names from place, animal, plant, unliving things in nature or natural phenomenon”. For example, in Chinese names, Yan Emperor(炎帝, one ancestor of Chinese people) lived near Jiang Water(姜水, a name of a river), so his tribe used jiang (姜) as their tribe name. In English, people used the natural phenomenon as family names, such as Frost, Rain, and Snow etc. And some names come from animal names, for example, Bird, Bull, Lion, Fox, Wolf and so on. Some come from plant names, for instance, Flower, Apple, Lily, Rose. This phenomenon reflects similar cultural connotation that names are associated with primitive totemism. Personal names in Chinese culture follow a number of conventions different from those of personal names in Western cultures. Most noticeably, a Chinese name is written with the family name first and the given name next, For instance, the basketball player Yao Ming should be addressed as “Mr. Yao”, not “Mr. Ming”.

UNIT 19

The Twelve Animal Signs

十二生肖

题记

中国传统文化中是用十二种动物做生肖来记录日期的循环。生肖的顺序是鼠、牛、虎、兔、龙、蛇、马、羊、猴、鸡、狗、猪。这十二种动物依次代表各个年份，每十二年循环一次。

In traditional Chinese culture, the 12 animal signs were used to record years. Chronologically, they are rat, ox, tiger, rabbit, dragon, snake, horse, goat, monkey, rooster, dog and pig. Every 12 years is a cycle.

There are many legends about why the little rat came in the first place in the 12 animal signs. A popular legend said that the Yellow Emperor wanted to elect 12 animals as animal signs by an equal competition. Many animals took part in the race. The ox at that time ran very fast and was going to be the first, but the cunning rat who was riding on the ox's back secretly, at the last moment jumped over the finish line first, so the ox only got the second place in the race. Another statement goes that in ancient time, it was the rat that bit the chaotic heaven and earth and separated it, therefore, it was ranked the first.

The ox that was ranked the second is a diligent symbol in China. Before farming machines were invented, it was the ox that helped the peasants to do the hard farming work, so they liked it very much. It is believed that the people born in the ox year are honest and stubborn, a strong sense of responsibility and great patience. They also have positive attitude toward life and care about their families.

The third of the 12 animal signs is tiger. Tiger is a symbol for dispelling evil and blessings. It is believed that the people born in the tiger year are confident and often work alone, they have better willpower and are adventurous. They are men of good leadership. Tigers are very popular among people. For instance, the women in the country like sewing colorful cloth tigers，tiger shoes, and tiger caps, as gifts to their relatives and friends. If a new baby is born, a cloth tiger will be given as a lucky gift to wish the child as strong and healthy as a tiger.

Another popular animal sign is monkey. Monkey is very lovely and has been regarded as a clever and bright symbol. It is also regarded as an auspicious symbol because it has the similar sound to "nobleman or marquis". So in ancient paintings, monkeys played a lucky role. For example, a monkey riding a horse in a painting meant someone would become a nobleman immediately: A monkey riding on the back of another monkey in a drawing suggested the members of the family would be granted titles and land for generations.

"Pig" is the last animal sign. Chinese people believe that pig is a frank animal and that people who are born in the year are honest, kind, generous and very popular. The "pig" has been a theme in paintings, paper cutting, embroidery, and other folk arts. Even in the modern times, more babies are born in the years of the pig.

Up to now, animal sign culture has greatly influenced the life of Chinese people in various fields. The ancients liked to use terracotta figurines of the 12 animal signs as burial articles. There were 12 animal sign clocks in Yuanming Yuan. The ancient bronze mirrors of 12 animal signs were made during the Tang Dynasty. Now, they are still the popular themes for many Chinese artists. For example, since 1980, China's Ministry of Posts and Telecommunications issued a set of stamps of the 12 animal signs every 12 years, which were novel and lovely and well received by many stamp collectors.

段落译文

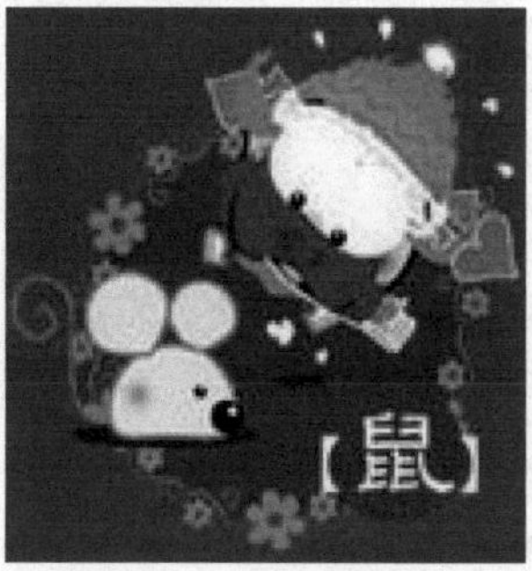

关于小小的老鼠排在 12 属相的第一位，有很多的传说。其中之一是这样的：当年黄帝要选 12 种动物做生肖。原则是平等竞争，择优录取。参赛的动物很多，当时的野牛不是现在慢悠悠拉车的老牛，它跑得飞快，遥遥领先。眼看牛就要第一个跑到终点了，一直跟在后面的老鼠偷偷地跳到牛背上，在最后一刻抢先跃过终点线，获得了第一名，牛只好屈居第二。另一种说法是，上古时候，天地混沌一片，是老鼠将这混沌咬破，使得天地分开，建此奇功，因此它当之无愧名列十二生肖榜首。

排名第二的牛在中国是勤奋的象征。在农业机器出现以前的漫长岁月里，一直是牛勤奋地帮助农民完成繁重的耕种工作，所以人们非常喜欢牛。并认为属牛的人性格正直倔强，责任感强、富有忍耐心。他们家庭观念浓厚，对生活抱有积极的态度。

老虎位居第三。老虎在中国人的心中是祛邪和祝福象征。人们认为属虎的人性格独立，自信心强，意志力和冒险性也胜过常人。他们是天生的领袖型人物。中国民间非常喜欢虎的形象。例如农村妇女们喜欢缝制色彩鲜艳，造型生动布老虎、虎鞋、虎帽等作为馈赠亲朋好友的吉祥物。谁家生孩子，送上一只布老虎，是祝愿孩子长得虎头虎脑，活泼健康。

另一个人们喜爱的属相是“猴”。猴子好动可爱，一直被人们视为聪明伶俐的象征。由于“猴”是“侯”的谐音，因此使“猴”也成了祝福吉祥的符号。古人绘画，猴就是以吉祥的角色入画的。例如，一幅猴子骑马的画，寓意马上当官封侯；一只猴骑在另一只猴的背上，其寓意是辈辈封侯。

“猪”是十二生肖中的最后一位。中国人认为猪是坦诚的动物。属猪的人诚实可靠，心地善良，慷慨大方，做事认真，人缘极佳。“猪”一直是十分受欢迎的年画、剪纸和刺绣等民间艺术的题材。甚至到了现代化的今天，每逢猪年，都会有很多“猪宝宝”出生。

古往今来，生肖文化已深深地融入到中国人民生活中的各个领域。古人喜欢用十二生肖陶俑来随葬作为避邪的神物。北京圆明园有十二生肖钟，唐代有十二生肖的古铜镜。至今，十二生肖仍然是很多艺术家们喜爱的选题。1980 年以来，我国邮电部每十二年发行一套生肖系列的邮票，由于构思新颖，形象惹人喜爱，受到了广大集邮者的欢迎。

实用词汇

十二生肖 the 12 Zodiac animals; the 12 animal signs
鼠 rat
牛 ox
虎 tiger
兔 rabbit
龙 dragon
蛇 snake

马 horse
羊 sheep
猴 monkey
鸡 rooster
狗 dog
猪 boar; pig
黄道十二宫 the signs of the zodiac
白羊座 Aries
金牛座 Taurus
双子座 Gemini
巨蟹座 Cancer
狮子座 Leo
处女座 Virgo
天秤座 Libra
天蝎座 Scorpio
人马座 Sagittarius
魔羯座 Capricorn
宝瓶座 Aquarius
双鱼座 Pisces

名言俗语

三人成虎。

Three men make a tiger. A lie, if repeated often enough, will be accepted as truth.

狡兔三窟。

A hare with only one hole is soon caught. A wily hare has tree burrows.

画虎类犬。

Tiger and dog: try to draw a tiger but end up with the likeness of a dog.

好马不吃回头草。

An able horse will never come back to feed in the same stable.

马儿跑得快慢在于鞭策的力度。

All the speed is in the spurs.

山中无老虎，猴子称霸王。

Among the blind the one-eyed man is the king.

会叫的狗不咬人。

A barking dog was never a good biter. / A barking dog never bites.

对公鸡而言，麦谷胜于钻石。

A barley corn is better than a diamond to a cock.

宁为鸡首，不为牛后。

Better be the head of a chicken than the tail of an ox.

狗是人类最好的朋友。

A dog is a man's best friend.

狗不嫌家贫，儿不嫌母丑。

A dog won't forsake his master because of his poverty; a son never deserts his mother for her homely appearance.

兔子急了也会咬人。

Even a rabbit will bite when it is cornered.

不入虎穴，焉得虎子。

Nothing venture, nothing gain.

打草惊蛇。

Stir the grass and alert the snake.

虎头蛇尾。

A tiger's head and snake's tail / A good beginning with a lousy ending.

词语注解

鸡犬升天：比喻一个人得势，同他有关系的人也跟着沾光。

Chickens and dogs also ascending to heaven: now it is often cited to describe anyone who promotes his relatives or friends to high positions simply because he has the clout and power.

老马识途：比喻阅历多的人富有经验，熟悉情况，能起到引导作用。

An old horse knows the way: today people often use it to describe someone with experience knows the ropes and has the knowledge of a veteran.

骑虎难下：比喻事情中途遇到困难，为形势所迫，又难以中止。

He who rides a tiger finds it hard to get off. Now, Chinese people often use the idiom to describe someone who is in a difficult situation but still must carry on.

塞翁失马 焉知祸福：比喻坏事在一定的条件下可以变为好事。

A lost mare means when the old man on the frontier lost his mare，who could have guessed it was a blessing in disguise. It is often cited by people when they try to console someone who has suffered an unexpected loss or mishap.

九牛一毛：比喻极大的数量中微不足道的一部分。

A single hair out of nine ox hides. It is a metaphor used to describe something is trivial and unimportant.

猴年马月：指不可知的年月或遥遥无期。

The year of monkey and month of the horse , which means a time that will never come.

纵虎归山：比喻放走敌人，留下祸根。

Let the tiger escape; let the tiger return to the mountain. Now it is cited to describe any decision which may cause calamity for future.

初生牛犊不怕虎：比喻青年人勇敢大胆，敢作敢为。

The newborn calves are not afraid of tigers: young people dare do anything and fear nothing.

中西合璧

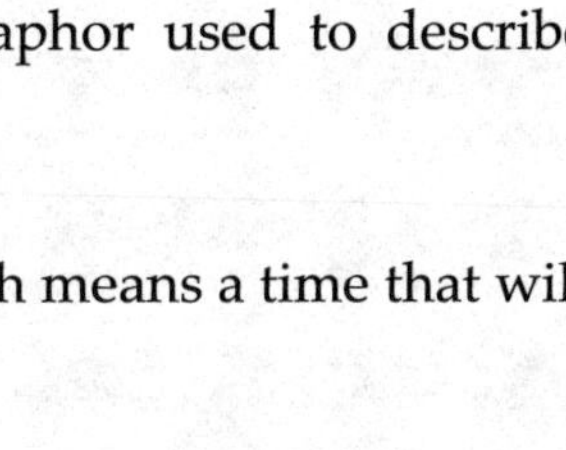

除了中国有十二生肖之外，其他国家也有生肖文化。例如，墨西哥的十二生肖与中国的生肖很相似，其中虎、兔、龙、猴、犬、猪与中国完全相同，其余六种则是当地的常见动物或古代常见动物。埃及与希腊的十二生肖(十二兽历)完全相同。它们是牡牛、山羊、狮、驴、蟹、蛇、犬、猫、鳄、红鹤、猿、鹰。

中国人有十二生肖，西方人有黄道十二宫(星座)。例如一月份出生的人属摩羯星座，其余按月依次为水瓶、双鱼、白羊、金牛、双子、巨蟹、狮子、处女、天秤、天蝎、射手星座。西方人认为，不同星座属相的人可能会有不同的性格、行为和命运，这与中国生肖文化有很多相似之处。事实上，中国的生肖文化是年生肖，西方的十二宫文化是月生肖。

In addition to Chinese animal signs, other countries also have animal sign culture. The 12 animal signs of Mexico are very similar to those of China, including tiger, rabbit, dragon, monkey, dog, pig and other six common local animals. The animal sings of Egypt and the Greece are exactly the same. They are ox, goat, lion, donkey, crab, snake, dog, cat, crocodile, flamingo, ape and eagle.

Westerners have the signs of the zodiac (constellations) as the Chinese animal signs. For example, the people who are born from Dec. 23 to Jan. 20 belong to Capricorn and followed by Aquarius, Pisces, Aries, Taurus, Gemini, Cancer, Leo, Virgo, Libra, Scorpio and Sagittarius. Westerners believe that people with the different signs of the Zodiac may have different personalities, behavior, and destinies. This is similar to Chinese animal sign beliefs. In fact, the Western zodiac is a calendar of months, and Chinese animal signs are a calendar of years.

UNIT 20

Chinese Marriage Customs

中国婚俗文化

题记

中国幅员辽阔，历史悠久，曾经出现很多不同的婚俗。在现代的中国，许多传统婚礼的习俗已经不再盛行了。不过近几年传统婚礼习俗在中国很多地方再次兴起，并且越来越吸引人们的视线。

China has a long history with various marriage customs in the vast land. In modern China, various traditional wedding customs and ceremonies were out of date. However, in recent years they have become more and more popular and attractive.

Wedding ceremonies have been considered an important life matter both home and abroad throughout human history. "Three Letters and Six Etiquettes" were the basic principles of traditional Chinese marriage customs in ancient times.

Three Letters include a Betrothal Letter, a Gift Letter and a Wedding Letter. The Betrothal Letter is the formal document of the engagement, a must for marriage when the bridegroom presents the betrothal gifts (engagement). The Gift Letter is delivered to the bride's family and is a document necessary before the wedding, in which will be enclosed lists of the types and quantities of gifts for the wedding. The Wedding Letter refers to the document, which will be prepared and presented to the bride's family on the day of the wedding, to confirm and commemorate the formal acceptance of the bride into the bridegroom's family.

The Six Etiquettes are namely: Proposing (A matchmaker discusses marriage with the potential bridegroom and bride), Birthday matching (the matchmaker will ask for the girl's birthday and birth-hour record to assure the compatibility of the potential bride and bridegroom), presenting betrothal gifts (Once birthdays match, the bridegroom's family will then arrange the matchmaker to present the betrothal letter, to the bride's family), the defining of an auspicious wedding day (the groom's family delivers appointment letter bride's side family), presenting wedding gifts (after the betrothal letter and betrothal gifts are accepted, the bridegroom's family will later formally send wedding gifts to the bride's family enclosing the Gift Letter), picking a wedding date (an astrologist or astrology book will be consulted to select an auspicious date to hold the wedding ceremony), and the wedding ceremony (The bridegroom departures with a troop of escorts and musicians to escort the bride).

The modern wedding ceremony generally refers to the activities which are held on the wedding day, but in ancient times "Three Letters and Six Etiquettes" included the marriage etiquette with a series of activities of matchmaking, engagement and the wedding ceremony. If the men and women did not follow the process, the marriage was then not acknowledged. In of these activities, wedding ceremony is the most over elaborate. It refers to the activity in which the bridegroom departures and escorts the bride to the bridegroom's home, the wedding ceremony begins.

The historical books record the earliest traditional Chinese wedding ceremony:

On the early morning of the wedding day, the bride puts on the new outfit in a pair of red shoes after a bath in grapefruit water, waiting for a lucky woman to comb her hair. The bride will put on Feng Guan (phoenix coronet) in red silk bridal veil and listen to a married woman who tells her how to be a good wife, while waiting for her future husband.

The fun is that when the groom comes to the door of the bride's, the bridesmaids and her sisters try not to let him in! The purpose is to let the bridegroom experience difficulties to enter the door. Usually the groom can overcome the difficulties with his wisdom and courage and the help of his friends. Then, the groom sings for the bride and finally he can see the bride, but the groom must offer red packages with money to the bridesmaids and the sisters to be allowed to take his bride home. The bride is accompanied into the sedan by a lucky woman. The bride's sister support a red umbrella, while another sprinkles some rice in the sedan with a metal mirror hanging behind, which people think it can protect the bride from evil spirits. The bride must cry while departing, showing her unwillingness to leave her parents.

People began to set off firecrackers to ward off evil spirits while the bride sitting into the sedan. And people will try to avoid unlucky things all the way: the curtain of the sedan was closely plastered in case the bride may see widows, well, cats which are considered as unlucky things. Firecrackers meet the bridegroom's team, the bride will walk a red cushion and pass a burning pan to ward off evil spirits before entering the groom's.

The wedding ceremony is the climax of the whole process. The bride and groom are shown into the ancestral temple. They first worship the heaven and earth, the ancestors and parents and then themselves, finally they enter the bridal chamber. An emcee narrates the story, accompanied by the wedding guests with applause and cheers. Friends and guests are entertained at a big wedding banquet. The newlyweds drink the cross-cupped wine, drink to thank the guests and get their blessings.

Three days back door practices. Traditionally the newlyweds return to visit the bride's parents in three days. The groom is teased by the bride's relatives and friends out of kindness, of course.

As time goes on, the traditional ceremony based on "Three Letters and Six Etiquettes" is gradually simplified. But wedding ceremony is completely passed down. Of course some fashions are melted into the tradition. Sedan chair, for instance, is replaced by heavily flower-decorated car to greet the bride.

Nowadays in modern China, traditional wedding ceremonies seem not so popular though still in fashion in the countryside. But people have become more and more interested in it and are paying much attention to traditional wedding ceremonies in recent times.

段落译文

在人类历史中婚礼仪式被世界公认为是一件重大事情。在中国古代传统婚俗必须遵循“三书六礼”的基本原则。

三书是指聘书、礼书和迎亲书。聘书是正式的婚约书，是婚事必备的。礼书也是必备的。一旦双方同意了这桩婚事，它将被送往女方家，列出所有婚礼礼品的品种和数量。迎亲书是为了在婚礼上呈给女方家人的，以确认并正式接纳新娘为新郎家庭的一员。

六礼是指纳彩(媒人提亲)、问名(看男女生辰八字是否相配)、纳吉(男方将订婚书送到女方家)、纳征(男方送女方婚礼礼品)、请期(择良辰吉日完婚)、亲迎(新郎带队迎新娘)。

现代婚礼通常指在结婚当天所举行的活动，但在古代“三书六礼”包括一系列结婚礼仪活动：如媒人做媒、订婚及婚礼。如果男女双方在这一过程中有不遵守礼仪，婚姻得不到承认。在这期间，婚礼最复杂，需要精心准备：新郎迎请新娘到家、婚礼开始。

历史上记录最早的传统的中国婚礼是这样的:

在婚礼当天的清晨，新娘将在加了柚子的水中沐浴，再穿上新的嫁衣和红鞋，等候一位幸运的女人来为她梳头。新娘将戴上垂有流苏的凤冠，在蒙上红色丝制的盖头。然后一边听着已婚妇女告诉她如何做一个好妻子，一边等待她未来的丈夫迎娶她过门。

……

有意思的是新郎进新娘的家门了，女傧相和新娘的姐妹们严守家门。这一习俗是让新郎在门前经历重重困难。通常新郎的智慧和勇气以及他的朋友们会帮他成功地通过考验。新郎过了这一关后为新娘高歌，最后才能见到新娘。然而，还有一关，新郎还必须塞给女傧相和姐妹们红包，红包里装着吉利钱，这样她们才允许他将新娘带回去。

新娘由一个幸运的女人背进花轿。新娘的妹妹为她撑着红伞，另一个妹妹撒一些米在花轿里。花轿的背后挂上筛子和一面金属做的镜子，人们认为这样可以保护新娘免受邪灵的伤害。新娘必须哭着离去，表示她不愿意离开父母。

在新娘坐进花轿的同时，人们开始燃放鞭炮，以驱除邪灵。一路上人们都会尽力避免不吉利的事情发生。比如花轿门被门帘挡得严严实实，不让新娘看见诸如寡妇、井、猫等不吉利的东西。迎亲的队伍来到新郎家时，新郎家会燃放鞭炮迎接新娘的到来。在花轿前铺上红色的垫子，为的是不让新娘直接接触到地面。进门前，新娘要跨过一个烧旺的火盆，以驱除邪灵。

结婚仪式是整个过程的高潮。新娘和新郎被迎进祠堂。先拜天地，再拜祖先和父母最后夫妻对拜。进入洞房。整个过程都有司仪的旁白，并伴有参加婚礼的客人们的掌声和喝彩。

接着是丰盛的婚宴，招待亲友以及帮助筹备婚礼的人。在席间新婚夫妇要喝交杯酒，然后新人向来宾敬酒——表示感谢。同时也得到他们的祝福。

三天回门的习俗。传统的新婚夫妇在婚后三天回到娘家，拜访新娘的父母。这次是新郎被新娘家的亲戚朋友们戏弄了。

随着时间的推移，这种基于“三书六礼”的传统仪式逐渐简化，但婚礼得到了彻底传承，当然人们将时尚融入了传统的婚礼，如用鲜花装饰的轿车来代替花轿。

在现代的中国，许多传统婚礼的习俗已经不再盛行了。但在农村还能看到传统的婚礼。不过近几年传统婚礼习俗在中国很多地方再次兴起，并且越来越吸引人们的视线。

实用词汇

聘礼 betrothal gifts

三书(聘书、礼书和迎亲书) Three Letters (Betrothal Letter, Gift Letter and Wedding

良辰吉日 an auspicious date

结婚请帖 wedding invitation card

结婚典礼 wedding ceremony

迎亲 to escort the bride

轿子 sedan

花车 festooned vehicle; bridal car; flower-decorated car

盖头，蒙首 bridal veil

喝喜酒 to drink happy wine

闹新房 teasing the newlyweds on the wedding night; teasing games in the bridal chamber;

交杯酒 wedlock wine

双喜字 double happiness

喜糖 wedding sweets

喜酒 wine offered to guests at a wedding

结婚证 marriage certificate

新郎 bridegroom

新娘 bride

嫁妆 dowry; trousseau

回门 returning home

白头偕老 live to ripe old age in conjugal bliss; remain a devoted couple to the end of their lives

半路夫妻 couple married halfway through life

比翼连枝 like birds that pair off wing to wing or trees that have their branches intertwined—deep affection of a devoted couple

比翼鸟 fabulous birds that had only one wing each and thus had to fly in pairs—used as an epithet for a loving couple in poetry

彩轿 bridal sedan chair

彩礼 betrothal gifts

出阁（of a woman）leave her boudoir—（of a woman）get married

盖头 bridal veil

纳彩 (of present bridegroom's family) present gifts to the girl's family at time of betrothal

青梅竹马 green plums and a bamboo horse—a girl and a boy playing innocently together

休书 letter by a husband unilaterally announcing his decision to divorce his wife

嫁汉嫁汉，穿衣吃饭 A women marries for food and shelter.

有福同享，有难同当 Share happiness and hardship.

妻管严 henpecked

甩手掌柜 hands-off

大男子主义 male chauvinism

娃娃亲 infant matrimony

指腹婚 belly-pointing marriage

从一而终 not remarry after one's husband dies

集体婚礼 group wedding

蜜月旅行 honeymoon; marriage trip

合婚 exchange of horoscopes of the two parties before formal betrothal to see whether they are compatible or not

红媒 matchmaker

红娘 maid in the play the Western Chamber, whose good offices help bring about the union of the lovers, her mistress Yingying and Student Zhang; go-between; matchmaker

花红 gift for a wedding,etc.; bonus

花烛 candles with dragon and phoenix patterns used in the bridal chamber on the wedding night

花烛夫妻 husband and wife by the first marriage

欢喜冤家 quarrelsome and loving couple

婚检 physical check-up before marriage

婚丧喜庆 marriage and funeral—important occasions of a family

婚外恋 extramarital affair

婚约 marriage contract

佳偶天成 ideal marriage divinely arranged

佳期 wedding day

嫁出去的女儿，泼出去的水 a married daughter is like spilt watter—a married daughter is no longer a member of the family

嫁鸡随鸡，嫁狗随狗 follow the man you marry, be he fowl or cur

交杯酒 drink the nuptial cup(part of an old-fashioned marriage ceremony, in which the bride and the bridegroom drink out of goblets tied together by red thread, exchanging cups and drinking again)

结发夫妻 husband and wife by the first marriage

结婚登记 marriage registration

开脸 (of a girl on the eve of marriage) remove the fine hairs on the face and the neck and tidy up hairline at temples

开亲 become engaged or betrothed

名言俗语

家有贤妻万事兴。

The wife is the key of the house.

妻惠夫贤。

A good wife makes a good husband.

走遍天下，家最好。

East or west, home is best.

金窝银窝不如家里草窝。

Every bird likes his own nest best.

爱屋及乌。

Love me, love my dog.

情人眼里出西施。

Beauty is in the eye of the beholder.

男人盖屋，女人持家。

Men make houses; women make homes.

佳偶天成。

Matches are made in heaven.

美满的婚姻是人生的新开端，是幸福和有益的新起点。

A happy marriage is a new beginning of life, a new starting point for happiness and usefulness.

幸福的婚姻是生活能够奉献的最佳礼物。

A happy marriage is the best thing life has to offer.

“善待对方”这是婚姻的金科玉律，也是让爱相随终生的秘诀。

"Be kind to one another." This is the Golden Rule of marriage and the secret of making love last through the years.

我了解一些美满的婚姻——都是双方互助互爱，同甘共苦地生活。

I know some good marriages—marriages where both people are just trying to get through their days by helping each other, being good to each other.

爱情是一种永恒的信仰。

Love is an eternal belief.

词语注解

指腹婚：指着怀着胎儿的腹部，双方父母达成了子女的婚约。此习俗自汉代开始，流行时间很长时间，现已杜绝。

Belly-pointing marriage: a marriage agreement made by parents for the children still in the womb by pointing at the pregnant abdomens. The custom started in the Han Dynasty, but has been abandoned by now.

抛彩球：用抛彩球的方式来选择配偶，在中国的文学作品中常指女子抛绣球选择夫婿。

Tossing colorful balls: It is a way of picking one's mate. In Chinese literary there are many stories about women throwing the ball to select their future husbands.

回门：新娘嫁到丈夫家称为“进门”，从丈夫家回到娘家称为“回门”。含有女儿不忘父母养育之恩，女婿感谢岳父母，以及表示夫妻恩爱的意思。

Returning home: When a bride is married, it is customarily called "entering home"; therefore, when the newlyweds pay a formal visit to the bride's parents after the wedding, it is called "returning home", which signifies the daughter's not forgetting her parental upbringing, the son-in-law's gratitude to his parents-in-law, and conjugal love between the newlyweds.

父母之命，媒妁之言：父母对婚姻的建议看法和媒人的看法决定婚姻的成败。

the command of parents and the advice of a go-between (in former times) the proper way of contracting a marriage

丑媳妇也得见公婆：表示中国古代的媳妇难做，要过的第一关是婆婆关。

an ugly bride will sooner or later have to come face to face with her parents-in-law.

白马王子：女孩梦想中理想的结婚人选。

Mr. Right: a white horse is not a horse—a man to whom a girl dreams to get married.

中西合璧

中西方的婚俗有相似的地方。例如，中国古代有抛绣球迎亲的习俗；而西方的新郎新娘在教堂举行婚礼后，会把手中的鲜花抛向空中，如果有人接到的话就预示着他将很快结婚。中国人比较保守、爱热闹的性格在中国传统婚礼中得到了充分的体现。在婚宴结束以后，新人的亲朋好友会去新房中闹洞房。认为在新房中越热闹，新人在婚后的生活越幸福。西方人婚礼的高潮则是在教堂中：随着神圣的《婚礼进行曲》，新娘手挽着父亲捧玫瑰步入鲜红的地毯，慢慢向新郎走去，新娘的父亲将女儿的手放在新郎的手上，将女儿的一生托付给他，神父说："你可以亲吻你的新娘了……结婚是一生的盟约，你是要为之坚守一辈子的誓言。"然后新郎新娘或是去晚宴地点或是去度蜜月，并没有中国传统婚俗的种种礼节。中国是以佛教为主，而西方则是以基督教为主。所以西方的婚礼是在教堂中举行，主婚人是神甫。中方的传统婚俗中最重要环节就是拜天地，拜了天地以后就算是礼成了。

There are many similarities in marriage Customs between China and the west. For example, Chinese bride throws the Hydrangea (a ball made of strips of silk) to the girls and the western bride hands the flowers into the air, if someone gets the ball or the flowers, she or he will soon get married.

Chinese people are conservative, but fun loving, which is fully displayed in the Chinese traditional wedding ceremony. At the end of the wedding ceremony, the friends and family would go to newly-weds' chamber to celebrate it by all means. We believe that the more lively the new home is, the happier the newly-weds will be. In the west, the climax of the wedding is in the church: As the couple march to the Wedding music along the bright red carpet with the bride accompanied by her father, and then the bride is handed to the groom by the father putting his daughter's hand into the groom's hands. The priest says: You can kiss your bride ... Then the bride and groom go to their honeymoon. Westerners believe in God, so the wedding is held in the church by the priest. One of the Chinese traditional marriage customs is Baitian Di to show respect and thanks to the heavens and earth as they become husband and wife.

UNIT 21

Chinese Money

中国钱币

题记

中国是世界最早铸造金属钱币的国家之一，同时也是世界上最早发行纸币的国家。中国钱币不但具有自己独特的制作风格，并且影响到周边许多国家和地区。从天然贝币到方孔圆钱，从银元到纸币，各种钱币伴随着中国走过了四、五千年的历史进程。钱币也反映了中国各个朝代的政治、经济、商业、科技和文化的发展和变迁。

China is not only one of the earliest minting countries, but also the earliest country issuing paper money. There were a lot of unique minting skills in China, which influenced many countries and areas in the neighborhood. From shell money to copper coins, silver coins to paper currency, many kinds of money have accompanied China for 4000~5000 years. The money has also reflected the development and changes of the politics, economy, finance, commerce, technology and culture during different dynasties.

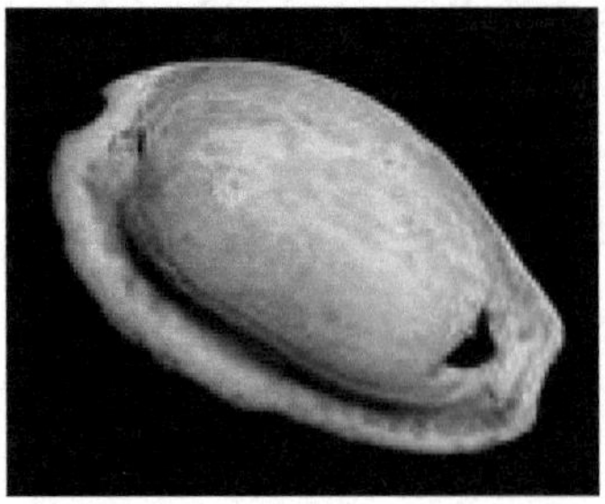

It is hard to say how many kinds of money there have been throughout Chinese history, but it is estimated that there are more than a hundred thousand of them. Chinese money can be divided into two categories: coin and paper. The coins were made of different metals including gold, silver, copper, iron, lead, aluminium, and nickel. Sometimes bamboo, wood, bakelite, pottery, and porcelain were also used as substitutive money. Paper currency included those which had been printed on cotton paper, mulberry paper, and Daolin paper. People also used currency which was printed on cloth, such as canvas, sailcloth, and oilcloth, etc.

The earliest currency in China was shells. In China's late New Stone Age period, the barter trade had failed to meet the needs of social life so shells were regarded as a medium for exchange at that time as they were small, portable and easy to calculate. Besides, farm tools, spinning wheels, jade, grain, and livestock were also once used as money. Then, gold, silver and bronze appeared as weighing money.

During the Spring and Autumn and Warring States Periods, a great amount of coins were founded which were made of lead, silver and gold, besides bronze. After Qin Shi Huang, the first emperor in Chinese history, had unified China, he unified the written form of Chinese characters, measurements, as well as money. He abolished all the old money that once circulated in the other kingdoms of the Warring States, and introduced the new Ban Liang Qian based on the money of the Kingdom of Qin. Since then, the Ban Liang Qian coins became the country's lawfully circulated money.

Because Ban Liang Qian was too heavy to carry and inconvenient to use, the emperor Wudi of the Han Dynasty founded Wu Zhu coins which were light enough to use and met the requirements of the social economy. Therefore, they were continually produced for many dynasties after Han. It had been the standard currency in circulation for 739 years and was the money with the longest period of foundry.

The first emperor of Tang Dynasty abolished the old monetary system based on "zhu" and "liang", and issued a new currency called "Kai Yuan Tong Bao". Since then, the metal money was called "Tongbao" or "Yuanbao", breaking away from old way of naming money in accordance with its weight. The decimal system of weight units of liang, qian, fen, and li replaced the old unit of Zhu, which was 1/24 of one liang.

Song Dynasty saw the peak of China's ancient minting period, by quantity, selection and artistry. But in Yuan Dynasty, notes were the main currency and the amount of coins decreased greatly. Although the governments of Ming and Qing still founded coins with reign titles, each emperor had only one reign title, so there were less kinds of coins than those of Song Dynasty.

It is well known that China was the earliest country using paper currency. During Tang Dynasty, a kind of paper currency which was called "Feiqian" appeared. It could be exchanged for cash in different areas or places. Then, it became the main currency of Yuan Dynasty, and was issued by the government. The paper currency from Ming Dynasty was named "Da Ming current Bao Chao". In Qing Dynasty, the main currency was copper coins and silver. They issued the paper currency in the reign of Xian-Feng, which was divided into two categories: one was "Da Qing Bao Chao", which was used to evaluate the money, the other was called "Hu Bu Guan Piao", which could evaluate silver. That is why Chinese money is also called "Chao Piao" now.

In the middle of the 19th century, a great deal of silver dollars had entered China and the Chinese government had copied them. Since 1949, China has issued many sets of Renminbi. Now, Chinese money minting and printing technology are advanced.

段落译文

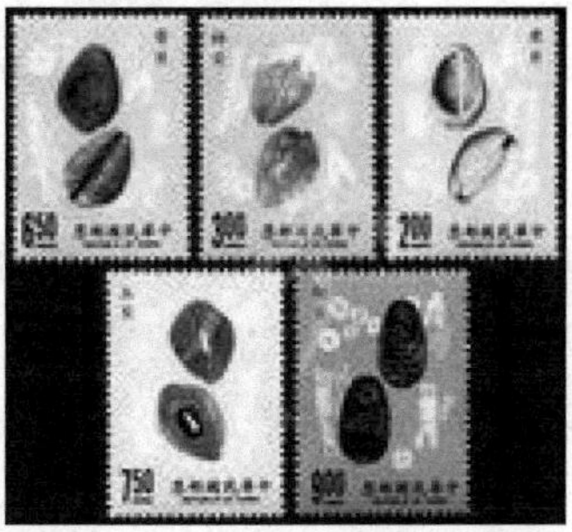

有史以来中国钱币有多少种？很难说出准确数字，有人估计在10万种以上。中国的钱币主要分硬币、纸币两类。硬币包括金、银、铜、铁、铅、铝、镍等各种铸币，还有竹、木、胶木、陶、瓷等各种代用币。纸币则包括全棉纸、桑皮纸、道林纸等印制的各种纸币，还有帆布、油布等布料印制的布币。

中国最早的货币是贝壳。在新石器时代晚期，以物交换的方式已不能适应社会生活的需要，由于贝壳小巧玲珑，坚固耐用，携带方便，又容易计数，因此贝壳就自然成了交换的媒介——货币。除贝壳之外，农具、纺轮、玉石、谷帛、牲畜也曾充当过货币。后来黄金、白银、青铜也以称量货币形式出现了。

金属铸币的大量出现是在春秋战国时期。除了青铜铸币外，春秋战国的货币还包括铅币、银币、金币等。秦始皇统一中国以后，在统一文字，统一度量衡的同时，也着手统一了货币。他废除了原各国的旧币，以秦币为基础推行新的“半两”钱， 从此，“半两”钱就成了全国统一的法定货币。

但是由于秦“半两”太重，使用不便，汉武帝时铸造了“五铢”钱。“五铢”钱轻重适中，合乎古代社会经济和价格水平对货币的要求，因此汉武帝以后的很多朝代都铸造使用五铢钱，五铢钱历时739年，成为我国历史上铸形时间最长的一种钱币。

唐高祖废除了历代以“铢”、“两”为钱的名称的货币制度，开始铸行名为“开元通宝”的新钱。至此，中国的金属铸币脱离了以重量为钱币名称的体系。而称之为“通宝”、“元宝”。重量计算单位也改用两，钱、分、厘的十进位法代替了二十四进位法的“铢”。

两宋是中国古代铸币的顶峰时期，钱币的数量和种类最多、艺术性也最高。

后来的元代以纸币为主，铸币的数量明显减少。明清两代虽仍铸造年号钱，但是每一个皇帝只有一个年号，所以种类远不及宋朝。

中国也是世界上使用纸币最早的国家，早在唐代就有可以在异地兑现的“飞钱”了。元代，纸币成为主要通货，由国家统一印发。明代纸币统一名称为“大明通行宝钞”。清朝早期主要通货是铜钱和白银，到咸丰朝才又发行两种纸币。一种是“大清宝钞”对钱作价，另一种是“户部官票”对银作价，现在钱币也被称为“钞票”，就源于此。

18 世纪中叶，西方银元大量流入中国，中国开始仿制银元。道光年间(1821～1850 年)在东南沿海地区就出现了自铸银元。自 1949 年以来，中国已发行了多套人民币。现在中国的造币和印钞技术都已跨入世界先进行列。

实用词汇

贝币 shell money
秦半两 Ban Liang Qin (half liang money) of the Qin Dynasty
金属铸币 metal mint
黄金 gold
白银 silver
铜钱；铜板 copper coin; copper
金币 gold coin
铁 iron
锡 stannum
铅 lead
铝 aluminium
镍 nickel
锑 antimony
竹 bamboo
木 wood

胶木 bakelite
陶 pottery
五铢 Wu Zhu coin
元宝 ingot
开元通宝 Kai Yuan Tong Bao
代用币 substitutive money
纸币 paper currency; bank note; folding money; note
布币 cloth money
刀币 knife money
金元宝 shoe-shaped gold ingot
银元宝 shoe-shaped silver ingot

名言俗语

金钱万能。
A golden key opens every door. / Money answers all things.
不可精于便士，昏于英镑。不可小事聪明，大事糊涂。
Don't be penny wise and pound foolish.
钱烧口袋漏，一有就不留。/ 挥金如土。
Your money burns (a hole) in your pocket.
金钱不做你的仆人，它就会做你的主人。/ 你不会支配钱，钱就会支配你。
If money be not thy servant, it will be thy master.
生财容易，守财难。
It is easier to get money than to keep it.
借出你的钱，朋友翻了脸。/ 借钱失友。
Lend your money and lose your friend.
金钱是万恶之源。
Money is the root of all evil.
金钱并不是一切。/ 金钱并非万能。
Money isn't everything
有钱走遍天下。有钱处处受欢迎。

Money makes a man welcome everywhere.

金钱最有发言权。钱能通神。

Money talks.

智力投资决不会投错。

Money spent on the brain is never spent in vain.

有钱就能赚钱。/ 钱能生钱。

Money would be gotten if there were money to get it with.

平时存钱，防备雨天。/ 富裕时省钱，防患于未然。

Save money against a rainy day.

时间就是金钱。/ 一寸光阴一寸金。

Time is money.

金钱可以收买小人，却不能收买真理。

Money can buy off a mean person, but it can never buy off truth.

钱财来得容易去得快。

Easy come, easy go.

骗来的钱烫手。

Gain got by a lie will burn the fingers.

金钱的价值不在其本身，而在于你用它做什么。

Don't value money for its own sake, but for what you can do with it.

正当得到的一分钱，胜过偷来的一块钱。

The honest penny is better than the stolen dollar.

一分钱难倒英雄汉。

A man without money is no man at all.

有钱使人担心，没钱使人伤心。

To have money is a fear, not to have it a grief.

词语注解

一诺千金：形容诺言信度极高。

Golden promise: It is described anyone whose promise is weightier than one thousand pieces of gold.

一贫如洗：形容穷的一无所有。

Penniless is used to describe a man who is utterly destitute.

金字招牌：商店用金粉涂字的招牌，也指商店资金雄厚，信誉卓著。

Gold-lettered signboard of a store, which also means that a store is abundant in capital and having good credit

有钱能使鬼推磨。指有钱可以买通一切。

Money can buy the devil himself means money can buy everything.

中西合璧

世界货币分为两大体系，一是以中国为代表的东方货币，另一个是以希腊为代表的西方货币。东方的货币是以铜、铁等金属为材料，以文字为币文，制造技术是铸造。而西方的货币是以金银等贵重金属为材料，以图形为币文，制造技术是打压。但是历史上也曾出现过中西文化和技术融合的钱币。这就是著名的“汉佉二体钱”，此钱是圆形无孔，用铜为材料，却用源于希腊的打压法制造。钱上有马的图案，周围是佉卢文，另一面却写着汉字，两种文化和地域特点都融合在一枚钱币上了。现在中国的钱币不但继承了传统的造币技术，同时也借鉴了西方的造币技术，事实上，现今人民币是中西造币技术融合的产物。

The world currency system can be divided into two monetary systems. One is the east currency system, represented by China, and the western currency system represented by Greece. The eastern currencies were made of copper and iron, the characters were used as adornment and foundry technology was used. Meanwhile, western currencies were made of precious metals, such as gold or silver, figures were used as adornment, and pressing technology was used. But one kind of coin was made by both east and west cultures and technologies had appeared once. It was the famous "Han Qu Erti Qian", which was made of copper, however, later pressing technology was used. The money was round without a hole in its centre. It is the coin with the respective cultural and geographical features, which had a horse pattern on one side surrounded by Kharosthi, and Chinese characters written on the other side. Now the Chinese money has not only inherited the traditional minting techniques, but has also learned from western minting technology. In fact, RMB is a product of the combination of eastern and western minting technologies.

UNIT 22

Chinese Food Culture

饮食文化

题记

中国的饮食文化在全世界首屈一指。长期以来，人们对“吃”有着特殊的偏爱，由此摸索出了很多至精完美的烹调术，形成了京、川、苏、粤、鲁等各具特色的地方菜系及数不胜数的民间风味小吃，从而吃出了中国特有的饮食文化。

The food culture in China is the top of the world. People love “eating” and eating has become our favourite pastime. Chinese people spent a lot of time perfecting cookery, thus formed the local cuisine in Beijing, Sichuan, Jiangsu, Guangdong, Shandong and so on, and their unique characteristics as well as numerous folk flavored snacks. Chinese food culture came into being by eating.

Chinese cuisine includes a variety of different flavors due to China’s vast geography and diverse nationalities. Their specific cooking techniques and dishes are distinctive and each has its own specialties. Chinese cuisine is a collection of them all.

There are many cooking schools of Chinese cuisine. The most influential and representative ones also recognized by the community are: Shandong, Sichuan, Guangdong, Fujian, Jiangsu, Zhejiang, Hunan, and Anhui cuisine, which are often regarded as the "Eight regional cuisines" in China.

Shandong cuisine is the general term, mainly composed of Jinan and Jiaodong local food. Jiaodong were good at blasting, being deep-fried, fried and steamed, leavened, and steamed. The dishes are fresh and somewhat mild. Jinan is known for its soup supplemented by frying, roasting, and deep-fried dishes which are clear, fresh, crisp and tender. Famous dishes are: Jiuzhuandachang, sweet and sour Yellow River carp, braised chicken and so on. Shandong cuisine became "North Dishes" and played a leading role since Han and Tang Dynasties and its special features remain to the present.

Sichuan Cuisine is one of the most famous Chinese cuisines in the world with the spices used diversely and distinctively. The famous ones are the "three peppers" in particular: Chinese prickly ash, pepper, hot pepper and the "three incense": onions, ginger, garlic, vinegar, which is beyond the others' reach. Sichuan Cuisine owns many tastes such as sweet, sour, spicy, bitter, salty, etc., and "eight flavors" which are fish-flavored, hot and sour, both spicy and pungent, smelly, spicy, with marked oil, ginger juice,and home-style. There are as many as 38 cooking methods, so the world knows the saying "food in China, taste in Sichuan". There are more than 300 kinds of dishes as Dengying beef, boiled beef, Fuqi feipian, Mapo Tofu and Spiced Fish Stew.

Guangdong Cuisine or Cantonese cuisine is made up of Guangzhou, Chaozhou and Dongjiang Cuisines. Guangzhou cuisine is creative with an emphasis on artistic presentation of multiple ingredients and is enjoyed for its light, crisp and fresh flavor and has been known for seafood cooking, soup, vegetables, and sugar beets which are its most distinctive features are fine shapes and pure taste. Dongjiang cuisine, namely the Hakka cuisine, is mainly cooked with meat, very little seafood. The ingredients of the dishes are comparatively various with strong fragrance, heavy salty taste, the casserole is a unique local flavor. Cantonese cuisine is especially good at cooking snakes, raccoon dogs, cats, dogs, monkeys, rats and other wild animals. Specialty is "Suckling Pig", Frozen Meat, "Melon Cup", Daliang Fried Milk. Cantonese cuisine originated from the Western Han Dynasty, "eating in Guangzhou" is an old saying.

Fujian cuisine is a general term which includes Fuzhou, Xiamen, Quanzhou cuisine. The cooking methods are broth, Deep-frying and stir-frying seasoning with red wine, sugar and vinegar, and with emphasis on soup ingredients in particular. Famous dishes are: "Fo tiao qiang", "wine-pickled chicken" and "grain-pickled boiled mejillon", "snowflake-like chicken" and "chrysanthemum fish ball", etc.

Su cuisine is of Jiangsu local flavor dishes, SU Xi vegetables, Nanjing, Huai Yang cuisine. The main features are the stew, the simmered, the steamed, roasting, frying; with emphasis on the styles, appearance and gorgeous colors. The specialties are Jiaohua chicken (*Beggar's Chicken* (jiào huā jī 叫化鸡)), lotus leaf chicken, pork ball stew , squirrel-like mandarin fish and so on. In Tang and Song Dynasties, Jiangsu cuisine, and Zhejiang cuisine were two important ones in the south of the country.

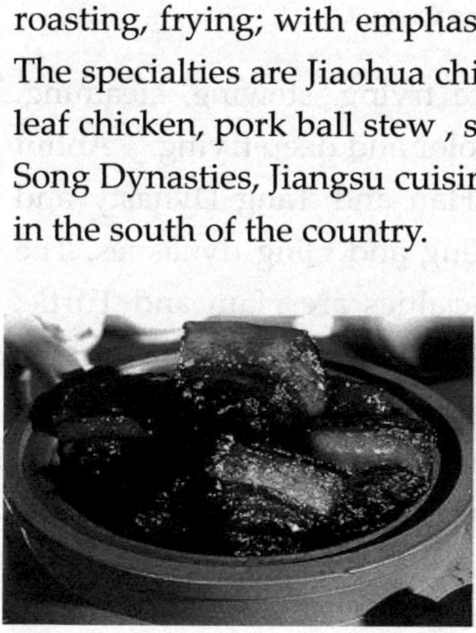

Zhejiang Cuisine: Made up of Hanzhou, Ningbo and Shaoxing Cuisines, Zhejiang cuisine is enjoyed for its freshness, tenderness, and mellow flavor. Hangzhou, Ningbo, Shaoxing represent three kinds of local-flavored dishes which have early fame. Cooking methods are mainly frying and braising. Ningbo cuisine is fresh and salty, featured as steaming, roasting, stewing and known for its seafood, which is tender, soft and slippery, with the original juice flavor. Shaoxing is specialized in cooking river food, and poultry, which are made crisp and glutinous, with a rural flavor. The specialties are "West Lake Vinegar Fish", "Dongpo Meat", "homemade meat", "lotus leaf Steamed Meat", "West Lake Brasenia soup", "Longjing Shrimp", "Hangzhou stewed chicken", and so on.

Hunan cuisine, made up of Xiangjiang cuisine, Dongting Lake flavors and dishes in mountainous areas in western Hunan. The cooking methods are mainly smoking, steaming, deep frying characterized by heavy oil, and thick color, which is spicy and sour, inexpensive but substantial. The specialties are "Dongan chicken" and "Red simmer shark's fin", "Bacon co-steam", "breaded whole duck," "Spicy Bamboo Shoots", "Chestnut Cooking Vegetables" and "Wuyuan chicken" and "spicy Chicken" and so on.

Anhui cuisine (Hui Cai for short), one of the eight most famous cuisines in China, features the local culinary arts of Huizhou. It comprises the specialties of South Anhui, Yanjiang and Huai Bei. The highly distinctive characteristic of Anhui cuisine lies not only in the elaborate choices of cooking materials but also in the strict control of cooking process.

Cooking skills are frying, stewing, steaming, with heavy oil, thick color and deep frying. Anhui cuisine started from Han and Tang Dynasty and became popular in Ming and Qing dynasties. The traditional Anhui specialties are Ham and Turtle, Stewed civet Cats, Wuwei Smoked Chicken, Huangshan Braised Pigeon and so on. The "Ham Stew Snapper" also known as "Water Chestnut Consommé Turtle".

段落译文

中国菜是由各地名特小吃组成的。它们的具体烹调技术和菜点风味又各具特色。正是这些多姿多彩的地方菜，构成了风味独特的中国菜。

中国菜肴在烹饪中有许多流派。其中最有影响和代表性的也为社会所公认的有：鲁、川、粤、闽、苏、浙、湘、徽等菜系，即被人们常说的中国“八大菜系”。

鲁菜是山东菜的总称，主要有济南和胶东地方菜组成。胶东派擅长爆、炸、扒、熘、蒸；口味以鲜夺人，偏于清淡。济南派则以汤著称，辅以爆、炒、烧、炸，菜品以清、鲜、脆、嫩见长。名菜有九转大肠、糖醋黄河鲤鱼、德州扒鸡等。鲁菜自汉唐，成为“北菜”主角，至现代仿膳仍有鲁菜特色。

川菜是世界上最著名的中国菜系之一，所用的调味品既复杂多样，又富有特色；尤其是号称“三椒”的花椒、胡椒、辣椒，“三香”的葱、姜、蒜等的使用频繁及数量之多，远非其他菜系能相比。川菜有“七滋八味”之说，“七滋”指甜、酸、麻、辣、苦、香、咸；“八味”即是鱼香、酸辣、椒麻、怪味、麻辣、红油、姜汁、家常。烹调方法共有38种之多，故国际烹饪界有“食在中国，味在四川”之说。名菜有灯影牛肉、水煮牛肉、夫妻肺片、麻婆豆腐、水煮鱼等300多种。

粤菜是广东菜的总称，由广州、潮州、东江三种地方菜组成。粤菜配料多，讲究鲜、嫩、爽、滑。以烹制海鲜见长，汤类、素菜、甜菜最具特色。刀工精细，口味清纯。东江菜又名客家菜，菜品多用肉类，极少水产，主料突出，讲究香浓，下油重，味偏咸，以砂锅菜见长，有独特的乡土风味。尤以烹制蛇、狸、猫、狗、猴、鼠等野生动物而负盛名。名菜有“烤乳猪”、冻肉、“冬瓜盅”、大良炒牛奶等。粤菜源于西汉，今名播中外，有“吃在广州”之说。

闽菜是福建菜的总称。以福州、厦门、泉州等地方菜发展而成，烹调方法以清汤、干炸、爆炒为主，调味常用红糟，偏重甜酸，尤其讲究调汤。名菜有：佛跳墙、“醉糟鸡”、“糟汁氽海蚌”、雪花鸡、菊花鲈鱼球等名肴最负盛名。

苏菜系即江苏地方风味菜，由苏锡菜、南京菜和淮扬菜组成。擅长炖、焖、蒸、烧、炒；其菜肴注重造型，讲究美观，色调绚丽。名菜有叫化鸡、荷叶鸡、狮子头、松鼠桂鱼等。唐宋时，苏菜和浙菜同为“南食”两大台柱。

浙菜系以杭州、宁波、绍兴三种地方风味菜为代表，成名较早。烹调方法以爆、炒、烩、炸为主，清鲜爽脆；宁波菜以“咸鲜合一”，蒸、烧、炖制海鲜见长，讲求嫩、软、滑；注重大汤大水，保持原汁原味。绍兴菜擅长烹饪河鲜、家禽，入口香酥绵糯，富有乡村风味。名菜有“西湖醋鱼”、“东坡肉”、“家乡南肉”、“荷叶粉蒸肉”、“西湖莼菜汤”、“龙井虾仁”、“杭州煨鸡”等。

湘菜系即湖南菜，以湘江、洞庭湖区和湘西山区等地方菜发展而成。手法以熏、蒸、干炒为主，重辣酸。其制作精细，用料广泛，品种繁多，其特色是油多、色浓，讲究实惠。湘西菜擅长珍野味，烟熏腊肉和各种腌肉。名菜有“东安子鸡”、“红煨鱼翅”、“腊味合蒸”、“面包全鸭”、“油辣冬笋尖”、“板栗烧菜心”、“五元神仙鸡”、“麻辣仔鸡”等。

安徽菜简称为徽菜，是安徽菜的总称，也是中国八大菜系之一，以徽州菜为主要特色，兼有淮南、沿江及淮北特色。皖菜注重烹饪过程的细节以及对烹饪原料的精心选择。在烹调技艺上擅长烧、炖、蒸，重油、重色、重火工，以烹制山珍野味著称。徽菜起于汉唐，盛于明清。其名菜有火腿甲鱼、红烧果子狸、无为熏鸡、黄山炖鸽等。其中“火腿炖甲鱼”又名“清炖马蹄鳖”，是徽菜中最古老的传统名菜。

实用词汇

艾窝窝 steamed cake made of glutinous rice with sweet filling
八宝菜 eight-treasure pickle
八宝饭 eight-treasure rice pudding
八珍鸡汤 ba-zhen chicken soup
拔丝山药 hot candied yam
白汤 clear soup

白斩鸡 tender boiled chicken with soy sauce
百合红枣莲子汤 lotus seed soup with lily bulb and red dates
北京烤鸭 roast Peking duck
菠萝鸡丁 diced chicken with pineapple
菠萝苦瓜鸡 bitter gourd chicken with pineapple
槽子糕 cake made with moulds
糙米鸡 stew chicken with unpolished rice soup
柴米油盐 fuel, rice, oil and salt—chief daily necessities
炒米 parched rice; millet stir-fried in butter
炒面 parched flour; fried noodles with shredded meat and vegetables
炒什锦 fried vegetables
炒腰花 stir-fried kidneys
炒鱿鱼 stir-fried squid—boot sb. out
川菜 Sichuan cuisine
葱爆虾 sauted shrimp with scallion
葱油鸡 scallion chicken
冬瓜薏仁炖排骨 stew spareribs with wax gourd and yiren
发菜三丝汤 sea moss soup
翡翠鲍鱼 abalone mushroom with vegetable
粉蒸肉 pork steamed with ground rice flour
粉蒸鲜菇 steam black mushroom
高汤 (meat or chicken) soup-stock; thin-soup
宫爆鸡丁 kunpao chicken
咖喱鸡 curry chicken
荷叶饼 thin packle
红案 red board—cooking that prepares dishes
红豆薏仁汤 yiren soup with red beans
红烧豆腐 simmer bean curb
红烧烤麸 simmer baked bran
红烧苦瓜 simmer bitter gourd
红烧栗子鸡 simmer chestnut chicken

红烧牛腩 stewed beef

红烧排骨 pork ribs braised in soy sauce

红烧肉 simmer meat

红烧狮子头 pork ball stew

荤菜 meat dish

火锅 chafing dish

火树银花 fiery trees and silver flowers—dazzling displays of fireworks and lanterns (on a festival night)

火腿蛋 ham and egg

火腿玉米浓汤 ham corn soup

火腿月饼 ham-stuffed moon cake

家常便饭 homely meals

家常菜 home-cooked dishes

家常豆腐 ordinary plain bean curd

叫花子鸡 Beggar's Chicken (whole chicken baked in a mud coating)

空心汤团 hollow dumpling (one without filling)—empty promise or favour

绿豆糕 mung-bean cake

油茶面 flour fried in beef fat with sugar and sesame

油条 deep-fried twisted dough sticks; sly person

油炸鬼 deep-fried dough strips or rings

鱼香茄子 fry eggplants

鱼香肉丝 flavored sliced meat

名言俗语

萝卜青菜，各有所爱。

A man's meat is another man's poison.

富人口里的美味，是穷人的辛酸血泪。

The dainties of the great are the tears of the poor.

味如鸡肋："tastes like chicken ribs", which is often used to describe anything that is of little value but would be a pity to throw away.

吃是为了生存，但是生存不是为了吃饭。

Eat to live, but not live to eat.

巧妇难为无米之炊。

Even a clever daughter-in-law finds it hard to cook without rice.

天下无不散的宴席。

Eventually, all bosom friends will drift apart. /The longest day has an end.

衣食足而后知荣辱。

First secure an independent income, then practice virtue.

鲜肉由天赐，劣厨乃鬼遣。/ 厨师常将菜烧坏。

God sends meat and the devil sends cooks.

佳肴应配美酒。

Good eating deserves good drinking.

贪多嚼不烂。

Many irons in the fire, pare must cool.

吃饭做弥撒，对人无妨碍。

Meat and Masse, never hindered man.

吃饭时，不应开口说话。

The mouth which eats does not talk.

饥不择食。

Nothing comes amiss. / Wrong to a hungry man.

一颗豆子称不上一顿正餐。

One bean does not make a whole meal.

因噎废食。

One cannot refuse to eat just because there is chance of being choked.

自食其力。

Paddle your own canoe.

吃饭时要快，做事时也要快。

Quick at meal, quick at work.

太多厨师反而烧坏汤。

Too many cooks spoil the broth.

吃得最多的人一定最胖，书读得多的人不一定最聪明。

Those who eat most are always fattest, those who read most are not always wisest.

吃得好喝得好的人往往醉的最糟。

Those who eat best and drink best often do worst.

词语注解

满汉全席：中国正式的宴席

A full, formal banquet, combining Manchurian and Chinese delicacies

八仙桌：大的四方餐桌，人们可以围坐用餐

Eight Immortals table—big square table around which people can sit at each side

百家饭：从很多家收集的米和面粉做的饭

meal prepared with rice and flour collected from many families

粗茶淡饭

plain tea and simple food

当家菜：每天必备的最基本的、有代表性的菜

basic, common vegetables essential for daily consumption

中西合璧

中西方的饮食风俗大相径庭，尤其在饮食观念方面。中国人认为丰富的食物是好客的表现及对美食的强调。宴会上的食物和酒应该丰富多彩、必须美味、昂贵。吃饭时，主人要求客人喝得尽兴、吃得尽兴，并用自己的筷子经常为客人添食物以表示真诚。西方人则认为食物的营养价值最重要，而不强调色香味美。他们强调健康的饮食。有时为客人准备食物十分简单。他们希望客人感到快乐，认为邀请吃饭是维持友谊的机会，通过吃饭交流信息、传达友情。用餐时不会像中国人反复劝酒劝菜，最多一次或两次。他们认为劝得太多是将自己的观点强加于人。当然现在的年轻人可能有不同观念。

Western and Chinese customs and tastes are quite different，in concepts particularly. The Chinese think much of their friends and of the richness of the food representing one's hospitality. Also emphasizing the meal itself when treating friends, The food and wine at the banquet should be rich and colorful and it must be delicious and expensive. When the feast starts, the host urges guests to drink and eat more and pick up food for their guest frequently with their own chopsticks. In the host's opinion, the aim to entertain is to let guests drink and eat to their heart's content. Western people hold the opposite opinion. They think nothing is more important than the nutrition of the food when they are dinning. They pay great attention to the nutrition of the food rather than its color, flavor, shape, etc. Their diet mainly focuses on health, as if they don't care about the enjoyment of its tastes, sometimes the dishes prepared for guests are extremely simple. The Westerners hope their guests feel joyful. Meanwhile, they think that invitation is a chance of the maintenance of friendship. And the most important is to get much useful information by entertainment. When the feast starts, Westerners are also warm to the guests, urging guests to drink and eat, but only once or twice. They consider saying too much would force their views on others. Of course the young may have different ideas and different way of life.

UNIT 23

Chinese Alcohol

酒文化

题记

世界有三大古酒——黄酒、葡萄酒和啤酒，其中黄酒的源产地是中国绍兴。中国有着五千多年的酿酒历史，技术不断发展，品种繁多。除黄酒外，还有白酒、果酒、药酒等，同时也形成了丰富多彩的酒文化。

There are three kinds of ancient alcohol in the world. They are yellow rice wine, wine, and beer, among which yellow rice wine was originally made in Shaoxing, China. With a 5000-year history of wine-making, China has been improving its technology. In addition to yellow rice wine, there are many different wines, such as distilled spirits, fruit wine, and medicinal liquor, and rich wine culture.

Chinese alcohol has always been associated with the famous poems and great men. The poem "only Dukang wine can allay misgivings" written by Caocao has enjoyed great popularity for thousands of years, which also shows Chinses people an understanding of wine. Most Chinese alcohol belongs to "distilled spirit" made from different cereal crops. Thousands of years ago, the Chinese had made a unique grain alcohol by using special brewing technology. And the unique culture was formed.

There has been an indissoluble bond between wine and Chinese people. When they are happy, wine is used to celebrate; when sad, it can eliminate their gloom; when they are lonely, it can be their best friend. No matter young or old, in high or low status, people usually become frank and sincere when they drink some alcohol. An old saying, "Ale in, truth out", describes this thinking. In the world of liquor, people tend to reveal their natural, innocent, and pure nature. The ancient poets and writers believed that they would have abundant imagination and often produce unexpected inspiration when they were slightly drunk. It was said that the famous Chinese poet, Li Bai, who is known as a saint poet and Jiu Xian (the god of wine / winebibber), could not even write any poems without drinking some alcohol.

Although wine is not a necessity in the daily life, But on important occasions, such as weddings, giving birth to a child, and birthday parties, alcohol is used to entertain guests. It is also the best thing to entertain friends and add to the fun when getting together, especially during festivals.

Many ethnic minorities have their own drinking habits. Almost all Tibetan people like to drink Qingke barley wine. When the guests receive a toast, they must show the respect to gods first, and then finish the drink in three sips. Mongolians like to drink horse milk liquor with a big bowl but not a goblet or cup. It is polite to drink up when they toast to you. The Yi people in Liangshan, Sichuan province drink buckwheat or corn wine. In a friendly and harmonious atmosphere, the hospitable hosts would make sure that the guests can enjoy themselves. Therefore, many ethnic minorities use songs and dance to make their guests drink more.

It is worth mentioning that the Chinese medicinal liquor which is also well known all over the world, can improve people's health and cure many diseases.

段落译文

中国酒常常与名人的诗句相联系。"何以解忧，唯有杜康"，古代曹操这脍炙人口的诗句，千百年来一直为人们所称颂，它也道出了人们对酒的一种理解。中国酒大多是由谷物经传统工艺酿造而成的"白酒"。早在几千年前，中国人就在世界酿酒技术史上独辟蹊径，用酒曲酿出独树一帜的谷物酒。同时也形成了中国特有的酒文化。

酒与人们的生活结下不解之缘。欢乐时，人们用它来表示庆祝；忧愁时，人们用它清除心中的郁闷；孤独时，它可以成为人们的知己。往往在酒的氛围中，人们无论是高低贵贱，男女老少，都能敞开心扉，赤诚相待。中国的俗语"酒后吐真言"就是描绘这种境界。在酒的世界里，人们往往能显露出自然、天真、纯洁的本性。古代文人与酒的关系也非常密切。他们认为在微微酒醉的境界里，想象力会更加丰富，此时的文人墨客常常会产生意想不到的灵感，创造出精美的诗篇。例如著名诗人李白，据说在他的生活中，无酒不能作诗，因此被后人称为"诗圣"和"酒仙"。

尽管"酒"不是人类生活的必需品，但是在人们生活中的所有重大活动，诸如结婚、生子、贺寿等都要摆酒祝贺。在中国逢年过节，亲朋好友相聚，酒是最能助兴添情的东西。

中国各民族都有饮酒的习惯。藏族人喜欢饮青稞酒。客人接受敬酒时，先用右手无名指沾酒向身后上方弹三次，表示敬上苍神灵后，再分三口饮尽。蒙古族喝马奶酒。一般敬酒都用酒碗不用酒杯，不喝干是不礼貌的。四川凉山的彝族喝荞麦、玉米酿的酒。在友好融洽的气氛中，主人要热情周到，让大家都尽情尽兴。因此很多民族都有敬酒的歌舞，用来劝酒。

值得一提的还有中国的药酒，它具有保健强身、治疗疾病的功效，早已驰名海内外。

实用词汇

酒 alcohol
酿酒 make wine; brew beer
白酒 distilled spirit; white spirit
茅台酒 Maotai
黄酒 yellow wine
果酒 fruit wine
白葡萄酒 white wine
红葡萄酒 red wine
人参酒 ginseng liquor
啤酒 beer
罐装啤酒 canned beer
鲜啤酒 draught beer
香槟 champagne
威士忌 whisky
白兰地 brandy
清酒 pure rice wine; sake
鸡尾酒 cocktail
药酒 medicinal liquor
名诗 famous poem
诗圣 saint poet
喜酒 wedding feast
迎客酒 welcome wine
干杯 drinking a toast
酒歌 drinking song
酒过三巡 wine going round three times
祝酒 drinking a toast; toasting
斟酒 decanting wine, filling a wine cup

嗜酒如命 slavish drinker
畅饮 drinking one's fill; carousing
酒量大 heavy drinker
酒量小 little / small drinker
酒友 drinking companion
品酒 wine tasting
酒令 drinker's wager game
酗酒 wine drunk
猜拳 finger-guessing game
戒酒 giving up drinking
醉眼蒙眬 drunken and bleary-eyed

名言俗语

酒后吐真言。/ 老酒下肚，实话说出。
Ale in, truth out.
酒神巴克思比海神尼普顿淹死的人还多。/ 美酒害死的人比海水害死的人还多。
Bacchus has drowned more men than Neptune.
大口吃饭，少量喝酒。
Eat at pleasure, drink with measure.
酒香客自来。
Good wine sells itself.
酒肉朋友不长久。
Table friendship soon changes.
陈酒味醇，老友情深。
Old friends and old wine are best.
自己酿的酒自己喝。/ 自作自受。/ 自食其果。
One must drink as one brews. / As you brew, so must you drink.
酒陈味香醇，人老阅历深。
Wine and judgement mature with age.
美酒酿酸醋；极爱结深仇。

As the best wine makes the sharpest vinegar, so deepest love turns to the deadliest hatred.

镜照人面酒映心。

In the mirror we see the face; in wine, the heart.

无酒不成欢。

There is no gladness without wine.

酒是叛徒：先是朋友，后是敌人。

Wine is a turn-coat, first a friend, then an enemy.

酒是魔鬼攻击青年人的第一件武器。

Wine is the first weapon the devils use in attacking the young.

酒逢知己千杯少，话不投机半句多。

Drinking with a bosom friend, a thousand shots are too few; talking with a disagreeable person, half a sentence is too many.

今天花天酒地，明日潦倒穷途。/ 乐极生悲。

Drunken days have all their tomorrow.

今朝有酒今朝醉。

Eat, drink, and be merry, for tomorrow we die.

词语注解

酒囊饭袋：比喻无能的人。

Wineskin and rice-bag: It also means someone good for nothing.

酒肉朋友：指只在一起吃喝玩乐，不干正经事的朋友。

Wine-and-meat friends: It is often used to describe the fair-weather friends.

敬酒不吃吃罚酒：比喻好好地劝说不听，用强迫手段却接受了。

To refuse a toast only to drink a penalty, which also means to submit to sb.'s pressure after first turning down his request.

酒令：饮酒时所做的可分输赢的游戏。输了的人罚饮酒。

Drinkers' wager game, in which losers are punished by having to drink wine.

醉翁之意不在酒：表示本意不在此而在别的方面。

The drinker is really not interested in wine. It means some one talks about one thing, but tries to do another.

醉生梦死：像喝醉了酒和睡梦中那样糊里糊涂地活着。

Living as if drunk or dreaming, which means to lead a befuddled life.

中西合璧

世界各国也都有各自喜欢的美酒和独特的酒文化。法国以香槟和葡萄酒著称于世。法国人喝酒喜欢细品慢饮，而且还有很多讲究，例如红酒配红肉，白酒配鱼等。俄罗斯人最喜欢喝伏特加，并且喜欢干杯。据说俄罗斯人喝伏特加时，必须先从喉咙里发出“咕噜”声。相传这是几百年前彼得大帝时留下来的传统。德国以啤酒著名，德国人喜欢用大杯喝啤酒。英国人使“威士忌”闻名于全世界。

Every country in the world has its own favorite wine and unique wine culture. France is famous for champagne and wine. In France, people like drinking wine slowly and gently. There are some tasteful rules, such as that red wine goes with red meat, and that white wine goes with fish, and so on. The favorite drink for Russians is vodka, a kind of liquor. It is said that before they drink it, they gurgle it in their throats first, a tradition handed down from “Peter the Great” hundreds of years ago. Germany is famous for beer. Germans prefer using large cups to drink beer. The British make “Whiskey” known all over the world.

UNIT 24

Chinese Tea

茶文化

题记

中国是茶树的原产地，也是世界上发现和饮用茶叶最早的国家。茶是中华民族的举国之饮，劳动人民在栽培、加工茶叶方面有丰富的经验。中国的茶叶一直以品质优良、种类繁多著称于世。现在世界上各产茶国家，都直接或间接从中国引种过茶树或茶籽。因此，许多国家的现代语言中“茶”字的发音，都和中国闽粤一带“茶”字的发音相似。

Tea was originally found and produced in China. In China, tea is the most famous beverage. And Chinese have had rich experience in planting, utilizing and processing tea. Chinese tea is famous worldwide for its high quality and many varieties. All of the tea-producing countries have brought in tea plants and seeds from China directly or indirectly. Hence, the pronunciation of "tea" in different countries is similar to that of the pronunciations in the provinces of Fujian and Guangdong in China.

Tea, coffee and cocoa are the three beverages which enjoy the great reputation throughout the world.

Tea originated from China and it was the first nation that discovered and drank it as a beverage. There are many stories about the origins of tea. The character of "tea" emerged in approximately Tang

Dynasty. When LuYu, (the saint of tea) compiled his masterpiece—*The Scripture of Tea*, he decided that it was necessary for tea to have a unified term, at this time the Chinese character 茶 (*cha*) was adopted, and it has been ever since. It has been said that tea was found much earlier from Shennong or in Qing and Han Dynasty.

Chinese tea can be sorted into six types with its characteristics of processing and fermentation.

Green tea is not fermented and it has the widest producing regions, the largest output and finest quality. Among them are some relatively famous types as follows:

The West Lake Longjing tea, Guizhou Duyun Maojian, Jiangsu Biluochun the Sichuan Mongdinganna, the Mount Lushan Cloud and Fog, the Mt. Huang Mao fong, the Even Water Pearl, Southern Rain tea, Anhui Green Snow, Sichuan Bamboo Leaves, Henan Xinyang Hair Point, and so on.

The effects of green tea are better than any other tea. As for the anti-cancer functions, the green tea surpasses black tea. It is believed that the senior citizens should not drink green tea, especially for those who have habitual constipation, as it may make it more serious. But young boys and girls in the development period can drink green tea. Those who are engaged reading and writing should often drink green tea.

Black tea is fully fermented and is the second most famous tea in China. The most famous black teas are Qimen Kung Fu, Wu Hung Kung Fu, and Dian Hong fall. With tea buds as the raw material, they are withered, twisted, oxidized and fermented indoors, finally being dried to produce the final black tea. Black tea is good for our stomachs and helps urinary output, dieting and, slows down aging. Black tea is the best choice for physical laborers and is also very good for women after child-birth to drink with brown sugar.

White tea is slightly unfermented. White tea is classified as "Great White", "the Narcissus White" and "Young White". The Fujian White Hair Acupuncture Needle, the White Peony and Shoumei all belong to the white tea family. It is very rare and valuable because the tea buds, completely covered with white hair, as white as snow. White tea is famous for its elegance with a more than 880 years of history.

The yellow tea is also slightly fermented tea, with its crafts producing similar to Green tea, but the colour is yellow, therefore product has the yellow leaf, yellow tea soup, the fragrance is clearly sharp, and the taste is sweet. The best are Mt. Jun silver needle, Mongding yellow bud.

Heicha is unique and only produced in China. It is a post-fermented tea. It is produced from the old tea leaves. There are Hunan Heicha, Hubei Old Green tea, Sichuan Biancha, Guangxi Liubao tea and Yunan Pu'er tea and so on. Heicha is glorious because of its long history. Generally they are from Huan, Hubei, Sichan, Yuanan and Guangxi. Yunnan Pu'er is especially famous all over the world.

Oolong tea is also called Qingcha, which is produced by combining the craft of black and green tea production. It is known as a collection, as half fermented tea. The representatives are Oolong tea in the north of Fujian, Mt. Wu Yi Roch Tea, Narcissus, Dahongpao (the Scarlet Gown), the Anxi Oolong tea, the Guangdong Oolong tea and so on. Oolong tea has the functions of black tea and green tea, it is as fresh and thick as green tea, while as clear and delicate as red tea. Oolong tea contains less caffeine, and thus everybody can drink it. It also has the obvious function of diuresis and is a good medicine to help reduce weight.

In addition there are two types of re-processed tea, pressed tea and scented tea (flower tea). Pressed tea is convenient for long-distance transport and storage, and dry compressed tea is generally produced from black tea or Heicha, while scented tea is made of green tea or black tea with fragrant flowers such as jasmine, magnolia, etc.

The top ten of the famous tea in China are the West Lake Longjing tea, Tie Guan Yin, Huangshan Tippy, Junshan silver needles, Huang Shan Mao Feng, Keemun black tea, Lushan clouds, Xinyangmaojian, Wuyi yancha, Dongting Biluochun, and Luan seeds.

Chinese tea has been playing a great part in qualifying ourselves, supporting friendship, showing the ceremony, character cultivation and beautifying our life. Tea has been able to adapt to different sectors and many occasions, the nature of tea is in line with the nature of the simplicity and honesty of Chinese people.

Chinese people love tea, which formed the foundation of the Chinese tea ceremony and its ethnic characteristics, the art of tea, tea drinking customs and the unique Chinese tea culture. Chinese tea culture has specific content, and a strong national character, which has made it globally famous. During its development Chinese tea culture continues to spread to neighboring countries and influence their food culture.

段落译文

茶叶、咖啡和可可，是举世公认的三大最佳饮料。

中国是茶叶的故乡，也是世界上发现和饮用茶叶最早的国家。中国饮茶起源众说纷纭，年代不一。但唐代以前无“茶”字，而只有“荼”字的记载，直到茶经的作者陆羽，才将“荼”字减一画写成“茶”字，因此才有茶起源于唐代的说法。

还有茶起源于神农、秦汉等说法。

中国茶多以加工和发酵的工艺来分类的，主要分为六类：绿茶、红茶、乌龙茶、白茶、黄茶和黑茶。

绿茶是不经过发酵的茶，是中国产区最广、产量最多、品质最佳的一类茶叶。西湖龙井、江苏碧螺春、庐山云雾茶、黄山毛峰、安徽六安瓜片等属于这一类茶。绿茶抗癌作用优于红茶，但是老年人不宜饮用，特别是有习惯性便秘的老人，不宜饮绿茶，因为饮绿茶后往往加重便秘。而青春发育期的青年男女，适宜饮绿茶。文字工作者更应常饮绿茶。

红茶是在制作加工时全发酵的一类茶。祁门功夫、湖红功夫、滇红功夫等属于这一类。以一芽二或三叶为原料，经过萎凋、揉捻，在室内充分氧化、发酵，最后再进行干燥处理四个工艺程序而制成，是中国第二大茶类。红茶能暖胃，利尿，抗衰老。体力劳动者饮红茶最适宜，妇女产后饮红茶加红糖最好。

白茶属轻微发酵茶，是中国茶类中的特殊珍品。因茶树品种不同又分为“大白”,“水仙白”和“小白”。福建白毫银针、白牡丹和寿眉都属于白茶。主要有银针白毫、白牡丹、贡眉这三个品种。白茶的历史悠久，其清雅芳名的出现，迄今已有八百八十余年了。

黄茶，属于轻微发酵茶类，基本工艺近似绿茶，因为是黄色的茶叶、茶汤，黄茶因此成名。黄茶具有黄叶黄汤、香气清锐、滋味醇厚的特点。主要有君山银针、蒙顶黄芽、广东大叶青等。

黑茶，属于后发酵茶，是中国特有的茶类，由老茶叶制成。主要品种有湖南黑茶、湖北老青茶、四川沱茶、广西六堡散茶、云南普洱茶等。其生产历史悠久，主要产于湖南、湖北、四川、云南、广西等地。云南普洱茶古今中外久负盛名。

乌龙茶，又称青茶，是红茶、绿茶加工技术的结合，是半发酵茶类的总称。代表茶品有武夷岩茶、武夷水仙、大红袍、安溪铁观音、广东乌龙茶等。乌龙茶兼有红茶和绿茶两者之长，男女老少都适宜饮用，且有明显利尿作用，也是减肥的良药。

另外有再加工的两类茶是指紧压茶和花茶。紧压茶是为了长途运输和长时间保存方便，将茶压缩干燥，一般由红茶或黑茶制作。花茶是以香花如茉莉、玉兰等和绿茶(有时也用红茶)制作的。

中国公认的十大名茶是西湖龙井、安溪铁观音、黄山毛尖、君山银针、黄山毛峰、祁门红茶、庐山云雾、信阳毛尖、武夷岩茶、洞庭碧螺春、六安瓜子。

中国茶能养性、联谊、示礼、传情、育德、陶冶情操、美化生活。茶之所以能适应各阶层，众多场合，是因为茶的情操、茶的本性符合中华民族的平凡实在、合诚相处的民族精神。

中华民族酷爱饮茶，形成了具有民族特色的茶礼、茶艺、饮茶习俗，及独具特色的茶文化。中华茶文化在丰富发展的过程中不断地向周边国家传播，影响各国的饮食文化。

实用词汇

采茶戏 tea-pickers' opera
茶博士 teahouse keeper
滇红 Yunnan black tea
砖茶 brick tea
茶糕点 tea cake, tea snacks
茶菜 tea cuisine
茶道 Chadao, the Way of Tea, tea ceremony
花茶 scented tea
茉莉花茶 jasmine tea
品茗 sip tea
普洱茶 Pu'er tea
祁红 keemun, black tea produced at Qimen of Anhui Province
压制茶 pressed tea

珠茶 a kind of green tea（the tea leaves looking like beads）
领略饮茶情趣 take delight in tea-drinking
品茶 savoring tea
紧压茶（tightly-pressed）tea lump

名言俗语

宁可三天无盐，不可一日无茶

Rather live without salt for three days than without tea for a single day.

开门七件事：柴米油盐酱醋茶

"Seven things in daily life are required: firewood, rice, oil, salt, soy sauce, vinegar and tea"

"水是茶之母，器是茶之父"

"the water is the mother of tea and the pot its father"

茶能提神、驱散疲倦、减轻疲劳、警醒思想、防止困倦

"Tea tempers the spirit, harmonizes the mind, dispels lassitude and relieves fatigue, awakens the thought and prevents drowsiness."

宁可一日不食，不可一日无茶。

"Better to be deprived of food for three days, than tea for one."

客从远方来，多以茶相待。

"When a guest comes to my home from afar on a cold night, I light bamboo to boil tea to offer him."

朋友之最可贵，贵在雪中送炭，不必对方开口，积极主动相助。朋友中之极品，便如好茶淡而不涩，清香但不扑鼻、缓缓飘来，细水长流。

The value of friends lies in the timely help; your friends will come to help you in a hurry automatically without being asked. The best friend is good tea, weak but not puckery, fragrant but not strong, slow but lasting long.

词语注解

碧螺春：原产太湖地区的一种绿茶

green tea originally produced in the Taihu Lake area

炒青：炒茶叶一道工序

process of curing tea-leaves

珠茶：茶叶象圆珠的一种茶

a kind of green tea (the tea leaves looking like beads)

看茶：上茶，给客人端茶

(to the servant when a guest arrives) serve tea

茶道：泡茶、品茶的礼节合称，有时还包括茶具及泡茶的动作，茶道是茶文化的体现。

Chadao, the Way of Tea , the rituals and processes of making and savoring tea, A tea ceremony is a ritualised form of making tea. One can also refer to the whole set of rituals, tools, gestures, etc. used in such ceremonies as tea culture. All of these tea ceremonies and rituals contain 'artificiality, abstractness, symbolism and formalism' to one degree or another.

中西合璧

中国是文明古国，礼仪之邦，很重礼节。凡是来了客人，沏茶、敬茶的礼仪是必不可少的。当有客来访，可征求意见，选用最合来客口味的茶叶和最佳茶具待客。在饮茶时也可适当佐以茶食、糖果、菜肴等，达到调节口味和点心之功效。

英国是世界上第二大茶叶消费国，平均每年每人消费 2.1 公斤，通常是红茶加牛奶或糖。“茶歇”是英国普通人每天下午活动的一个重要组成部分。下午茶不只是饮料，而是带饮茶的便餐。

China is a country with a time-honored civilization and a land of ceremony and decorum. Whenever guests pay a visit, it is necessary to make and serve tea to them. Before serving tea, you may ask them for their preferences as to what kind of tea they fancy and serve them the tea in the most appropriate teacups. Snacks, sweets and other dishes may be served at tea time to complement the fragrance of the tea and to allay one's hunger.

The British are the second largest tea consumers in the world, with each person consuming 2.1 kg per year on average. Usually black tea is served with milk and sometimes with sugar. For the working class of the United Kingdom. “Tea break” is an essential part of a day. Tea is not only the name of the beverage, but of a late afternoon light meal, irrespective of the beverage consumed.

UNIT 25

Chinese Clothing

中国服饰

题记

中国服饰有着悠久的历史。人们在北京周口店山顶洞人的文化遗存中发现了骨针，说明早在旧石器时代晚期我们的祖先就会用针缝衣了。到了新石器时代晚期，不同地区和民族人们的服饰款式已有很大的不同。

Chinese clothing has a long history. The bone sewing needles found in the culture remains of Zhoukoudian, Beijing, show that the people of the Paleolithic Age had learned to make clothes. At the late Neolithic Age, people from different regions and nations had already worn many different styles of the clothes.

The earliest style of ancient Chinese clothing is the upper outer garment and the skirt. During Shang Dynasty, the people began to wear crossing-collar-out garments and skirts on the lower part of the body, loincloths in the middle, and curled up shoes. After Qinshihuang united the whole China, clothes displayed distinct differences. The working people wore short garments made of coarse cloth, they were called "Bu-yi" or plebes; the rich usually wore long and loose fitting dresses. Since then the basic shapes of Chinese clothing have been established.

In Spring and Autumn Period and Warring States period, the appearance of Shen-yi and Hu-fu (pien-fu) were the greatest changes in Chinese clothing. At that time people would sew the tunic and a skirt together to make a new kind of garment called shen-yi. It was worn by the people from the Warring States period to the Western Han Dynasty and could be worn by both men and women in all ranks. Hu-fu was the dress of a ethnic groups (a non-Han nationalities) living in the north of China. In order to ride easily, they usually wore short garments, trousers and boots. Since the clothes worn by the people of Han were not convenient for working, Wu-ling, one of Kings of state Zhao at that time, encouraged his people to wear Hu-fu. He became the earliest reformer in Chinese clothing history. At the same time, the Han clothing was enriched and improved.

The policies of recuperating, multiplying and building the economy during Han Dynasty strengthened the communion between the nations and changed the social fashion so the people dressed more extravagantly. For example, Shen-yi worn by women during Han Dynasty had several layered skirts with many triangular ornaments weighing them down and long ribbons. After Eastern Han Dynasty, men no longer wore Shen-yi, but women still wore it. Shen-yi influenced Chinese women clothing so greatly that Qipao (cheongsam) and one-piece dress all evolved from it.

During the Western Zhou period, ranking systems were established gradually and the integrated clothing system for government officials came into being. From then on, there were different color clothes for different people, defining the emperor from plebes. For example, during Tang Dynasty, the color of the emperor was yellow, and the color of the officials' clothes was different from the first to the ninth rank, such as purple, red, green, blue or black and so on. Later, no one was allowed to wear yellow clothes, except the emperor, yellow and gold clothes became the emperors' only, which continued until Qing Dynasty.

In ancient China, the gowns worn by emperors were called "Long-pao" or "dragon gowns", which are mainly yellow and embroidered elegant dragon patterns. For example, the Long-pao of Qing Dynasty was embroidered with three dragons both in the front and back separately, two on the shoulders, and one inside the front of it, so there were nine dragons in total. Five of them can

be seen from the front or back. In ancient China, the emperors were also reserved the numbers nine and five, as these two numbers symbolized dignity. In addition, other things such as spray or spindrift, hills and treasures would be embroidered at the lower hem of the gown. These patterns show good fortune as people wished that the emperor would unify the land of the country and keep it peace forever.

The men's clothing in Qing Dynasty was the gown and Magua. Magua also known a mandarin jacket was usually worn outside of the gown, which originally was the riding clothing for the Manchu. After the Xin-hai revolution, although people still wore gowns and mandarin jacket, Sun Yat sen's uniform was popular and gradually became the main style for men. It has a combination of advantages of Western style, Chinese style and Japanese students' uniforms. Mr. Sun liked this uniform very much and was the first one to wear it, so it was named after Sun Yatsen.

The Qipao (Cheongsam) is an elegant type of Chinese dress. This close-fitting dress comes from Manchu nationality. It was so long that could reach the insteps with its wide cuffs. Later, Qipao became popular among women in China and underwent many changes. In fact, it is said that Qipao is a combination of many national cultures including Manchu, Qidan, Mongolia and Han. Nowadays, Qipao is still one of the first choices for many Chinese women when they attend important social gatherings.

段落译文

上衣下裳是中国古代最早的服装款式。商代人上身穿交领衣，下身着裙裳，腰间束带，脚穿翘尖鞋。秦始皇统一中国后，产生了阶级。劳动人民穿短衣粗布，因此“布衣”成了庶民(普通老百姓)的代称。有些富人养尊处优，穿宽衣大袖，从此奠定了中国服饰的基本形制。

春秋战国时在服饰方面最重要的变化是深衣和胡服的出现。深衣是将过去的上下不相连的衣和裳连接在一起，下摆不开衩口，而是将衣襟接长，向后拥掩。从战国至西汉，深衣一直是人们穿着的一种主要服式，不分尊卑，不论男女，都可以穿着。胡服是指我国北方草原民族的服装。他们为了游牧时骑马的需要，多穿短上衣，长裤和靴。当时汉族人所穿服装衣宽袖广，劳动不方便，战国时期赵武灵王推行胡服，成为中国服装史上最早的一位改革者，促进了民族交往和融合，丰富了汉族人民的穿着。

汉代的“休养生息”及“经济繁荣”加强了各民族之间的交流，导致社会风尚的改观，人们对服装的要求越来越高，穿着打扮日趋华丽。汉代华丽的女式深衣在下身要缠绕好些层，并在衣裾的斜缘上下坠许多三角形物及长飘带。东汉以后，男子不再穿深衣，妇女仍以深衣为礼服。这对后来的服饰产生了极大的影响，旗袍和连衣裙都是其沿革的结果。

西周时代，等级制度逐渐确立，完整的官服制度也随之产生。从此，贵贱分等，衣服颜色各有区别，从天子到庶民，服制各有等差。例如，在唐代，皇帝的服色为黄色，官员从一品至九品，服色以紫、绯、绿、青为差别。后来规定，除天子以外，其他人一律不准穿黄色衣服，黄色衣服成了皇帝的专用服饰，此规定一直延续到清朝。

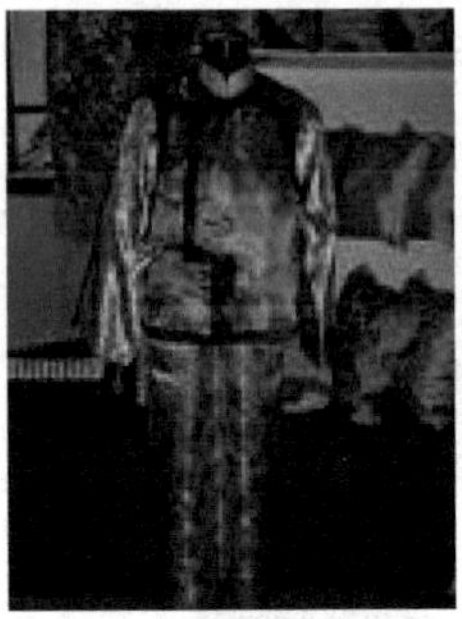

古代皇帝穿的衣服被称为“龙袍”，颜色以中黄色为主，其上绣有非常讲究的龙型图纹。例如清朝皇帝的龙袍，前身和后身各绣三条龙，左、右肩上各绣一条龙，衣襟里面再绣一条龙，这样，龙的总数为九；从正面或背面看是都是五条龙，正好与九五之数相吻合。因为中国的帝王之位，被称为“九五之尊”，九与五两个数字象征着高贵。龙袍下端还要绣一些浪花和山石宝物等，这些图案表示吉祥如意，绵延不断，隐喻一统山河，万世升平。

清朝的男子一般穿长袍马褂。马褂穿在长袍外面，长不过腰，短衣短袖，本来是满族人骑马的服装，因此得名。辛亥革命后，长袍马褂虽然继续存在，但是中山装逐渐风行起来。中山装一直是现代中国男子的主要衣服式样。它结合西式服装的轻便，中式服装的舒适，又借鉴了日本学生装立领单排扣的风格，演变而成。孙中山先生非常喜欢这种服装，并带头穿用，因此称为“中山装”。

旗袍是一种具有丰富的中国民族文化韵味的服装。旗袍开始是满族妇女的长袍，袍长可掩盖住脚，袖口平而大。后来演变为汉族妇女的主要服饰之一，可以说旗袍是满族、契丹、蒙古、汉族等民族文化融合的产物。时至今日，旗袍依然是中国妇女最常穿着的礼服之一。

实用词汇

上衣 upper outer garments; jacket
下裳 skirt
直筒长裙 full-length straight skirt
肥腿长裤 baggy trousers

长袍 gown, robe
旗袍 Qipao, cheong-sam
连衣裙 dress
便装 plain clothes; informal dress
花衣服 bright-colored clothes
内衣 underwear; underclothes
奇装异服 outlandish clothes
盛装 rich dress; splendid attire
睡衣 pyjamas
套装 suit
童装 children's clothes
校服 school uniform
时装 fashionable dress; the latest fashion
中山装 sun yat sen's uniform; Chinese suit
布衣 cloth gown
中式服装 garments in Chinese style
坎肩 sleeveless jacket
马裤 riding breeches
恰袢，对襟长袍 Qiapan
宽松袖的 loose-sleeved
环扣 looped-button
无领 collarless
无袖 sleeveless
花边 lace
鞋面 instep
裤腰 waist of trousers

名言俗语

人靠衣服马靠鞍。/ 衣着予人风采。

Clothes make a man. / Fine clothes make man. / Fine feathers make fine birds.

脏衣服应在家里洗。/ 家丑不可外扬。

Wash your dirt linen at home.

最适合我穿的衣服才是最好的衣服。/ 适合的就是最好的。

That suit is best that best suits me.

看布裁衣。/ 量体裁衣。

To cut the coat according to the cloth.

人的一切——面貌、衣着、心灵和思想，都应该是美好的。

Everything ought to be beautiful in a human being: face, and dress, and soul, and ideas.

君子在德不在衣。

It's not the gay coat that makes the gentleman.

穿着整齐本身就是一种职业，一味追求穿着就没有时间做别的事情了。

Being a well-dressed man is a career, and he who goes in for it has no time for anything else.

服饰得体的人你永远也不会注意到他的穿着。

The well-dressed man is he whose clothes you never notice.

门不挡衣着华丽的人。

Good clothes open all doors.

只重衣衫不重人。

A smart coat is a good letter of introduction.

借来的衣衫不合身。

Borrowed garments never fit well.

宁可衣衫褴褛上天堂，不要绫罗绸缎下地狱。

Better go to heaven in rags than to hell in embroidery.

词语注解

天衣无缝：传说天上仙女穿的衣服，不用针线制作，没有缝儿。比喻事物没有一点破绽。

A heavenly dress; A heavenly dress without seams. Chinese people often use it when they want to describe something that is flawless, particularly well-designed plans, or a water-tight legal case.

衣锦还乡：古时候指做官后，穿着锦绣的衣服，回到故乡向亲友夸耀。

One goes back to his/her old home in silken robes after acquiring wealth and honour.

衣冠禽兽：指行为卑劣，如同禽兽的人。

Beast in human clothing; which is often used to describe the person as vile as a brute.

衣不解带：形容日夜辛劳，不能安稳休息。

Sleep without taking off one's clothes, which means someone is too tired to have proper sleep due to hard work.

衣冠楚楚：形容穿戴整齐，漂亮。

Neatly and immaculately dressed.

中西合璧

同中国服装的演变相似，西方的服装也是在生活和工作中慢慢形成的。据说西服上装原来是渔民的着装，他们终年在海上谋生，穿敞领少扣的衣服很方便，适合于捕鱼工作，后来逐渐演变成现在的式样。而最讲究的燕尾礼服，其实是中世纪欧洲马车夫的服装。马车夫穿着后面开衩的衣服，是为了方便骑马。

With the same evolution of Chinese clothing, western-style clothes evolved from daily life and work too. It is said that the suit was originally fishermen's clothing, which was worn at sea all the year round and was very convenient for fishing work with open-necked collar and less buttons. Finally it evolved into the current style. The most dainty, swallow-tailed coats turned out to be a coachman's clothing from medieval Europe, which was very convenient to ride horse.

UNIT 26

Chinese Embroidery

中国刺绣

题记

刺绣是中国优秀的民族传统工艺之一，早在四千年前《尚书》记载的章服制度里，就规定“衣画而裳绣”。因此刺绣服装的风气，也逐渐在民间广泛流行。如今，中国的刺绣工艺几乎遍及全国，并且融入到我们生活当中。我们的一些日用品如被面、枕套、靠垫、鞋面之类，很多都是刺绣品。

Embroidery is one of the outstanding traditional crafts of Chinese people, as early as four thousand years ago, “Shangshu” (the book of history) recorded that “clothing should be designed and embroidered." As a result, the embroidered clothes became a fashion, which was widespread. Today, the embroidery is very popular in the whole country and become a daily necessity, used for quilt cover, pillow, cushion, etc.

Embroidery is a craftwork which deals with different kinds of fabric with various materials to weave different patterns, and it is a brilliant wonder of Chinese art. From the magnificent Dragon Robe worn by Emperors to the popular embroidery seen in today’s fashions, embroidery adds so much pleasure to our life and our culture. Meanwhile, it has also a key impact on international cultural life.

Chinese embroidery is a long established art form in China and possesses many sorts of categories, namely: hand-silk thread embroidery, metallic yarn embroidery, beaded, mechanical embroidery, cross-stitch, and appliqué. The oldest embroidered product from China on record dates from the Shang Dynasty while it reached its peak during the Autumn and Spring period. Embroidery in this period symbolized social status, as it did with i range during Qin and Han period. Furthermore, it was not u development of national economy, that embroidery entered the lives of the common people.

Though Chinese embroidery has a long history, it was never classified as a solely female activity, but men and women, the old and the young have been involved in embroidery. The items embroidered are quite diverse including daily clothes, theatrical costumes, tablecloths, pillow cases, cushions and other daily necessities, screens, and other furnishings of the wall as well.

According to the stitches used, there are two main divisions of embroidery, one uses the long and one the short stitch, while the other involves the seed stitch used in Beijing which is also known as the French knot. The stitches most commonly used by the Chinese include: 1) satin stitch, which is further classified into long and short; 2) Beijing stitch or French knot; 3) Stem stitch; 4) Couching; 5) Chain stitch; and 6) Split stitch. All of these stitches are known in the west. Many westerners find Chinese embroidery a little over done. The Chinese satin stitch when done to perfection is exquisite in its fine detail. When it comes to Chinese embroidery, we have to mention the four major traditional styles: Su, Shu, Xiang, and Yue.

Su Embroidery. There are many kinds of embroidery products in Suzhou, which are referred to as Su Embroidery. Suzhou is a typical southern water town, abundant with silk, so it is renowned that "every family breeds silkworms and every household does embroidery". As early as the Song Dynasty, Su Embroidery was already well known for its elegance and vividness. It is said that during the Three States Period, the wife of the emperor Wu—Sun Quan, Mrs. Zhao did well in embroidery, her embroidery work, "the map of states" was praised as "the 10000 embroidered states in a brocade". She then got the fame as the "matchless needle". Later in Qing Dynasty Su embroidery products had been widely used in clothing, pillows, cushions and other daily necessities. Su embroidery is famous for its beautiful patterns, elegant colors, variety of stitches, and consummate craftsmanship. Its stitching is meticulously skillful, and its coloration subtle and refined.

Historically, Su Embroidery dominated the royal wardrobe and even today, Su Embroidery occupies a large share of the embroidery markets in China as well as in the world.

Shu Embroidery refers to the embroidery in the west of Sichuan. Shu Embroidery, influenced by its geographic environment and local customs, is characterized by a refined and brisk style. The earliest record of Shu Embroidery was during Western Han Dynasty. At that time, embroidery was a luxury enjoyed only by the royal family and was strictly controlled by the government.

In Qing Dynasty, Shu Embroidery entered the market and an industry was formed. The composition of Shu Embroidery, which can be seen as paintings by masters, patterns by designers, landscapes, flowers and birds, dragons and phoenix, tiles and ancient coins, is diverse and colorful. Folk stories like *the Eight Immortals Crossing the Sea,* and other auspicious patterns such as magpies on plums and mandarin ducks playing on the water were also favorite topics. Patterns with strong local features were very popular among foreigners at that time. These local features included lotus and carp, bamboo forests and pandas. Thus Shu Embroidery is famous for its smooth line piece, rigorous stitches, gentle hue, vivid strength and tact for the situation.

Xiang Embroidery is collectively referred to as the embroidery products that are based on the central Changsha, and Hunan regions. It is the origin of Hunan ancient folk embroidery, and formed the mature technique during the Zhanguo period.

Over two thousands years, Xiang Embroidery became a special branch of the local art. Xiang Embroidery gained popularity day by day. Besides the common topics seen in other styles of embroidery, Xiang Embroidery absorbed elements from calligraphy, painting and inscription. Therefore Chinese paintings take place of the traditional painting draft, retaining the traditional charm of Chinese painting, while exerting the elaborate stitches and the intense color of Xiang Embroidery. It used a needle as a pen, lines as the color. That is why Xiang Embroidery can be widely appealing and long lasting. In Xiang Embroidery, a flower seems to be able to send off fragrance, a bird seems to sing, a tiger seems to run, and a person seems to breathe. Everything is alive, that is Xiang Embroidery.

Yue Embroidery, which encompasses Guangzhou Embroidery and Chaozhou Embroidery, has the same origin as Li Brocade. Portraits, flowers, and birds are the most popular themes of Yue Embroidery as the subtropical climate favors the area with an abundance of these plants that are rarely seen in central China. In addition, Yue Embroidery tends to use dark colors, widely used are red and green to strongly bring out their spectacular and lively atmosphere. The composition of Yue Embroidery is complicated but messy, including splendid color, changeable stitches, clear texture, and strongly decorative aesthetic. There is another kind of Nasi embroidery, which uses gold embroidery and leather for lining, and its products appear golden and brilliant. The masterpiece of Yue style embroidery is hundreds of Birds.

Besides the "four famous Chinese embroidery styles", there are still others, such as Jing Embroidery of Beijing, Gu Embroidery in Shanghai, Miao Embroidery of Miao nationality and so forth. Produced in different states, they all own their peculiar styles. Nowadays Chinese embroidery has been spread all over the world. So far, it has become one of China's strong exports and very popular with foreigners.

段落译文

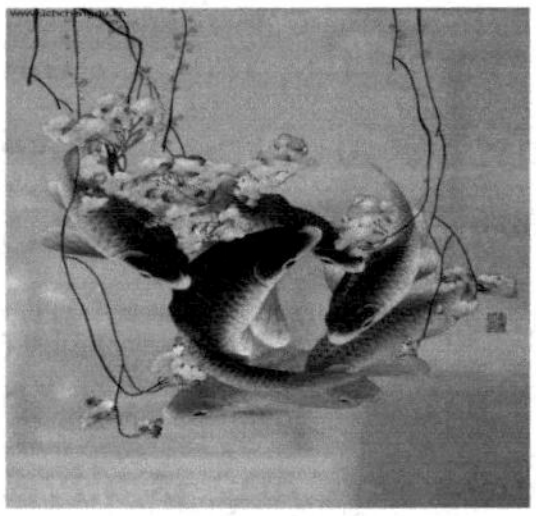

刺绣是一种在织物上用各种线料织出种种图案的工艺，是中国传统工艺中的一颗璀璨的明珠。从皇帝身上穿的豪华的龙袍到今天的刺绣时装，刺绣给我们的生活和文化增加了无穷的姿色，同时在国际文化生活中也产生了很大的作用与影响。

中国刺绣历史悠久，品类繁多，有手工丝线刺绣，金银线绣，珠绣、机绣、挑花、补花等，图案工整美丽，针法变化多端，技艺细腻精巧。据记录，中国最早的刺绣品产于商朝，春秋时期绣品已极精美。刺绣品在这个时期象征着身份地位，到秦汉刺绣品应用范围更广，随后刺绣逐渐进入了平民百姓家。

刺绣不仅仅是女性参与的活动，男女老少都可以从事这一行业。绣品更是包罗万象：生活服装，歌舞或戏曲服饰，台布、枕套、靠垫等生活日用品及屏风、壁挂等陈设品。

中国刺绣根据针法主要分为两种，一种是长短针交替缝合，而另一种是被称为法国结的北京种子针。中国刺绣通常使用的针法包括：(1)缎子缝——这是从长短针中进一步分出来的；(2)北京针或法国结；(3)干缝；(4)横卧绣；(5)链形绣；(6)分裂针。所有这些针法都是西方人所熟悉的，许多西方人认为中国刺绣真是巧妙之至。我国最著名的刺绣是苏绣、蜀绣、湘绣和粤绣。

苏绣：苏绣是苏州地区刺绣品的统称。苏州位于中国南部水乡，盛产丝绸，素有“家家养蚕，户户刺绣”之说。早在宋朝，苏绣就以它的高雅和生动闻名。三国吴主孙权夫人赵五妃擅绣，所绣“列国图”有“绣万国于一锦”，被当时人称为“针绝”之说。清代苏绣品已广泛用于衣饰、被枕、椅垫等日常用品。苏绣的特色在于它上好的样式，配色调和、绣工雅洁、，针法多变和装饰性强等。在历史上，苏绣掌控着皇家壁橱。今天，苏绣在中国市场乃至在世界市场占有着一大份额。

蜀绣：蜀绣指川西的刺绣。受地理环境和地方风俗的影响，蜀绣描绘的是一种精巧且轻快的风格。蜀绣最早期的记录是在西汉时期。当时，刺绣仅供皇室享用的奢侈品并且由政府严格控制。

清朝时蜀绣进入市场，从而形成了刺绣工业。蜀绣的构图从大师创造的绘画，设计师构想的样式，到风景、花鸟、龙凤、瓦片和古老的硬币，应有尽有，丰富多彩。民间故事如“八仙过海”以及“喜鹊报李”、“鸳鸯戏水”等象征吉祥的素材均是蜀绣喜纳的图案。传统的图案还有莲花和鲤鱼，竹森林和熊猫等。蜀绣以线片平顺光亮、施针严谨、色泽柔和、劲气生动、虚实得体而著称。

湘绣：湘绣是以湖南长沙为中心刺绣品的统称，起源于湖南古老的民间刺绣，在战国时期就有了较成熟的技艺。经过长达两千年的发展，湘绣逐渐成为地方艺术的一个特别的分支，并且随着时间的推移赢得了声望。湘绣的独特之处在于它吸收了书法、绘画和题字中的元素，其画稿融合了中国画题材，替代了传统画稿，既保留国画神韵，又发挥了湘绣针法及色彩强烈之特长，以针代笔、以线代色、雅俗共赏、历久不衰。在湘绣里，花似乎在送芬芳，鸟似乎在歌唱，老虎似乎在奔跑，人似乎在呼吸，一切都活灵活现。这就是湘绣。

粤绣：包含广州刺绣和潮州刺绣。画像、花、鸟动物，如鱼、龙虾、佛手柑和荔枝等是粤绣最普遍的题材，这些亚热带富饶的动植物在中国中部是比较稀有的，因此别具一格。另外，粤绣倾向于使用深颜色，广泛应用红色、绿色来强烈地衬托出其壮观和热闹的气氛。粤绣构图繁而不乱，色彩富丽夺目，针法多变，纹理分明，装饰性强。另有一种纳丝绣，以皮金绣作衬，绣品金光灿灿，分外精艳。粤绣中的代表作是百鸟朝凤。

中国刺绣除“四大名绣”外，还有北京的京绣、上海的顾绣、苗族的苗绣等等。产地不同，风格各异。如今中国刺绣遍及全国各地，名扬四海，成为中国出口大宗，颇受外宾欢迎。

实用词汇

刺绣绣花针织机 needle machine
单针刺绣机 single needle embroidery frame
针距 needle passage
横针板导针 needle pitch
刺绣工 embroiderer
纺织品刺绣 textile embroidery
编织物 braided fabric
变形；走样 deformation
不褪色；色泽牢固 fast colours
抽绣；刺绣品 punch work embroidery
醋酯纤维 acetate fibre
大麻 hemp
纺织品 textiles
钩编编织物 crochet
光泽 gloss, lustre
黄麻 jute
黄麻布（袋）gunny cloth (bag)
混纺织物 mixture fabric, blend fabric
机织织物 woven fabric
绢丝 spun silk
麻织物 linen
毛织物（品）woolen fabrics
棉纺织品 cotton textiles
棉绒 cotton velvet
棉织物（品）cotton fabrics
耐绉的 non-crushable
黏胶纤维 viscose acetal fibre

配色 matching, colour
人造丝织物 combinations rayon fabrics
人造纤维 artificial fibre
绒线刺绣 crewel work
桑蚕丝；家蚕丝 mulberry silk
丝织物 silk fabrics
丝纺 silk spinning
手帕亚麻纱 linen cambric
素色 plain
提花丝织物 figured silk

名言俗语

革命不是绣花。
Revolution is not made with rose water.
小洞不补，大洞吃苦。
A stitch in time saves nine.
绣花枕头
Pillow with an embroidered case

词语注解

男人看田边，女人看花边：苗族妇女中，盛装是苗族妇女的珍爱，也是她们刺绣人生的精品和缩影。在过去的岁月里，一生当中只穿两次，一次是当新娘时作为陪嫁品，另一次则是她们生命终结作为陪葬到另一个世界。

The man looks at the edge of a paddy field, while the woman looks at the lace: the women in Miao national minority, the splendid attires are Miao national minority women's treasure, and they are also the high-quality goods and the miniature. In the past years, they only put on the splendid attires twice, one was with the bride's dowry, the other was at the end of their life which is buried in the tomb.

鸳鸯绣：常指恩爱夫妻，是亚洲的一种亮斑冠鸭。学名 Aix galericulata。是经常出现在中国古代文学作品和神话传说中的鸟类。鸳鸯绣常常赠送给新婚夫妇，代表他们恩恩爱爱，白头偕老。

The mandarin duck embroiders: The mandarin ducks are the affectionate couples, refers to one kind of duck in Asia, systematic name is Aix galericulata. They appear frequently in China ancient literary work and they are the myth of the fable birds. The mandarin ducks frequently are given to the newlyweds, which represent their forever love.

百鸟朝凤：也称百鸟朝王、仪凤图等，其文化内涵十分丰富。在中国古代，凤是用来比喻帝皇的，因此《百鸟朝凤》泛喻君主圣明，河晏海清，天下归附，亦可用来表达人们对太平盛世的无限期盼。

A Hundred Birds Worshiping the Phoenix: its cultural connotation is extremely rich. In the Chinese ancient times, the phoenix symbolized the ruler. Therefore "A Hundred Birds towards Phoenix" shows the common people's expectation of the prosperity of the world, and expresses the infinite hope of peace.

中西合璧

乱针锈，是 1930 年代刺绣家杨守玉所创造的刺绣针法，这种针法融合了中国传统刺绣的技术以及西洋艺术的特色，是中西合璧的新兴艺术。乱针绣按照西方油画中光和色的变化规律，以丰富多变的针线来体现作品的线条美与立体质感。乱针绣作品看上去像一幅油画，但它比油画的色彩更艳丽明快，形成绣的独特风格。因此乱针绣适合用于绣制油画、摄影和素描等稿本的作品。

十字绣是一种起源于欧洲的手艺，具有悠久的历史。公元四世纪，十字绣从土耳其经由意大利在欧洲传播开来，最初是在宫廷中风行，后来传入民间，广泛流行于欧洲和美国以及亚洲等国家和地区。十字绣在二三十年代曾经是欧洲女性的至爱，如今再度受到瞩目，近年来传入中国，因为它是一项易学易懂的手艺，受到不同年龄层的人的喜爱。

Random stitch was created by an embroideress Yang Shouyu in 1930s.

This kind of stitch combines the Chinese traditional embroidery technology with the Western art characteristic, which is a newly-born art. According to the light and the color change of the western oil painting, random stitch manifests the work by the rich changeable needle work to show the embroideries' beautiful lines and the three-dimensional sense of reality. The random stitch embroidery looks like an oil painting, but it is more gorgeous than that for its bright color, which forms its own unique style. Therefore random stitch is widely used in embroidering the oil painting, photography and sketch works.

Cross-stitch was a craft originated in Europe with a long history. In 4 A.D., it came from Turkey to Italy and then to Europe. Cross-stitch was initially popular in court and the folk followed suit and later spread all over Europe, America, Asia, and other countries. It was once the favourite of the European women in 1930s and nowadays has been heated. In recent years cross-stitch has been introduced into China. People of different ages love it because it is a craft easy to master.

UNIT 27

Chinese Furniture

中国家具

题记

在历史悠久的中国文化艺术宝库中，历代家具作为其重要组成部分之一，不仅与中国历史一样源远流长，而且独具民族特色及文化内涵。中式家具以其古朴典雅的造型吸引了不少人士，尤其是热爱中国传统文化和喜欢清幽环境的人们。

Being an important part of the treasure house of Chinese art and culture, furniture has not only had a very long history, but also a peculiar national characteristics and cultural connotations, with its simple and elegant designs. Chinese furniture attracts lots of people, especially those who love Chinese traditional culture and enjoy tranquil environment.

Chinese furniture, which is closely associated with social ideology, customs, life styles and aesthetic ideas in different periods of Chinese history, generated from mats which was used to sit on the ground, then gradually developed to sitting furniture that feet can be set on land (the furniture which on sitting with legs hanging). Based on different designs, Chinese scholars divided Chinese furniture into four groups: Chu Style Furniture (from Zhou Dynasty to Southern and Northern Dynasty), Song Style Furniture (from Sui and Tang Dynasty to the early Ming Dynasty), Ming Style Furniture (from the middle Ming Dynasty to the early Qing Dynasty), and Qing Style Furniture (after the middle Qing Dynasty).

Chu Style Furniture was developed from low size to high size in height of the furniture, with obvious Chu cultural characteristics, and became matured gradually through its development. During the Shang and Zhou Dynasties, Zu and Jin made of bronze, the most representative furniture, which was sacrificed to the heaven and the earth, to favorable weather and bumper grain harvest, reflects characteristics of the Times and technology level. Then in the Spring and Autumn and the Warring States Periods, tables to lean, screens, and hangers were made. Lacquer was very popular at that time, and lacquer furniture, of which main feature was painting, brightly coloured and plain gorgeous, was mainly made from Heidi, with red coloured patterns, reaching its palmy days in Qin and Han Dynasty. With the development of society, various low-type furniture had been springing up, such as beds, couches, tables, desks, cupboards, boxes, and hangers, etc. In the Wei, Jin, Southern and Northern Dynasty the people's living mode changed, high-type furniture was made, such as chairs and square stools. Lacquer furniture was not only the mainstream of Chinese furniture system, but also the main representative of Chu Style Furniture.

The appearance and growth of Song Style Furniture was deeply influenced by social politics, economy, and cultural consciousness. Before Song Dynasty, there were both low-type and high-type furniture, while their styles were light and simple but not thick and heavy; elegant and straight but not wholly rounded. Then during the Song Dynasty, the varieties of furniture increased, and their types became more beautiful. Sitting with legs hanging took the place of sitting on the ground during this time. High-type furniture had been the main form in people's lives during that time, such as desks and chairs, drawers and cupboards, dressing table, hangers,

towel rails, etc. The structure of most Song Style Furniture was simple, and its decorative style was simple and elegant, which presented people's aesthetic values in Song Dynasty—thrifty and neat. The Song Dynasty, which is generally considered as the most important developing period linking the past and future history of Chinese furniture, established the foundation for Ming Style and Qing Style Furniture.

Ming Style Furniture, which was based on traditional Song Style Furniture, took import high-quality timber (e.g. padauk wood, red-sanders, siame senna cassia, and combodia, etc.) as predominant materials to produce hardwood furniture which was made use of in halls, bedrooms, pavilions, and study-rooms, etc. Then a concept of furniture in whole set was formed. Ming Style Furniture referred to furniture developed from the middle Ming Dynasty to the early Qing Dynasty, the period that Chinese classical furniture reached its glorious age and was considered as the golden age of Chinese classical furniture. The style of the furniture was neat and pleasingly simple, and its style was modest, lines were tender and straight, with proper proportion, varied decoration, scientific structure, and high quality in materials, strongly reflecting national style. It combined materials, production, usage and aesthetic so skillfully that achieve the high integration of artistry and practicability. The book *"The Development of Furniture Home and Abroad"* made comments on it as follows: Ming Style Furniture was the high period of accomplishment of Chinese classical furniture. Chinese Confucianism which was broad and profound, ran through the development process of it that made it have strong characteristics of the Times and prominent national style. Not only was it the pride of the nation, but brilliant achievement in

the history of world furniture, also played a considerably important role in the development of world furniture. Qing Style Furniture refers to furniture that inherited style characteristics of Ming Style Furniture, however its form and tone is widely different from the Ming Style. Provided favorable conditions for furniture production by Kong and Qian Eras, Qing Style Furniture used various consummate technologies, mainly with thick and heavy designs, enormous contours, and complicated adornment. The major characteristic of the Qing style was making good use of materials; another one was varied decoration with high level craftsmanship. In addition, its decorations, concentrated in the pick of all dynasties, mainly were carving, inlays, and lacquer painting, such as the old-fashioned wooden armchair. In the late Qing Dynasty, folk furniture began to emerge and three furniture systems with strong local characteristic were formed, they were from Beijing, Suzhou, and Guangzhou. Beijing Furniture directly inherited the court living style in Qing Dynasty, but not so brilliant as of the court. Suzhou Furniture, produced in Suzhou, mainly showed the characteristics of Ming Style Furniture while varied slightly in style, and was considered as the typical representative of Ming Style Furniture. Guangzhou Furniture, as the representative of Qing Style Furniture, maintained Chinese traditional style. Its variety increased gradually and the caving of series works was complicated, and influenced by the West.

The above four furniture design styles show the course and heritage of Chinese classical furniture, chiefly reflecting the thoughts and harmony between man and nature. It was an integral part of inheriting and promoting Chinese traditional culture and furniture design.

段落译文

中国家具与中国历史不同时期的社会意识形态、风俗习惯、生活方式及审美情趣分不开。从最

早起源于“席地而坐”的席，逐渐发展到“垂足而坐”的坐具。中国学者根据不同的设计风格将中国古典家具分为四类：楚式家具(周代至南北朝)、宋式家具(隋唐至元代及明朝早期)、明式家具(明朝中期至清朝早期)以及清式家具(清朝中期以后)。

楚式家具经历了由低到高的演变过程，其家具形式带有明显的楚文化特征，并随其产生、发展而逐渐成熟。商周时期，最具代表性的家具要数青铜器的俎和禁，它们集中反映了时代特征与工艺技术水平。人们用其祀天地，以求风调雨顺、五谷丰登。春秋战国时期，出现了凭靠的几、屏风、衣架等，漆器在这一时期达到了普及。漆家具以黑地为主，配以红色彩绘图案，色彩艳丽，朴素而又华美。在秦汉时期，达到了兴盛的高峰，其主要特点是彩绘。随着社会的发展，逐渐涌现了各样低型家具，如床、榻、几、案、柜、箱、衣架等。到了魏晋南北朝时，起居方式也随着发生改变，出现了椅子、方凳等高型家具。从周代至南北朝，漆家具一直是中国家具体系的主流，也是楚式家具的主要代表。

宋式家具的产生与发展深深受到了当时社会政治、经济、文化意识等方面的影响。在宋代前，中国家具仍是高型与低型家具并存，但其风格却从以往的厚重变为轻简、浑圆变为秀直。到了宋代，家具品种越来越多，样式也越来越美观，垂足而坐的起居方式代替了历史几千年席地跪坐的起居方式，高型家具已成为人们起居作息的主要家具形式。桌椅类、抽屉橱、架台类(镜台、衣架、巾架等)开始进入平民百姓家。宋代家具大多都呈现出简约的结构，形态上表现出素雅的装饰风格，从而也体现了宋人节俭、简洁的审美观念。宋代被普遍认为是我国家具史上承前启后的重要发展时期，并为明清家具达到鼎盛奠定了基础。

明式家具在宋元家具传统样式的基础上发展起来，明代以进口优质木材(如花梨木、紫檀木、鸡翅木、酸枝木等)为主要材料制作硬木家具并出现了厅堂家具、卧房家具、亭台家具、书斋家具等，从而有了成套家具的概念。从明中期至清前期，中国古典家具发展到了顶峰，被称为是中国古典家具的黄金时代，这一时期的家具被称为明式家具。其家具风格特点为造

型简捷、素雅端庄、比例适度、线条挺秀舒展、装饰手法丰富多彩又恰到好处、结构科学、用材讲究、质地优美，形成了具有民族风格的明式家具。明式家具将选材、制作、使用和审美巧妙地结合起来，达到艺术性和实用性的高度统一。《中外家具发展史》一书中是这样评价明式家具的："明式家具是我国古典家具成就的高峰，博大而深远的中国儒家思想自始至终贯穿于明式家具发展的始末，使它具有浓厚的时代风骨和显著的民族风格。明式家具在世界家具史上写下了炎黄子孙引为自豪的辉煌篇章，并对世界家具的发展起着不可估量的影响。"

清式家具沿袭与继承了明式家具的风格特征。康乾"盛世"的局面为家具的制造提供了良好的条件。清朝家具追求运用各种精湛的工艺技术，大多以造型厚重、形体庞大、装饰繁琐为主，在形式和格调上与明式家具的秀丽雅致大相径庭，形成了有别于明代风格的独特面貌，故称为"清式家具"。清式家具的最大特点是用料毫不吝惜，用材厚重、奢靡挥霍。另一特点是装饰丰富、技艺高超。其装饰手法集历代精华于一朝，主要有雕刻、镶嵌和漆饰(如清代太师椅)。到清末，民间家具开始兴起，出现了"京做"、"苏做"、"广做"三大地方特色浓厚的家具体系。"京做"直接继承清宫廷家居风格，但不及其豪华；"苏做"家具产于苏州，集中反映了明式家具的特点，在风格上稍有变化，被看做是明式家具的典型代表；广式家具是清式家具的主要代表，受西方影响，品种增多，作品系列成套雕刻繁缛，保持了中国的传统风格。

以上四种重要的家具设计风格体现了中国古典家具的历程与风貌，集中反映了"天人合一"的思想，是中华民族传统文化艺术和传统家具艺术不可或缺的重要组成部分。

实用词汇

几 table
屏风 screen
衣架 hanger
漆器 lacquer

黑地 heidi
彩绘 painting
雕刻 carving
镶嵌 inlays
漆饰 lacquer painting
古式家具 antique furniture
仿古家具 antique reproduction furniture
扶手椅 armchair
茶几 tea table
长凳 long bench
长方凳 rectangular stool
橱 Cabinet
床衣镜 full-length mirror
搭板书案 board and stand desk
大方扛箱 large square box carried on a pole
方凳 square stool
方桌 square table
橱柜 cupboard
梳妆台 dressing table
花梨木 padauk wood
鸡翅木 door frame
紫檀木 padauk
山毛榉木 beech
樱桃木 cherry
黄花梨木 Huanghuali wood

名言俗语

没有其他家会像自己家一样好。
There is no fireside like your own fireside.
自己铺的床要自己睡。

You've made your bed, now lie in it.
割席断交。
Seats break off diplomatic relations cut.
早睡早起会使人健康、富有和聪明。
Early to bed and early to rise, makes a man healthy, wealthy and wise.
金窝银窝不如咱的狗窝。
There is no place like home.
朽木不可雕。
Fools grow without watering.

词语注解

席地而坐：坐在地上
Xi Di Er Zuo: to sit on the ground
垂足而坐：腿自然下垂而坐
Chui Zu Er Zuo: to sit with legs hanging
天人合一：人与自然和谐相容
Tian Ren He Yi: the thought of harmony of man with nature

中国古典家具：它包括两个方面，一是具有收藏价值的旧式家具，主要指的是明代至清代四五百年间制作的家具，二就是仿明清式家具，是现代的技术工人继承了明清以来家具制作工艺生产和销售的家具。

Chinese Classical Furniture includes two kinds of furniture, one is old-fashioned furniture which has a four or 500-year history, having collection values from Ming Dynasty to Qing Dynasty; the other one is imitated Ming or Qing Style furniture, made by modern technical workers who inherit furniture manufacturing technology from Ming Dynasty to Qing Dynasty.

中西合璧

在艺术上，尽管特色各异，中西方家具都具有辉煌华丽的特点；在装饰上，中国的漆饰很有特色，而西方则以雕刻为主。中国家具受儒、道、禅宗等思想以及礼教的影响，西方家具则受实用思想、权力主义、神秘主义、人文主义以及理性思想的影响。即使它们两者存在不同之处，但却都要符合人们当时的物质生活水平、社会生活内容以及对艺术品位的追求等，且不断以新的形式去适应时代的发展。

Even though characteristics are different in arts, furniture is gorgeous both in China and in Western countries. In terms of decoration, lacquer painting is a characteristic in China, while carving in Western countries. Chinese furniture was influenced by Confucianism, Taoism, Zen, and rules of propriety, etc. And Western furniture was influenced by pragmatism, authoritarianism, mysticism, humanism, and idealism, and so on. Although there are many differences in Chinese furniture and Western furniture, their development needs to fit with requirements of material living standard, of social life contents, of pursuit of arts, and keep abreast of the times with new forms.

UNIT 28

Traditional Folk Arts

民间工艺

题记

中国民间工艺是民间艺术创作中的一种重要形式，表现了百姓的审美观和民间艺术的特性。我国民间实用工艺品反映了中国人民的勤劳智慧以及浓厚的民族文化。

Chinese folk arts and crafts are important folk art forms, which illustrate Chinese people's aesthetic standards and folk art features. The popular and practical crafts reflect not only the Chinese people's diligence and wisdom, but a strong national culture as well.

Chinese folk art crafts are colorful and very rich in content with a long history. Most of these crafts are related to folk tales, which are of the contents based on lively spirit, good luck, long life, wealth, happy reunion with children and grandchildren and so on. Folk art crafts are also beneficial for folk festivals, traditional religious and ethnic decorations, and the folk crafts, lively and interesting, are widely spread, which represent the Chinese people's traditional culture and daily activities.

Shadow Play, a Chinese folk art form in China, is a unique and artistic combination of art and drama shining as a delicate pearl in Chinese arts. It is a folk art originating from rural areas of northwest China's Gansu, Shanxi and Ningxia provinces. This artistic form was popular between 14th and 19th Century, which was during the Ming and Qing Dynasties in China. Figures used in the play look pretty and charming and the carving techniques require a high level of skill. The material used for shadow plays is the skin of the ox, which is durable, soft, and just the right thickness. People first clean and dry the skin, then they draw the outline on the skin and carve it. Then they put it in water to add color to it and take it out, and iron it, which is the most difficult yet important step. Finally, the skin is dried and bound together for the performance.

The main colors of leather silhouette used are red, yellow, black and green. Yet the figure can display more subtle colors with complicated patterns. Simple figures and exquisite handicraft are its two features. People draw lines to depict the general figure. Most part of the figures is pierced, with the non-pierced part serving as complementary to each other. For different parts, different patterns are used. The parts of the body decomposition of Shadow people are reasonable, flexible portable, easy and convenient for the performance. They have rich and beautiful singing and exciting and moving performing. Shadow Plays emphasize on performance. By moving every part of the body while matching this with inspiring strains of songs, the whole plays display strong local characteristics.

Shadow Play has also played a certain role in the cultural development home and abroad. There are many new local Chinese operas that were derived from the ways of shadow singing. For thousands of years, Shadow Plays have been widespread and deeply loved by people.

Clay Modeling: Clay figure modeling is a malleable art, involving kneading with the fingers to create various figures, animals, flowers and plants out of clay. Chinese clay crafts are unique in their style because they are beautifully shaped, vivid, lively, and lovely. The history of painted clay crafts goes back to the Ming Dynasty more than 600 years ago. Fengxiang in Shanxi is the birthplace of clay modeling. The local unique white earth was used for billets, and the traditional folk handicraft was adopted in the production process of clay sculpture. In the past farmers enjoyed it in spare time or at night during busy harvest time. There are ten steps in making clay work. They include molding the clay, turning over the base, gluing it into the designed shape, polishing, painting, and so on. Clay crafts enjoyed a great reputation during Qing Dynasty, mainly because of the painted clay work done by "Clay Figurine Zhang" in Tianjin. He improved the traditional art and plastic figurines to garden plastic level. Decorated with colors and props, it was made a unique style. Chinese clay crafts have been to the World Expo many times and received a number of awards and are spoken highly of by people at home and abroad. The main clay works includes tigers, crouching cows, zodiac animals, toys, legendary figures like the eight immortals, and characters from the three Kingdoms, especially "Little pandas inviting the guests" as the best gift for children.

Kites, also called fengzheng, had a long history of more than two thousand five hundred years. They were known in ancient China as yao (wooden kites) in the south, and as yuan (paper kites) in the north. Kites are one of the well-known handicrafts beaming with national characteristics. The earliest kite was made by ancient philosopher Me zhai and soon they were used in wars. During Tang and

Song Dynasties kites were made of paper and quickly spread to the folk and became a favorite pastime and enjoyment among common people. It was said that kite flying could help get rid of disaster and now people still believe that flying kites can bring good luck and make their crops rich and tall. Kite flying is wide spread in China, especially in Beijing and Weifang which are both epicenters of kite manufacturing and flying. As for the variety of the kites, there are soft-winged, hard-winged, dragon-shaped and so on, with more than 100 themes. The kites manufactured in China have swept all over the world with their exquisite beauty and unique style occupying an important position in world history, science and culture.

Chinese folk handicrafts are various and colorful. In addition to the above, we have cloth, wood carvings, illumination, straps, lacquers, bamboo crafts, jade crafts, porcelain, paper cutting, and New Year pictures. These folk arts are the outcomes of thousands of years of wisdom and Chinese culture.

段落译文

中国民间艺术工艺品历史悠久，内容丰富多彩。这些工艺品大都与民间传说有关，内容大都是精神活泼向上、吉祥如意、长命健康、富贵有余、儿孙满堂等，常用于民间传统节日、传统宗教和民族饰品等。这些民间工艺品流传广泛、生动有趣，体现了中国人的传统文化和日常活动。

皮影戏是我国的一种民间艺术形式，它是工艺美术与戏曲巧妙结合而成的独特艺术品种，是中华民族艺术殿堂里不可或缺的一颗精巧的明珠。皮影戏起源于中国明清时（14至19世纪），是甘肃、陕西、宁夏农村地区的一种民间艺术。皮影戏中的平面偶人以及场面道具景物，通常是民间艺人用手工，刀雕彩绘而成的皮制品，故称之为皮影。艺人先用水洗净、晒干牛皮；然后进行画图雕刻、再入水加色，最难的是熨烫这个步骤，最后晾干供演出用。

红、黄、黑、绿是皮影的主要用色，但复杂的式样往往用色丰富多彩。简朴、精湛的工艺是皮影的两个特征。一般人物用线条描绘，大部分人物的肢体部分通过刺刻而成，与其他部分相得益彰；人物身体的不同部分所采用的图案各异。皮影戏重在表演。演员通过控制、操作皮影人物身体的每一个部分、配以振奋人心的歌曲或独白来演绎故事情节。皮影人肢体部分之间的组合分解合理，因此表演灵活。它的演出装备轻便，唱腔丰富优美，表演精彩动人，剧中的人物形象精美、迷人，富有强烈的本地特色。

皮影戏还对国内外文化艺术的发展起过一定的作用。有不少新的地方戏曲剧种，就是从各路皮影戏唱腔中派生出来的。千百年来，皮影戏深受广大民众的喜爱，所以流传甚广。

泥塑是一种造型艺术，是指用黏土和泥捏塑成各种人物、动物、花卉等形象的民间手工艺术。中国泥塑式样独特是因为它形状美丽、生动、可爱。彩塑的历史可以追溯到六百年前的明代。中国西部陕西的凤翔是中国泥塑的发源地。泥塑采用当地独有的白土作坯，采用传统的民间工艺品工艺制作。农民在农闲时或农忙时的夜晚休息为之。一件泥塑需要经过整理黏土、完成基本部分、粘合成设计的形、抛光、上漆等十道工序才能完成。泥塑在清代享有很大声誉，主要是天津“泥人张”的彩塑。他把传统的捏泥人提高到园塑艺术水平，装饰以色彩、道具，形成了独特的风格。中国的泥塑多次参加世界博览会，获多项大奖，受到国内外人士的高度评价。代表作品有老虎、蹲牛、十二生肖动物、玩具、传奇人物八仙、三国人物等等，特别是产品“小熊猫请客”被誉为中国儿童最佳礼物中的最佳产品。

风筝诞生于我国，至今已有 2500 年历史。古时我国南方称其为“鹞”，北方谓“鸢”。风筝是具有我国特色的民间工艺品之一。最早的风筝是由古代哲学家墨翟制造的。风筝问世后，很快被用于军事。唐宋时期，风筝改由纸糊，很快传入民间，成为人们娱乐的玩具。古时传说放风筝可以除灾，现在有些地方有“放风筝”为“放晦气”之说，是为了带来好运，或者是为了能使庄稼长得丰硕长得高。如今，放风筝在中国很流行，特别是在风筝制作及放飞中心地区的北京和潍坊。风筝有很多种：软翅类、硬翅类、龙形类……等多种类型、上百种题材。我国制作的风筝，以精巧美观和独特的风格驰名中外并已风靡全球，在世界科学文化史上占有重要的地位。

中国民间工艺品千姿百态，除以上所提之外，还有布艺、木雕、灯彩、吊饰、漆器、竹编、玉器工艺、瓷器、剪纸、年画……数不胜数。这些民间艺术都是千百年来中华民族智慧的结晶。

实用词汇

白陶 white pottery

彩釉陶 glazed colored pottery

黑陶文化 black-pottery culture

风筝 kite

景泰蓝 cloisonne

泥塑木雕 like an idol carved in wood or moulded in clay—as dead as a door-nail

漆器 lacquerwork

青铜器 bronze ware

陶瓷 pottery and porcelain

陶钧 potter's wheel mould

陶犬瓦鸡 rubbish

陶文 inscription on pottery

陶俑 pottery figurine

唐三彩 Tang tricolour

印纹陶文化 Stamped Pottery Culture

釉陶 glazed pottery

半身雕塑 bust

贝雕 shell carving

大理石雕 marble carving

雕花玻璃 cut glass

皮影戏 shadow show

名言俗语

艺术是自发性的幻想。

Art is the illusion of spontaneity.

隐而不露即艺术。

Art lies in concealing art.

艺术家四海为家。

An artist lives everywhere.

人生苦短，艺术源远流长。

Life is short, art is long.

一项技艺是取之不尽的财富。

A useful trade is a mine of gold.

俗语注解

泥塑木雕：用泥作模子雕在木头上，指大脑不灵活的人

like an idol carved in wood or moulded in clay: as dead as a door-nail

彩陶：出现在 600 多年前的明朝

painted pottery: The history of the painted pottery goes back to the Ming Dynasty, 600 years ago.

一技未熟，勿学他技。学艺不贪多，学一样就学好。

Never embark on what comes after without having mastered what goes before.

中西合璧

世界各民族都有各自独特的工艺品。比如木鞋是荷兰最具民族特色的工艺品，是民族风俗文化的缩影。俄罗斯套娃是俄罗斯的特产木制玩具，具有浓郁的地域风格，是俄罗斯民族特有的一种手工制作的工艺品。中国民间艺术的艺术形式再现了中国各民族各地区的民风民俗，通常不同省份存在差异。各种民间艺术都有

其悠久的历史，许多传统流传至今。中国民间艺术是我国丰富的文化和艺术遗产的重要组成部分，其种类繁多、对农村风貌的真实反映、丰富的生命气息以及鲜明的地方风格和浪漫主义的艺术方法赢得了全世界人民的赞誉。

Each nation in the world has its own peculiar handicraft. For instance, the clogs of the Netherlands are of the most national characteristics of its handicraft with the epitome of national culture and custom; Russian Matryoshka dolls (nesting dolls) are of special wooden toys with various regional styles. They are the peculiar handcrafts of Russian people. Chinese folk art crafts are artistic forms inherited from a regional or ethnic scene in China. Usually there are some variations among provinces. Individual folk arts have a long history, and many traditions are still practiced today. Chinese folk art is an important part of the country's extremely heavy cultural and art heritage. Chinese folk art has won recognition and praise from experts both at home and abroad for its great variety, sincere rural content, rich flavor of life, distinctive local style, and its artistic approaches of romanticism.

UNIT 29

Chinese Jade

玉文化

题记

中华民族是崇拜玉的民族，在世界上有着“玉石之国”的美誉。事实上，中国也是世界上最早发现玉和使用玉的国家。早在 8000 年前，中国的先人就开始用玉制作装饰品。中国人认为玉石是非常神秘的石头，也是集天地精华和灵气于一身的美石。

The Chinese people have worshipped jade, thus China has been called “the country of jade”. In fact, China is the first nation to discover and make use of it. 8000 years ago, Chinese people began to make ornaments with jade. They believe that jade is a mysterious and beautiful stone with wonderful spirit both from heaven and earth.

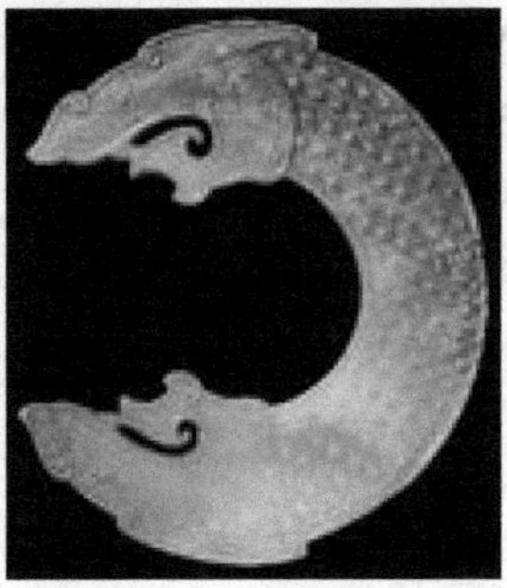

In China, jade is very popular and is a beautiful, sacred, precious and auspicious symbol. The Chinese even believe that jade has the five virtues as human. The five virtues of jade are the tough texture, smooth light, florid color, dense structure and comfortable sound that can be compared with benevolence, righteousness, wisdom, bravery, and cleaness—the five virtues of men. Jade culture has a profound influence on the spirit of the Chinese nation. They have always advocated the national integrity with the ideal, “Better a glorious death than a shameful life”

and "Turn swords into ploughshares". In ancient times, jade was also a symbol of hierarchy. In civil society, it was said that jade could create luck, avoid devils and prevent diseases. The Chinese people have worn beautiful jade for thousands of years. That's why they embodied their love of jade with the medals inlaid with jade of the Beijing 2008 Olympic Games.

7000 years ago, in the Neolithic Age, Chinese carved jade into semi-circular jade pendants, pearls, pendants and other decorations. The jade articles of Liang Chu culture in Jiangsu and Zhejiang provinces represent the highest level of primitive Chinese jade sculpture. At that time, it was popular for the noblemen to take jade objects as burial articles. There were more than 200 jade articles in one gave, among which included more than 20 kinds of jade articles such as jade tablets, bracelets, fish, birds, turtles. These jade articles are of excellent workmanship, complicated shapes and superb sculpture.

In the Xia Dynasty many jade articles that were high-quality made evolved from weapons and tools, such as dagger-axe, knives, battle-axe, etc. The jade objects of Shang Dynasty were represented by the ones unearthed from the tomb of Fu Hao. There were 755 jade articles in her tomb, among which there was a fine knelt jade figure meticulously carved with clear facial expression, dress and hair style.

During the Warring States Period the nobility liked famous Hetian jade very much, and the jade pendants were most popular at that time. The best jade articles were produced in Yuan, Ming and Qing dynasties. The biggest jade article (artificial mountain carving) "Da Yu Led People in Curbing Floods" displayed in Palace Museum is more than two meters high and 10000 kilograms in weight, which was finished in the 53rd year of Qianlong Period.

From ancient times, jade had been regarded as precious thing, so when the emperors and the nobles died they were usually dressed in jade clothes known as "jade burial suit sewn with fine gold thread". The one unearthed from the tomb of Liu Sheng, the king of Zhongshan was composed of 2498 pieces of jade and 1100 grams gold thread. It was said that according to the hierarchy only emperors could wear the jade clothes sewn with gold thread, the princes and princesses wore those sewn with silver thread, and the ones sewn with copper thread were worn by the other nobles.

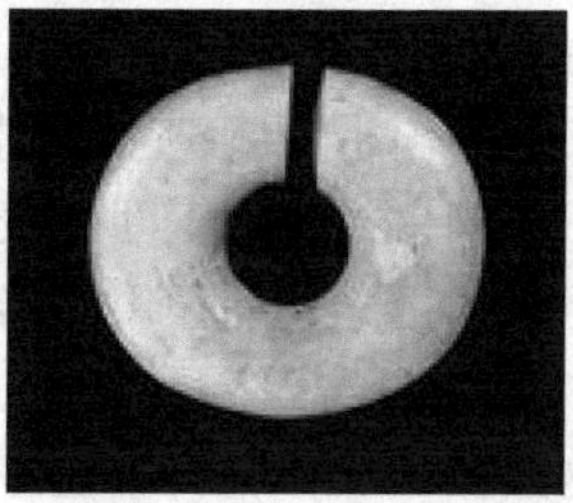

The most famous legend about jade should be "He Family Tablet". During the Spring and Autumn Period there was a man called Bianhe found a stone, which was a rare piece of precious jade according to his rich experience. But when he twice dedicated this piece of uncut jade to the kings, he was punished having his feet cut off because the jade carvers in the palace said he had cheated the kings with an ordinary stone. At last, he sent the stone to the third who believed him and let workers open the jade stone, a fine priceless piece of jade appeared.

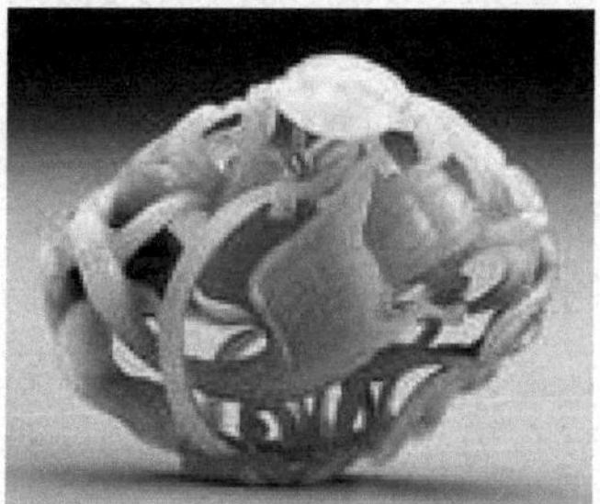

Later, many other kings wanted to possess this unparalleled jade. There was a famous story about the jade "Bring back the jade intact to the State of Zhao". The king of the Qin State said in order to get the jade he was willing to offer fifteen cities to the king of the State Zhao, the owner of the jade at that time. But when the king of Qin had accepted the jade, he refused to hand over the fifteen cities he had promised, so Li Xiangru, the emissary of Zhao, got the jade back in a clever way. However, when the king of Qin unified all other states of China, he possessed the jade at last and he turned the precious jade into his imperial seal.

段落译文

玉在中国是美好、神圣、贵重和祥瑞的象征，深受人们的喜爱。人们甚至认为玉和人一样都具有五德。玉的五德是坚韧的质地，莹润的光泽，绚丽的色彩，致密的结构和舒畅的声音可与人的五德——仁、义、智、勇、洁相媲美。玉文化也深深地影响中华民族的精神，中国人向来提倡“宁为玉碎，不为瓦全”的民族气节和“化干戈为玉帛”的友好团结风尚。在古代，玉是身份地位的象征物；在民间，玉有趋祥避邪、防病治病等传说。几千年来，中国人一直保持着佩戴美玉的习惯。2008年北京奥运会中国人又把爱玉的传统体现在镶玉的奖牌上。

早在7000年前新石器时代的中国古人就把玉雕刻成璜、珠、坠等装饰品。江浙一带的良褚文化玉器代表了中国原始玉雕的最高水平。当时的贵族墓盛行用玉器随葬，最多的随葬玉器达200多件，种类繁多包括玉壁、镯及鱼、鸟、龟等20多种。这些玉器制作精良、造型复杂、雕刻手法高超。

夏代的玉器有很多都是由兵器或工具演化的，如玉制的戈、刀、钺等，制作工艺相当的精美。商代玉器是以妇好墓出土的玉器为代表。妇好墓出土玉器达755件，其中有一个精美的跪坐的玉人。其雕刻精细人物的表情、衣冠、发型都表现得清清楚楚，一丝不苟。

战国时期的王侯喜欢使用著名的和田玉。玉佩是当时最常见的饰品。元、明、清三个朝代是中国玉器制造的鼎盛期。珍藏在故宫博物院的“大禹治水”就是乾隆五十三年完成的山子雕，它高达两米多，重达万斤，是至今为止世界上最大的一件玉雕工艺品。

从远古时期起，玉就被中国人视为珍贵之物，因此有些皇帝及贵族死后都要穿玉做的衣服。由于玉片间是用金丝编缀的，称为“金缕玉衣”。从中山王刘胜墓出土的金缕玉衣由 2498 片玉片组成，用掉金丝 1100 克。据说随葬玉衣是有等级之分的。只有皇帝才能穿金缕玉衣；诸侯王、贵人、公主穿“银缕玉衣”；其他贵族死后只能穿铜缕玉衣。

关于玉的最著名的传说应该是和氏璧了。春秋时期，楚国有位叫卞和的人挖矿时得了一块石头，根据经验他知道石头里面一定是一块罕见的美玉。但是当他两次把这块未经雕琢的璞玉献给君王时，却被不识货的宫廷玉工说成是普通石头，犯了欺君之罪，被砍去了双脚。直到他把璞玉献给第三个君主时，这次君主相信了他，让玉工截开石头，才使这块价值连城的美玉展现出来。

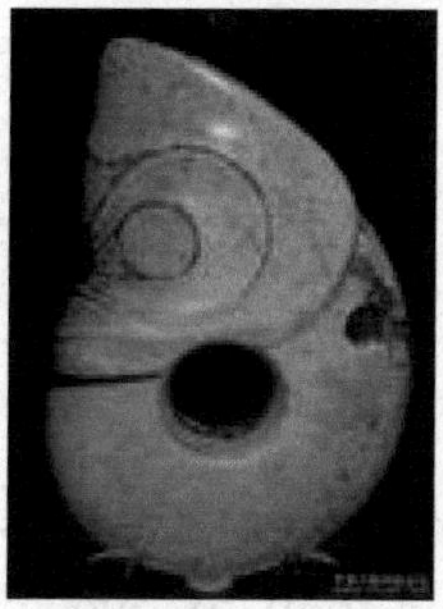

后来有很多君王都想得到这块举世无双的美玉，还演绎了中国历史上有名的“完璧归赵”的故事。传说当时秦王愿意用 15 座城市与赵国交换这块美玉，但是当秦王拿到美玉后，便不想把城市给赵国，而赵国的丞相蔺相如机智地把和氏璧拿了回去。但是当秦国攻灭了赵国等其他国家统一天下后，这块和氏璧还是落到了秦王的手里。秦王命令把和氏璧刻成了一方传世玉玺。由此可见美玉在中国的历史上是多么重要。

实用词汇

玉刻 jade carving
玉璜 semi-circular jade pendant
玉珠 jade pearl
玉坠 jade pendant
玉雕家 jade carver
玉器 jade article; jade object
玉圭 jade tablet
玉镯 jade bracelet

玉簪 jade hairpin
玉如意 jade ruyi
玉玺 imperial jade seal
镶玉的奖牌 medal with an inlay of jade
璞玉 uncut jade
金缕玉衣 jade clothes; burial suit sewn with fine gold wire or thread
佩 pendant
璧 a round flat piece of jade with a hole in its centre
玦 penannular jade ring
珰 ear-drop
山子雕 artificial mountain carving
趋祥避邪 tend toward luck and avoid devils
驱邪 cast out devils; exorcise evil spirits
和氏璧 He Family Tablet

名言俗语

宁为玉碎，不为瓦全。/ 死的高尚胜过活的卑劣。

Better a glorious death than a shameful life. / An honourable death is better than a disgraceful life. It is better to die with honour than to live in infamy.

抛砖引玉。

casting a brick to attract jade; throw out a brick to attract a jade.

玉不琢，不成器。

Without carving, a piece of jade cannot be turned into an ornament or be used as a sacrifice.

The finest diamond must be cut. The gem cannot be polished without friction.

瑕不掩瑜。

A speck on a jade stone won't obscure its radiance.

玉食锦衣

Eating delicacies and wearing gorgeous clothes

玉石俱焚

Destroy the good and the bad together; throw out the baby with the bath water.

金玉良言

golden saying and valuable advice

词语注解

化干戈为玉帛：比喻把战争或争斗变为和平、友好。

Turn swords into ploughshares, which means to turn war into peace or to cease hostilities and make peace; or turn hostility into friendship.

抛砖引玉：比喻用粗浅的、不成熟的意见引出别人高明、成熟的意见。

Casting a brick to attract jade is an illustration of the cleverness of the human mind can be found when a valuable trophy is netted at the expense of providing something cheap in advance. Today it is often used to mean that the introductory remarks are commonplace words offered so others can provide their more valuable opinions or comments.

完璧归赵：比喻原物完整无损地归还本人。

To bring back the jade intact to the State of Zhao. The saying is used to describe something being returned to its owner intact.

金口玉言：极难可贵的话，后来泛指不能改变的话。

Gold mouth and jaded words, which means the precious words or utterances that carry great weight.

玉叶金枝：指皇族和出身高贵的公子、小姐。

Jade leaves and gold branches, which is used to describe the persons of imperial lineage.

中西合璧

东方人天生喜欢玉石，而西方人喜欢钻石、水晶等宝石。事实上中国的玉石文化和西方宝石文化截然不同。但是令人称奇的是两者的共同之处是东方人祖先和西方人的始祖都本能地利用他们的宝石——玉石或水晶或其他宝石来占卜祭天，乞求吉祥和法力。

Asians are fond of jade, while Westerners love diamonds, crystal and other precious stones. In fact, there are different cultures about the precious stone between China and Western countries. But the amazing thing is that both of them, Asian ancestors and the ancestors of the West, instinctively offered their precious stones—jade or diamonds or crystal to God or Heaven, begging for good fortune and super natural power.

UNIT 30

Chinese Porcelain

中国瓷器

题记

瓷器的发明是中华民族对世界文明的又一伟大贡献。中国是瓷器的故乡，在英文中"瓷器"(china)一词已成为"中国"的代名词。中国早期的瓷器出现在公元前16世纪的商代中期；到唐代，瓷器的制作技术和艺术创作已高度成熟；宋代制瓷业蓬勃发展，名窑涌现；明清时代技术上又有进一步的提高。中国的陶瓷业至今仍兴盛不衰，质高形美，极受人们的欢迎。

The invention of porcelain is another great contribution of the Chinese nation to the world civilization. China is the hometown of porcelain. In English, "Porcelain" (china) has become a synonym of the word "China". Early Chinese porcelain came into being in the mid-16th century BC; and porcelain production technology and artistic creativity reached a high degree of maturity in the Tang Dynasty; Song Dynasty porcelain boomed and famous kilns emerged; and the technology was improved in the Ming and Qing Dynasties. Up to now, the ceramic industry has been flourishing and popular among the people from all over the world, due to its high quality and elegant shape.

According to the history of civilization, porcelain, like silk, with its distinctive ethnic flavor, serves as a unique contribution. From the word "china" (porcelain) and China, we can say that in the eyes of many foreigners, porcelain is subconsciously always associated with China.

The development of Chinese porcelain evolved from pottery, and the primitive porcelain that originated over 3,000 years ago. Till the Song Dynasty, famous porcelain and kilns had won their reputation over half of China and this became the most prosperous period. The development of Chinese porcelain basically can be divided into three stages: celadon—white porcelain—painted china. The period of celadon dated from the Warring States to Yuan Dynasty. Then in period of Wei Jin Southern and Northern times, porcelain technology was enhanced, and in Beichao, white porcelain appeared, which could be seen as a sensational invention in Chinese porcelain history. During the late North period, painted porcelain appeared. It was during the Tang Dynasty that Chinese porcelain reached its peak, furthermore, at this point its production had reached a very comprehensive level.

Celadon is fired by laying a green-glazed material, (iron is the coloring agent of the green glaze) on the body. With delicate texture, bright lines, smooth, dignified but simple shapes and pure color, celadon is famous over the world. "Green jade, bright as a mirror, sounds like a chime" and "porcelain flower", are all titles that made celadon worthy as a treasure of porcelain. In its day, celadon had the reputation of "surpassing porcelain and being similar to jade".

Based on celadon, white porcelain was eventually produced. During Tang Dynasty, the technology of producing white porcelain was very advanced, thus many kilns in the northern parts largely baked white porcelain. The white porcelain from the Xing kiln competed with the celadon, of which the southern region was the representative, so people always said that "south blue north white". The white porcelain produced in Tang Dynasty marked the true maturity with its glazed white skin resembling silver and the snow. The emergence of white porcelain paved the way for the blue and white porcelain and painted china.

Painted china had designs painted on its surface, and it was said that the painted china was at its most marvelous time in Tang Dynasty. The shift from Ming to Qing Dynasty was a prosperous period for the development of painted china. In this period, the most outstanding achievement undoubtedly would be the Jingde kiln. In addition, during Song Dynasty, at the porcelain capital, the Jingde kiln produced a kind of porcelain which was white but in which one could perceive the shadow of green color in it (also known as the blue porcelain). The blue-and-white and the glazed red porcelains were known for their bright and fresh red color. In Ming and Qing Dynasties, painted porcelain made unprecedented progress in its purity, texture, and diverse glazed color. In the Qing Dynasty, colored enamel appeared and pink was produced.

Porcelain serves as one of our nation's unique commodities and possesses a vast market overseas. Since Sui and Tang Dynasties, we had exported china to foreign countries such as Asia, Africa, the Middle East, Europe and the Americas. Even in Sudan and Egypt, you could inevitably find traces of Chinese porcelain. In Qing Dynasty (1684), porcelain began to be exported on a large scale. Chinese porcelain became the best seller in the world, there were even 52 shops to sell china in London. During this period, the upper class, as well as the ordinary people, took Chinese porcelain as a symbol of a fashion, pride, and wealth.

Moreover, the royal family possessed high-quality Chinese porcelain as a means of showing off their wealth. Even the Queen of Prussia did so, by trading Saxon cavalry with 600 teams consisting of four guards for 12 large Chinese porcelain vases which graced his wedding. Therefore, if you go into any of a European royal palace, museum, or small countryside castle, or even in a French friend's house, you can find some Chinese porcelain.

Since Tang and Song dynasties, porcelain has become one of China's bulk export commodities, and now many countries have unearthed or collected porcelain from China. Thus our country's major foreign transport channels have been nicknamed "The Porcelain Roads".

段落译文

在世界文明史上，瓷器与丝绸一样，也是中国一项带有鲜明民族色彩的独特贡献。瓷器与中国(china 与 China)的英文拼写相同：由此可见，在外国人心目中，始终把瓷器同中国联系在一起。

中国瓷器是从陶器发展演变而来的，原始瓷器起源于 3000 多年前。宋代时，名瓷名窑已遍及大半个中国，是瓷业最为繁荣的时期。中国的瓷器史基本上可分为三个阶段：青瓷—白瓷—彩瓷。从战国至元代为“青瓷”时期。魏晋南北朝时期，制瓷工艺又有所提高，北朝时成功烧制出了白瓷，堪称中国瓷器工艺史上的一大创举。北朝晚期又出现了彩瓷，时至唐代，中国瓷器工艺迎来了它的鼎盛时期，陶瓷的制作达到了相当完善的地步。

青瓷是在坯体上施以青釉烧制而成。青瓷以瓷质细腻、线条明快流畅、造型端庄浑朴、色泽纯洁而斑斓著称于世。有人将青瓷描绘成“青如玉，明如镜，声如磬”的“瓷器之花”不愧为瓷中之宝，珍奇名贵。时人有“越瓷类玉”的誉名。

白瓷是在青瓷的基础上出现的。唐代白瓷生产十分发达，北方许多窑口都大量烧制白瓷，其中以邢窑白瓷为代表，与南方地区越窑青瓷相匹敌，世称“南青北白”。唐代烧造的白瓷，胎釉白净，如银似雪，标志着白瓷的真正成熟。白瓷的出现，为青花瓷和色彩缤纷的彩瓷开辟了道路。

彩瓷是在器物表面中加以彩绘的瓷器。唐代的彩瓷更是素称美奂。明清时期开始出现釉上彩（粉彩），同时也是彩瓷发展的盛期，以景德镇窑成就最为突出。此外，宋代“瓷都”景德镇烧制出了白中泛青的影青瓷（又称青色瓷），誉满天下。元代的青花和釉里红色调清新明快；明清的彩瓷细腻纯净，釉色精美多样，成就空前。清代在康熙末雍正年间出现珐琅彩，之后又出现了粉彩。

陶瓷为我国独有的商品，海外有广大市场。从隋唐开始，我国的瓷器就已输出国外遍布亚洲、非洲各个区域——东达朝鲜、日本，南到东南亚的菲律宾、印度尼西亚等，远抵非洲的苏丹和埃及，都有隋唐瓷器的足迹。清朝康熙二十三年（1684 年），瓷器大规模外销。特别值得一提的是中国瓷器在欧洲市场十分畅销，仅在伦敦就有 52 家之多商店。在这期间，使用中国瓷器，在欧洲已蔚然成风。不仅上层社会以此为荣，普通民众也以此为时髦。

更有甚者，王室贵族把拥有中国优质瓷器作为夸耀豪富的手段。甚至普鲁士皇帝选皇后，也不惜代价地用六百名撒克逊骑兵组成的四队近卫军与邻近的君主换取 12 个巨大的中国瓷花瓶，为他的婚礼增辉。所以，当你进入欧洲任何一座皇宫、博物馆、失落在乡野间的古堡，或到法国朋友家里作客，都可以看到中国瓷器。

瓷器是唐宋以来我国出口的大宗商品之一，现在世界上许多国家都出土或珍藏我国的古瓷。所以，也有人把我国的对外交通渠道称为“陶瓷之路”。

实用词汇

官瓷 Guan porcelain (popular in the Song Dynasty); mandarin porcelain
官窑 Guan Kiln (cour porcelain kiln of the Song Dynasty)
青花瓷 blue and white porcelain
套瓷 try to establish a relationship with someone
影青瓷 shadowy blue porcelain
彩瓷 painted china

景德镇瓷窑 Jingde kiln
瓷制品 china-ware
釉 glaze
原材料 raw material
云母 mica
皂石，块滑石 steatite
陶瓷质地和类型 Qualities & Types of Pottery
白胎 White Body
碧玉细炻器 jasper
薄胎瓷 thin china / egg-shell porcelain
彩陶器，釉陶 faience
陈设瓷，摆设瓷 display china / ornamental porcelain
赤陶 terracotta, terracotta, red earthenware
德化陶瓷 Te-hua porcelain, Dehua pottery
高温陶瓷 refractory china
低温陶瓷 low-fired porcelain
工业陶瓷 industrial ceramics
工艺瓷，美术瓷，艺术瓷 art porcelain, art and craft china, art pottery, artistic china
骨瓷 bone china
古瓷 ancient porcelain
光瓷 lusterware
黑色陶器 basalt
裂变瓷 crackled porcelain
裂纹瓷 crazed china
米色陶器 creamware
青瓷 celadon
青花瓷 blue and white porcelain
轻质瓷、轻瓷 light china
日用瓷 household china, table ware
软瓷 soft porcelain

杀菌陶瓷 antiseptic pottery
绳纹陶器 Rope figure pottery
施釉陶器 slipware
粗瓷 stoneware
素彩瓷 plain porcelain
陶 earthenware
陶瓷 pottery
无釉陶、陶瓷素烧坯 biscuit, unglazed ware
锡釉陶 majolica
细瓷 fine china
硬瓷 hard porcelain
赭色黏土陶器 terra sigillata
紫砂 purple granulated, purple sand, terra-cotta
长石瓷 feldspar porcelain
瓷牙；牙科用瓷 dental porcelain
雕塑瓷；象牙色帕利安瓷 statuary porcelain
高铝瓷 high-alumina porcelain
锆质瓷 zircon porcelain
滑石瓷 steatite porcelain
化学瓷 chemical porcelain
尖晶石瓷 spinel porcelain
堇青石瓷 cordierite porcelain
镁橄榄石瓷 forsterite porcelain
镁质瓷；氧化镁瓷 magnesia porcelain
莫来石瓷 mullite porcelain
耐热瓷器 refractory porcelain
缥瓷 faint coloured porcelain
青白瓷 greenish white porcelain
钛质瓷 titania porcelain
天然原料制成的瓷器 natural porcelain
透辉石瓷 diopside porcelain

卫生瓷器 sanitary porcelain
鸭蛋青瓷 duck-egg porcelain
氧化铝瓷 alumina porcelain
原始瓷 proto-porcelain
皂石瓷 soapstone porcelain
中火度瓷 intermediate porcelain
IC 管瓷 IC packages
白云石瓷 dolomitic

名言俗语

没有金刚钻不揽瓷器活。
No diamond, no porcelain.
身有家财万贯，不如钧瓷一件。
Better have porcelain than property.
富人藏瓷，穷人藏陶。
The rich collect porcelain while the poor collect pottery.
瓮中之鳖。
Like a rat in a hole.
玉不琢，不成器。
The finest diamond must be cut.
粗瓷碗雕不出细花来。
You cannot make a silk purse out of a sow's ear.
友谊就像陶器，破了可以修补；爱情好比镜子，一旦打破就难重圆。
friendship is like earthenware: once broken, it can be mended; love is like a mirror: once broken, that ends it.

俗语注解

瓷：“中国”来自“china”，在英文中“中国”和“瓷”是同一单词
porcelain, china: China originated from “china”, the same word in English

“碰瓷”乃北京俗语，始于清末，本是古玩业的一句行话，指当时有人专门抱着劣质瓷器往马车和行人身上碰，然后高价索赔、借机讹诈。如今，是指一些人专门在大街上用身体或开着车去碰撞车辆，然后利用对方想尽快解决问题的心理，讹取钱财。

"Pengci" was an old saying in late Qing Dynasty in Beijing, this is a jargon indicating that some people were dedicated to holding low-grade porcelain to crush with carriages and pedestrians who touched, and then charged high-priced claim. Now, some people specialized in the street to use body or driving a car to crash other cars, and ask for money as a charge, which happens in Guangzhou, Beijing and other places.

瓷饭碗：指容易失业的工作，随时有可能失业

porcelain rice-bowl: insecure position or job

套瓷：不熟悉的试图和别人拉关系，套近乎

try to establish a relationship with someone

笨手笨脚的人：指像公牛闯进了瓷器店，打碎了所有的瓷器一样粗心大意、笨手笨脚的人

A bull into a china shop: some people are careless and rude just like a bull into a china shop and break the chinawares

瓷公鸡：指吝啬之人

china cock—a mean person

瓷婚：指结婚20周年纪念日

20th wedding anniversary: the celebration for being married for 20 years

中西合璧

中国历来被人们认为是陶瓷文化的发源地，因此，西方的陶瓷文化在一定程度上与中国有着某种联系，这种交流到了十八世纪尤为突出。不过在中西瓷器装饰文化的融合中，最为人津津乐道的就是洛可可风格了。我们也可以在瓷器装饰纹样上找到这种融合。一位西方学者曾说过：“洛可可艺术风格和古代中国文化的契合，其全部秘密就在于瓷器所体现出来的纤细入微的情调。”德国著名学者利奇温评论中国陶瓷时就认为瓷器象征了洛可可时代特有的光彩、色调和纤美的质感。中国瓷器光洁莹润的质感，中国式的绘画图案造型，淡雅的色彩、流畅写意的装

饰线条，恰是洛可可艺术纤巧、淡色，喜爱“S”形、“C”形曲线以及重自然逸趣的风格典范。

China has always been considered the birthplace of ceramic culture, therefore, the ceramic culture of the West has something to do with China to some extent, such was particularly obvious in exchanges in the 18th century. However, in western culture, the fusion of Chinese and western porcelain, is now most talked about is as Rococo style porcelain. Such a convergence can also be found in decorative patterns of porcelain. A Western scholar once said: “All the secret of the combination between Rococo art and ancient Chinese culture lies in the delicate porcelain, embodied in every possible way out of the tone." A famous German scholar Leach once commented that Chinese porcelain is considered as a symbol of the Rococo era porcelain because of its unique luster, hue and textural beauty. The smooth texture of Chinese porcelain, Chinese-style painting pattern shape, elegant colors, smooth lines freehand decoration, are precisely the Rococo art, like “S”-shaped, “C”-shaped curve styles, as well as the typical model of natural sense and leisurely delight.

UNIT 31

Paper-Cut

剪　纸

题记

剪纸是传统的、具有民族风格的工艺美术作品，俗称窗花，也是中国民间传统装饰艺术之一。民间剪纸，为聪慧的劳动妇女所创作。她以娴熟的技艺、朴素的技法，利用古今人物、吉祥动物、名贵花草等为素材创作出大量的艺术精品，中国剪纸可以把人们喜庆、快乐的感情表达得淋漓尽致，是极有欣赏价值的艺术品和礼品。

Paper-cutting, a paper-cut window decoration or a window flower, is one of the traditional folk arts with unique Chinese style. Created by intelligent rural females with their skillful and simple techniques, paper-cutting has created a lot of artistic works based on people, auspicious animals, beautiful flowers and plants. They can be valuable presents to show people's happiness and joyfulness.

Paper-cutting is one of the most popular and participated folk arts. According to research, ancient Chinese people began to make hollow carved ornaments with gold, silver, leather or silk fabrics during Shang Dynasty and this can be seen as the embryonic form of paper-cuts. Since the invention of paper by Cai Lun in Eastern Han Dynasty, it has been two thousand years and has become a popular art with widely used materials. Paper-cut often appears in religious ceremonies, decoration and plastic arts.

With a vast territory and multi-ethnic population, Chinese folk paper-cutting bears distinct national and geographical features. In art style, it is more straightforward in northern China; while more exquisite and delicate in the south. The rural female folk artists use only a pair of scissors and a piece of paper to convey their conceptual figures and color effect, which surpass time and space, while male-dominant career artists make paper cuttings with superb delicacy and graciousness in a more realistic style. The typical example is the character "寿 SHOU" represents longevity and will give delight to the whole celebration; and a big red paper character "喜喜 XI" (double happiness) is a traditional must on the newlywed's door for a wedding ceremony . During Spring Festival, people paste patterns on the window, door lintel or desks for the festival atmosphere.

Paper-cut can be produced as the monochrome and the color ones from the colors of the work. The ones engraved with one color are called monochrome paper-cut works as woodcut prints in monochrome, and it is the most common form. Such work may seem very simple but clear-featured. The color paper-cut is made in a different color, this kind of form is not commonly used, though it may seem more vivid and lively compared with the monochrome.

Paper cutting is all hand-made. It is easy to learn the rudiments. Non-craftsmen need only a knife or a pair of scissors and a piece of paper. For craftsman, they need knives and gravers of various types to make complicated patterns. It can be one piece of paper or many pieces. Simple patterns can be cut with a knife. For complicated patterns, people first pasted the pattern on the paper and then used various kinds of knives to make it. No mistake can be made during the process otherwise the work would be a failure.

There are several steps for us to follow when we have paper-cutting. First draft: when confirming the idea of the cutting, we must have a layout and draw it clearly and specifically to have an image in black and white; then we begin to cut or engrave; thirdly remove it carefully and gently one page after another; finally we copy and paste the work, with improvements sometimes.

It is easy to learn about cutting a piece of paper but very difficult to master it with perfection. One must hold the knife in an upright fashion and press evenly on the paper with some strength, flexibility is required but wiggling will lead to imprecision or damage the whole image. Paper cutters stress the cutting lines in several styles and there are basic lines that they endeavor to master. They attempt to carve a circle like the moon, a straight line like a stem of wheat, a square like a brick, and jaggedly like the beard.

©时代图片·图客 http://pt.tuke.com

In many parts of China, paper-cutting skill has become a must for men and women, old and young, and a symbol of a clever mind and nimble fingers. It has never stopped its stride since it came into being. Nowadays paper-cutting has long been out of the farmers' homes and into the modern designs as product packaging, trademark advertising, interior decorating, fashion design, cartoons, on stage, in magazines or in TV series etc. And as a carrier of the original Chinese culture, the art has been introduced to foreign lands and become the cultural wealth of humanity and art treasure in the world.

段落译文

剪纸是中国最为流行的民间艺术之一。据考证，从商代始就有人用金银箔、皮革或丝织品进行镂空刻花制作装饰品，这可以看做是剪纸的雏形。自东汉蔡伦发明造纸术以后，这种艺术形式因为找到了更易普及的材料而诞生了剪纸艺术。

可见，剪纸艺术距今已有两千多年的历史了。剪纸常用于宗教仪式、装饰和造型艺术等方面。

由于中国地域辽阔，民间剪纸艺术因地区不同而具有各自不同的特征。在艺术风格方面，北方的剪纸透露出直爽、俭朴；而在南方，剪纸艺术则表现了精致、优雅的艺术风格。农村妇女用一双巧手仅凭一把剪刀、一张白纸就能剪出表达她们思想的、跨越时空的艺术品；将剪纸作为职业的艺术家们则以现实主义风格创造出超级精致、优美的作品。例如剪纸“寿”字表达“长寿”之意，在生日宴会上是必不可少的，会给祝寿场面平添喜气；又如婚礼上的传统的大红剪纸“喜喜”更是任何其他饰品不可能代替的东西；还有春节期间，家家户户所贴的洋溢着节日气氛的窗花、门饰、桌饰，等等。

剪纸从色彩上分，有单色剪纸和彩色剪纸。用一种颜色的剪纸刻出来的作品就叫单色剪纸，它如同版画中的单色木刻一样，是最常用的一种形式，这类作品显得十分朴素大方但简洁明了。而彩色剪纸则是用不同颜色的剪纸剪出来的作品，这种形式并不常用，但看起来生动形象。

剪纸是一种纯手工活，入门非常容易。你只需要一把剪刀和一张纸就可以完成。如果要剪出更艺术、更复杂的作品，当然要用多种不同的剪刀和雕刻工具才可以。一次可以剪出一张纸或数张纸的作品。仅用一把刀就可以剪出简单的图案。要剪花样复杂的作品，必须先将要剪的图案贴在纸上，然后用各种剪刀剪出作品，这样剪制一般不会出错。

剪纸的制作步骤分为：起稿：构思确定后，起稿布局，对画面进行具体的描绘，画出黑白效果；剪、刻：如用刀子刻；揭离：剪刻完后需要把剪纸一张张揭开。揭离之前，必须先将刻好的纸板轻轻揉动，使纸张互相脱离；粘贴：将成品粘贴起来，便于保存。再经过修改复制等步骤即可完成。

剪纸学起来容易，但剪出完美的作品却是很困难的。剪纸的人必须将刀直立地握紧，水平、均衡地用力，刻纸的时候手必须灵活，不稳定刻的就不准确甚至毁了整个作品。剪纸艺术家一般要求必须努力掌握几种基本线条的刻法：圆形要圆得像月亮、直线必须像麦穗的杆一样直、方如砖、折线如须。

在中国很多地区，剪纸这种传统艺术已成为男女老少心灵手巧的象征。自这种艺术诞生以来，就没有中断过。如今，剪纸早已走出了庄户人的小院，走入现代设计的广阔天地，在产品包装设计、商标广告、室内装潢、服装设计、动漫、舞台、杂志及电视节目里到处可见等等。剪纸作为中国文化的载体，也走向了世界，名扬四海，成为全人类的文化财富与艺术瑰宝。

实用词汇

剪纸 paper-cut
剪影 paper-cut silhouette
剪纸艺人 paper-cutter
剪纸艺术 paper-cutting art
剪纸作品 paper-cuttings
剪纸风格 paper-cutting style
剪纸方法 paper-cutting method
式样设计 form design
单色画 monochrome
剪影画 silhouette art
服装设计 fashion design
艺术瑰宝 art treasure
折纸 paper-folding
装饰图案 decorative design
剪刀差 the margin between the prices of industrial products and agricultural product usually presented in the form of scissor's movement

名言俗语

美丽的东西赏心悦目。

A thing of beauty is a feast to the eye.

艺术使自然界更完美。

Art improves nature.

毫无价值

Not worth the paper it is printed

美术是揭示真实的虚假。

Art is a lie that tells truth.

俗语注解

剪烛西窗：指亲朋好友聚在一起亲密谈话

friends and relatives get together and talk intimately

窗花：将剪好的剪纸作品贴在窗户上作为装饰

paper-cut window decoration; window flower

剪单页剪纸：剪纸制作技术的一种，以剪刀为工具，一次完成一张纸的剪纸制作

one-page cutting: one of the paper-cutting techniques, to have one piece of paper-cut work a time with a pair of scissors

多页刻纸：用刀做工具，将设计好的图案贴在纸上，然后用刀刻出一次多张纸的作品的剪纸制作技术

multi-page engraving: one of the paper-cutting techniques, engrave multi-layers of paper with a knife

中西合璧

现存最古老的剪纸的是在中国新疆发现的公元 6 世纪的剪纸对称圆，8~9 世纪剪纸传入西亚，16 世纪传入土耳其。之后的一个世纪里剪纸艺术逐渐传入多数

欧洲国家。在德国和瑞士 Scherenschnitte 的意思是“剪纸”；剪纸自中世纪以来就成为犹太人的一种艺术形式，在约 17 世纪，作为宗教装饰而受欢迎。中国有许多剪纸艺术家从事剪纸艺术。剪纸艺术通常是祖传或在本地传艺。不同地区的剪纸风格不同。从前剪纸主要以中国传统为主题，如今则开始涉及西方现代艺术形象，洋为中用。

The oldest surviving paper cut out is a symmetrical circle from the 6th century found in Xinjiang China. By the eighth or ninth century paper cutting appeared in West Asia and in Turkey in the 16th century. Within a century, paper cutting was being done in most of middle Europe. *Scherenschnitte* means "scissors cutting" and is the German and Swiss art of paper cutting. Paper cutting has been a common Jewish art form since the Middle Ages. By about the 17th century, paper cutting had become a popular form for small religious artifacts. China has many paper-cut artists specializing in paper cut outs. The knowledge usually was passed on by generations of paper artists in their family or home town. There are different styles of rendering paper cuttings in each region of China. There used to be only traditional Chinese themes but today western images and modern art touches are found in certain paper cut outs.

UNIT 32

Chinese Seals

中国印章

题记

2008 年北京奥运会会徽的“中国印——舞动的北京”给人们留下了极其深刻的印象，它向全世界人们展现了大量的历史信息和独特的中国印章文化。

2008 Beijing Olympic Games emblem, “Chinese Seal—Dancing Beijing” made a profound impression on the people of the world. It portrayed the world a great deal of historical information and the unique culture of the Chinese seal.

The Chinese seal appeared in Spring and Autumn Period. It was a stamp that was used as a security tool in the process of the social communication. The seal began in “the lute” at first. When the ancient people sealed or transferred something, in order to prevent from opening it on the way, they always tied up the things first, then used the clod to seal the end of the rope, and finally stamped the seal on the lute. This kind of mark is the initial seal.

Ancient Chinses seals were mainly divided into two major categories: official seal and personal seal. The first one is the symbol of the rights and the latter is only a personal declaration. They both played a very important role in the social interaction and economy intercourse. Besides, the personal seals are also used for painting inscriptions, and become unique works of art.

In ancient China, there were many kinds of seals with different usages. They had a lot of other names. After Qin unified China, the seal of an emperor was called "Xi"; the seals of officials and civilians were known as "Yin", "Ji", "Guanfang", "contract", "seal", "Chuozi", etc.

努尔哈赤玉玺

Seal materials are various and with strict grades. For example, "Xi" is the emperor's seal, which was usually made of precious jade. Only emperors, empresses, princes and marquises could use jade seals and gold seals, high-ranking officials could use the silver ones, and the low-ranking officials must use copper seals. Most of the official seals are square and little larger. The personal seal is relatively smaller.

The seal cutting is the general designation of engraving seals. In ancient times most of the seals were firstly wrote down, then was cut. The text on the seals were called big seal character, small seal character and bird script separately. The bird script is a kind of character made of the shapes of birds and insects and they are decorative. In fact, it is considered to be a special type of calligraphy. The seal character "Jing" in the "Chinese Seal", the emblem of Beijing Olympic Games, fully demonstrated the charming art of Chinese seals.

Since the shapes and the inscriptions of seals are various in different periods, people now usually use them to identify the authenticity of the ancient bureaucratic establishment, geographical features, names and the historical relic for historical accuracy. For example, the prints of the private or official seals in the Warring States Period belong to big seal character and those of Qin Dynasty are small seal character.

Chinese seals are also divided into red character seals (Zhuwen seal), white characters seals, Yangwenyin, and Yinwenyin. The characters cut in relief are known as Yangwenyin, and the characters cut in intaglio are called Yinwenyin. In Chinese Calligraphy and painting, the characters with vermilion ink paste are red character seals and the characters carved in intaglio are called white characters seals.

Since the Tang Dynasty, the seal was not a symbol of the power or a security tool anymore. It became a type of art being collected along with the painting and calligraphy collections for scholars.

Until now, seals have remained not only the most important authenticators of the official documents or the trade contracts, but also an elegant work of art. They are collected and enjoyed by many people because of the seal cutting, drawing and calligraphy craftsmanship.

段落译文

中国早在春秋战国时期就有了印章。印章又称为图章，是人们在社会交往过程中使用的一种凭信工具。印章最初始于“封泥”，古人在封存或传递东西的时候，为了防止中途被人打开，往往先用绳子捆住物件，再用泥块把绳口封上，最后把印盖在封泥上，作为信验。这种印记就是最初的印章。

中国的古代印章，主要分为官印和私印两大类。官印是权利的象征，私章则是个人的凭信物。私章在人们的社会交往和经济往来中起到了非常重要的凭信作用。除此之外，私章还用于书画题识，后来发展成为一种特有的艺术品。

中国古代的印章形式有多种，用法各有不同，印章的名称也有所不同。秦统一中国后， 皇帝的印章称为“玺”，官吏和民间所用的印章称为“印”，或“记”、“关防”、“合同”、“图章”“戳子”等。

印章取材品种极多且有严格的等级之分。例如“玺”是帝王印，一般是以上等玉石制成。只有皇帝、皇后、诸王侯可以使用玉印和金印。高级官员使用银印，一般官员则使用铜印。官印多为正方形，较大。私印相对小些。

篆刻是镌刻印章的统称。古时印章多采用篆书，先写后刻。印章上的文字有大篆、小篆、鸟虫篆等。鸟虫篆是用鸟虫等形状组成文字，非常具有装饰意味。实际上，也是一种篆书美术字。北京奥运会会徽的“中国印”那个拟人化的篆书“京”字，充分展示了中国印章的艺术魅力。

由于不同时代具有不同的形制和铭文，现代人常用印章来考证古代的官制、地理、人名等或鉴别历史文物的真伪。例如战国时期无论官印还是私印，其文字属于大篆，而秦代印章文字属于小篆等。

中国印章还分朱文印、白文印、阳文印及阴文印等。阳文印是指在印章上镌刻的凸状文字，凹入的文字则称为阴文印。书画界一般用印章蘸有朱砂印泥盖在纸上，其印文为红色的称为朱文印，印文为白色的称为白文印。

自唐代以来，印章从权力的象征和取信的凭证逐渐发展进入文人士大夫阶层的文化生活中，成为用于书画收藏和玩赏的艺术品。

如今，印章仍然是官方正式文件或贸易合同中最重要的凭证。同时印章又是一种高雅的艺术品，由于它集篆刻、绘画、书法于一身，因此成为很多中外收藏家欣赏和收藏的艺术品。

实用词汇

国玺 seal of state
印章，图章 seal; stamp; chop
篆刻 seal cutting
象牙刻 ivory carving
玉刻 jade carving
石刻 stone carving
印章雕刻 seal engraving
玉玺 the emperor's seal
官印；公章 official seal
藏书印 the seal on the books kept
阴文 characters cut in intaglio
阳文 characters cut in relief
印材 uncut seal
印纽 seal knob
印泥 ink paste
印台 ink pad
印匣 seal case
篆刻家 sealcutter
印谱 book of ancient seals
大篆 big/greater seal character / style
小篆 small/less seal character / style
鸟虫篆 bird script
火漆印 seal
印章戒指 seal ring
篆刻材料 sealcutting materials
盖印 affix a seal; stamp a seal

名言俗语

爱的印记；爱的保证

Seals of love

言而有信

Be as good as one's word

心心相印

Have mutual affinity

信誉卓著

Outstanding prestige or reputation

信口开河

Talk at random; speak irresponsibly

丧失信用

Lose one's credit

俗语注解

印把子：指行政机关图章的把儿，比喻掌握政权。

It is the knob of the official seal of an administrative organ, which also means holding the authority.

朱文：印章蘸朱砂印在纸或书画上，印文为红色的称为朱文印

Characters carved in relief on a seal

白文：印章上的阴文。印文为白色的称为白文印。

Intagliated characters on a seal. It means the characters carved in intaglio are called white characters seals.

阳文：是指在印章上镌刻的凸状文字

Inscription or design of the seal cut in relief

阴文：是指在印章上镌刻的凹入的文字

Characters of designs cut or cast in intaglio on seals or other wares; intaglio

中西合璧

印章在亚洲使用得很普遍，特别是在中国和日本。西方人现在基本不用印章，只要签个名就可以了。但是在使用火漆印上，中西方是相同的。为了让传递的信件和物品防拆保密，中国古人发明了“封泥”和火漆印。后来中国的火漆印由印度传入欧洲，成为欧洲人保守通信秘密的法宝，西方人用火漆封信后，趁其未干，用刻有自己族徽的戒指在上面按压一下，生成标志密封信件，防止偷看。目前还有一些国家和地区在运送某些特殊物品(如文物等)时使用火漆印。

Seals are commonly used in Asia, especially in China and Japan. At present, there is no concept of seals in the west countries. It is all right for them to sign their own names. But they are identical in the use of wax / lute in order to prevent the letters and articles from being opened in transit, the ancient Chinese invented lute and sealing wax. Later the Chinese sealing wax spread to India, where it was introduced to Europe and became a trump to protect the secret letters. Westerners usually used their seal-rings to press on the wax before it hardened when they are sealing the letters to prevent the peeping eyes. Now, there are still a number of countries and regions using sealing wax in the delivery of certain special items such as cultural relics.

UNIT 33

Chinese Musical Instruments

中国乐器

题记

在文明古老的中国，为了丰富生活，我们的祖先创造了各种各样具有民族特色的乐器。例如，人们十分熟悉的琵琶、胡琴、笛子、锣、鼓等。

In the civilization of ancient China, our ancestors created varied instruments with national characteristics to enrich their life, which are very familiar, such as the pipa, Chinese fiddle, flute, gong, drum and so on.

The earliest instrument may be a percussion instrument. According to records, while people were working, they found that the dried tree trunks could emit different sounds, so they covered the hollow tree trunks with animal skins to make wooden drums. During Han Dynasty, different drums of various sizes, textures, and effects appeared not only for private entertainment, but also for strengthening their military in the battle. At present, traditional Chinese musical instruments are divided into blowing instruments, bowed string instruments, plucked string instruments, and hammered string instruments, which are short for “cui, la, tan, da”(blowing, pulling, plucking and hammering).

The flute is one of the most common wind instruments in Cha, it had already emerged in the late Spring and Autumn period. The flutes were popular among the people and came in the form of bamboo, wood, irons, and jade. Now most flutes are made of bamboo. Because of its beautiful sounds, much music has been handed down for over 2000 years.

Xiao or the vertical bamboo flute is an antiquated wind instrument from China and is suitable for solo or ensemble styles of music. In ancient tim was made not only of bamboo, but jade or porcelain. There were o sound holes at first, then two were be added. Xiao with 6 sound holes that is played by people now is made of bamboo. Before Tang Dynasty, there were no differences between the Xiao and flute. The one played horizontally was known as flute and the one played vertically was called Xiao after it.

In addition to xiao and flute, sheng, tube, and the suona also belong to Chinese wind instruments. Suona is a trumpet shaped instrument, which was one of the most popular musical instruments. It is said that it came from Persia and Arabia 400~500 years ago and that "suona" is the transliteration of "surna" in Persian. It is widely used in local operas and festive holiday celebrations because of its pitch and clear sound.

Huqin (Chinese fiddle) is the main bow-stringed instrument in China. There are many kinds of Chinese fiddles, such as Erhu, Beijing opera fiddles, and high-pitched Chinese fiddles, and so on. They are not only suitable for performing deep, plaintive melody, but are also able to demonstrate spectacular momentum, which is the main accompaniment in local operas. Matouqin, which is well known among the Mongolian belongs to bow-stringed

instrument family too.

Guqin is the oldest stringed instrument in China. It was very popular in the Zhou Dynasty. Chinese zither was also popular in the state of Qin during the Spring and Autumn period, so it was also known as "Qin Zheng". Chinese zithers with 12 to 25 strings were usually made of parasol wood. Modern players now like using 21 springs zheng. The tone of Zheng is vigorous and the lingering is long, which is good at expressing the artistic conception of floating clouds, flowing water and sentiment.

Pipa (Chinese lute) was the most common stringed instrument in ancient China. In legend, it was brought back from the Western Regions during the reign of Emperor Wu and became very popular in the Northern and Southern Dynasties. Sanxian, also known as Xian Zi, is also a kind of stringed instrument that was played by the people of Han, the Mongolians, and other minorities.

In addition to drums, the main traditional Chinese percussion instruments are as follows:

Bell chimes refer to the series of bronze bells hanging on a wooden frame, played with wooden clubs. From the Shang Dynasty, the bells are mostly in groups of three. The largest unearthed group has as many as 64 bells.

Generally, Chime stones were made of stone or jade, and hung on racks. At first, they were played for singing and dancing and later were used in sacrificial and other ceremonial activities, becoming a "ritual instrument".

Gong is one of the most widely used percussion instruments in China. It is said that it was brought to China from Central Asia and Central and South Asia in the 6th century A.D. Through continuous improvement, gong can now be played expressively, and has become an indispensable instrument in local operas, folk entertainments and celebrations.

There are also many instruments with the national characteristics in Chinese ethnic minorities such as the "Tamboura", "bongo" in Sinkiang area; Miao's "Lusheng", "bronzedrums", "Bamboo Flute" and Dai's "Mang Gong," and "Elephant-foot drum" and so on.

段落译文

最早产生的乐器可能是打击乐器。据记载，人们在劳动时，发现枯树干发出不同的声音，于是将空心树干蒙上兽皮，制成木鼓。到了汉朝，出现了各种大小、质地、作用不同的鼓。不但供民间娱乐时敲打，而且也成了军队打仗以壮军威的必备之物。目前，一般把中国传统乐器分为吹奏乐器、拉奏乐器、弹奏乐器、打击乐器四大类，简称为“吹、拉、弹、打”。

吹奏乐器

笛子是中国最常见的吹奏乐器之一，早在春秋末期就已经出现了。笛子在民间广泛流行，有竹笛、木笛、铁笛、玉笛等很多品种，现在的笛子一般都是竹制的。由于笛子音色优美动听，2000 多年来，有大量的乐曲相传下来。

箫也是中国古老的吹奏乐器。适于独奏或重奏。古时的箫除了竹制的外，也有玉制或瓷制的。当时的箫仅有 4 个音孔，后来又增加 1 孔。现代演奏的箫都是竹制的，有 6 个音孔。唐代以前，笛箫通常不分。到了唐代笛箫才基本分开，横吹为笛，竖吹为箫。

中国吹奏乐器还有笙、管和唢呐。唢呐是一种喇叭形乐器，是普通百姓最喜欢的乐器之一。据说唢呐在四五百年前流传于波斯及阿拉伯。“唢呐”是波斯语“surna”的音译。唢呐声音高亢明亮，在民间广泛应用，是地方戏曲及节日庆祝活动中的主要乐器。

拉弦乐器

中国拉弦乐器主要是胡琴。胡琴的种类较多，有二胡、京胡、板胡、四胡等。胡琴不但适合演奏深沉、悲凄的旋律，也能表现出气势壮观的意境，是地方戏曲的主要伴奏乐器之一。

蒙古族的马头琴也属于拉弦乐器。

弹弦乐器

古琴是中国最古老的弹弦乐器。相传已有3000多年的历史，在周朝时就已普遍流行。古筝早在春秋战国时期就已在秦国(今陕西)流行了，因此史称“秦筝”。古筝一般用梧桐木制成，12弦到25弦不等。现代演奏者多用21弦筝。古筝音色浑厚明亮，余音悠长，善于表现行云流水的意境和细腻委婉的情调。

琵琶是中国古代最常见的弹弦乐器。相传琵琶是在南北朝周武帝时期，有人从西域带回来的。琵琶一经传入，便很快地盛行起来。三弦，又称弦子，是汉族与蒙古族及其他少数民族共同使用的弹弦乐器。

打击乐器

中国传统的打击乐器除了鼓以外，主要还有以下几种：

编钟是指把一系列铜制的钟挂在木架上，用小木捶击奏的一种乐器。自商代起，编钟多数是三枚一组。目前所出土的最大的一组编钟多达64枚。

磬一般用石或玉制成，悬挂在架上，敲击而鸣。最早用于百姓的乐舞活动，后来用于祭祀宴请等礼仪活动中，成了“礼器”。

锣是我国最广泛使用的打击乐器之一。据说在公元6世纪由中亚和中南亚一带传到我国。经过不断地改进，锣已经成为地方戏曲以及其他庆典活动不可缺少的乐器。

我国的少数民族也有很多带有本民族特色的乐器。如新疆哈萨克族的“冬不拉”、“手鼓”；苗族的“芦笙”、“铜鼓”及傣族的“芒锣”、“象脚鼓”等。

实用词汇

中国乐器 Chinese musical instruments

拉弦乐器 bow-stringed instruments; bowed string instruments

胡琴 Chinese fiddle

二胡 two-stringed Chinese fiddle; Erhu

京胡 Beijing opera fiddle

板胡 high-pitched Chinese fiddle
弹弦乐器 plucked instruments; plucked string instruments
月琴 yueqin
琵琶 Chinese lute; Pipa
三弦 sanxian, a three-stringed plucked instruments
柳琴 liuqin
古筝 Chinese zither; Guzheng
古琴 Guqin
打弦乐器 hammered string instruments
扬琴 Chinese dulcimer
吹奏乐器 wind or blowing instruments
笛子 bamboo flute; Dizi
萧 vertical bamboo flute; Xiao
管 pipe
笙 Chinese reed pipe; Sheng
唢呐 suona
打击乐器 percussion instruments
锣 gong; Luo
铙 big cymbal
钹 cymbal; Bo
鼓 drum
腰鼓 waist drum
竹板 bamboo castanets
梆子 wooden clapper
古代乐器 ancient instruments
埙 pottery wind pipe
排箫 panpipe
罄 chime stone
编钟 bell chimes / stone chimes
箜篌 Chinese harp

名言俗语

旧琴也能演奏出好乐章。

There's many a good tune played on an old fiddle.

琴弦不可太紧，朋友不可太亲。

Friends are like fiddle-strings, they must not be screwed too tight.

音乐要用心灵去想，用头脑去感受。

In music one must think with the heart and feel with the brains.

爵士乐使你肌肉发痒，交响乐能舒展你的灵魂。

Jazz tickles your muscles, symphonies stretch your soul.

音乐能软人心。

Music has charms to soothe the savage beast.

音乐是医治心灵创伤的妙药。

Music is the medicine of the breaking heart.

笛子不吹，舞就不跳。/ 得了好处就忘了恩惠。

No longer pipe, no longer dance.

独木不成林，单弦不成音。

A single tree makes no forest; one string makes no music.

老调重弹

To harp on the same string

音乐是耳朵的眼睛。

Music is the eye of the ear.

俗语注解

对牛弹琴：比喻对不懂道理的人讲道理，对外行人说内行话。

Playing the lute to the cattle: It means someone is playing to the wrong audience, preaching to deaf ears or reading Shakespeare to a group of illiterate loggerheads.

滥竽充数：比喻没有真正的才干，而混在行家里面充数或拿不合格的产品充数。

Phony player means being there just to make up a number or to pass off as one of the players in an ensemble. Now it can also be used to describe substandard goods that are mixed with quality ones just to make up a round number.

吹拉弹唱：指可以进行各种乐器的演奏和歌唱表演。

Blow, pull, pluck and sing which means to perform various kinds of instruments as well as vocal music

吹吹打打：原指乐器合奏，借指对事渲染、夸耀，以张大声势，引人注意。

Put up an ensemble means to make a big fanfare

吹鼓手：原指旧式婚礼或葬礼中吹奏乐器的人。现比喻为某人或某事进行吹嘘捧场的人。

Players of wind music at an old-fashioned wedding or funeral. Now it means the eulogist of sb. or sth.

中西合璧

中西方的乐器有很多相同之处。西方的乐器中也有很多吹奏乐器和拉弦乐器。例如长笛，西方的长笛原来是一种竖吹的圆锥形木管乐器，到了中世纪才出现横吹的长笛。现在的长笛一般都是金属制作的。萨克管、黑管、小号都属于吹奏乐器。小提琴、中提琴、大提琴等是最常见的拉弦乐器；西方的弹拨乐器较少，吉他是其中一种。

There are many things in common between Chinese and Western musical instruments. There are a lot of wind instruments and bowed string instruments, too. For example the Western flute was originally vertical blown cone-shaped wooden instruments, the horizontal blowing flutes were not played until the Middle Ages and now flutes are usually made of metal. Saxophones, clarinets, and trumpets also belong to the wind instrument family. The most common western bowed string instruments are the violin, viola and cello. There are fewer plucked string instruments in the west, and guitar is one of them.

UNIT 34

Peking Opera

京 剧

题记

京剧是我国最大的戏曲剧种，流行于全国各地，影响甚广，有国剧之称。京剧走遍世界各地，成为介绍、传播中国传统文化的重要手段。京剧也是中国民族传统文化的重要表现形式，其中很多种艺术元素被用作中国传统文化的象征符号。

Peking Opera is the most important one among Chinese operas. It is so popular throughout the world that the opera is regarded as our national one and is of great influence and is an important means to spread traditional Chinese culture as well. Peking Opera is a culturally significant form, in which a variety of artistic elements are used as great symbols of traditional Chinese culture.

Peking Opera is regarded as China's cultural legacy. At the beginning of the late 18th century, music and performance skills were absorbed from the best Kun Operas (a local drama in Jiangsu Province) and Qin Operas (Shaanxi Provincial local opera), and were eventually developed into a unique performing style. The talented artists have created and developed opera for two hundred years. It is a subtle and harmonious combination of the various elements of traditional

music, poetry, singing, recitation, dance, acrobatics and martial arts.

The characteristics of Peking opera consists of singing and dancing, which tells a story with singing as monologue and dancing as acts. The dialogues in Peking opera are based on Beijing dialect, and the songs in it have a unique pronunciation.

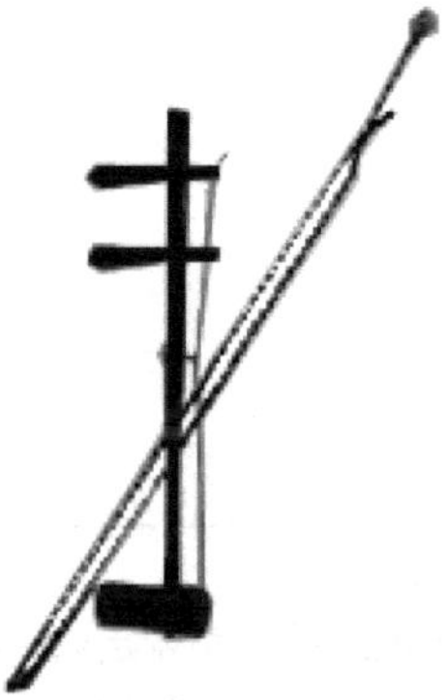

Peking opera abandons realism and attem pursuit of imagery. The actions in the opera are designed to beautify the scene. In addition to the singing, performers show their emotions by skillful movements, such as tiding the beard, adjusting the cap, waving with sleeves and lifting knees and raising feet. For example, the vibration of the performer's hand and body shows the extreme anger; actors put hands on their heads or reject the sleeves, which indicates surprise; if their faces are covered with the sleeves, they are revealing embarrassment.

Some movements in Peking opera are not very easy to be understood. For example, actors seize the sleeves and then quickly put the hands behind the back with a faster movement, which shows a person is decisive, strong, and can take heart in the face of danger. Sometimes, an action can be done for a long time. Martial arts fight scenes in Peking opera are a wonderful combination of dance and Wushu.

In Peking opera, the different roles represent different kinds of people in society, such as the loyal, the cunning, the good and beautiful and the ugly respectively. It also focuses on shaping the image, such as age, personality, gender, etc.

In general, the opera has four roles: Sheng, Dan, Hualian and Clown, which are decided by the age and the occupation. Sheng—Male roles, can be divided into three categories: the old, the young, and—the one good at martial arts. Dan—women's roles, including Huadan, Tsing Yi, Wu Dan and Lao Dan.

Jing—Hualian role, is regarded as frank and cheerful, with bright colored mask. Clown is marked with white paint on the nose. Clowns sometimes are on behalf of the positive, warm-hearted and humorous characters; while sometimes they also represent the dark, scheming, vicious, and stupid people. The singing and performing of the various roles in Peking opera are specialized with specific skills.

The facial makeup in Beijing opera is a special feature of a national cosmetics. As each historical figure or a certain type of person has an approximate spectral type, like singing, playing music, so "Lianpu" is called. It is said that facial makeup in Peking opera came from mask. The color of Lianpu is a characteristic of their role. The types of facial makeup in Beijing opera are based on certain personality, temperament or for some special types of figures, they use certain colors. Red, yellow, white, black, purple, green and silver are the main colors used for facial designs to represent different characters. For instance, red color stands for loyal, courageous and upright people; white color for sinister and cunning officials; Blue color shows vigorous, courageous and enterprising, while the yellow is reflected in the role of a resourceful, but not so extroverted person. Black tells about a pragmatic role, and brown is usually a symbol of the role of a stubborn-tempered person, and golden and silvery colors stand for gods and ghosts.

The costumes in Peking Opera have the characteristics of those in Ming Dynasty. The props, cloth walls, tents, cape, whip, paddle and weapons also have the Ming style. The props are real, although they are not enough, but in no way to reduce the way of the expression. Exaggeration and symbolism are the characteristics of Beijing Opera. For instance, the actor holding a whip shows that he is riding a quick horse; several soldiers appear on the stage, meaning a complete army. An actor on stage, moves back and forth means he is going on a long-distance journey.

According to statistics, there are more than 1,300 plays in Beijing Opera, and there have been many famous Beijing Opera artists. The well-known actors played as Xiaosheng are Tan Xinpei, Yang Xiaolou, Yushu Yan, Ma Lianliang, and Zhou Xinfang. The most famous actors of Dan roles are Mei Lanfang, Shang Xiaoyun, Cheng Yanqiu, and Xun Huisheng. With only 200 years of history, Beijing opera has become a profound artistic representative of China, and holds a great position as a performing art globally. In 1919, Mei Lanfang's performances went to Japan for the first time, and the opera has never stopped being spread abroad to promote international exchange and the performing arts of China.

段落译文

京剧，被视为中国的国粹，最初始于18 世纪晚期，以传统徽剧为基础，在曲目、音乐和表演技巧方面则吸收了昆剧（一种江苏省的地方戏剧）和秦腔（陕西省地方戏）的精华，最终发展成为一种具有独特风格的音乐表演形式。二百多年以来，很多才华横溢的艺术家创造和发展了京剧。京剧是由传统音乐、诗歌、演唱、朗诵、舞蹈、杂技和武术。

京剧的特色是以歌舞形态进行表演。唱念属于歌的部分，做打则是舞的部分。京剧的对话和念白采用北京方言，有一些唱词在剧中发音独特。

京剧在风格上舍弃写实而追求意象化，做打乃是意象美化后的动作。演员除演唱之外，还伴有娴熟的动作，譬如捋胡子、调帽、挥袖抬脚，来表达某一情感和意义。

如手和身体的颤动表明极端愤怒；如果演员将手放在头上和甩袖子，则表明吃惊或惊奇；用袖子盖住面孔则显露窘态。有些动作不是很容易被理解。例如演员以较快的动作抓住袖子然后又迅速地把他的手放回他的背后，表示果断、坚强，能够在危险面前振作起来。有时一个动作能持续 20 分钟。京剧的打斗场面是武术和舞蹈的一个美妙结合。

京剧里的角色代表着社会中形形色色的人物，对忠、奸、善、美、丑分别清晰。注重形象的塑造，如年龄、性格、性别。

一般来说，京剧有四个角色：生、旦、花脸和丑角，角色由年龄和职业决定。生——男性角色，可以被划分成三个类别：老生、小生和武生。旦——女性角色，包括花旦、青衣、武旦和老旦。

净——花脸角色，表现为坦率开朗，脸谱带着明亮着色。丑角由白色颜料轻拍鼻梁为标志。丑角有时代表正面的、热心肠的和幽默的人物；但有时也代表阴暗的、诡计多端的、恶毒的、愚笨的人。京剧的各个角色的唱腔和表演动作技巧都是特定的。

京剧的化妆同样风格独特。京剧脸谱，是具有民族特色的一种特殊的化妆方法。由于每个历史人物或某一种类型的人物都有一种大概的谱式，就像唱歌、奏乐都要按照乐谱一样，所以称为“脸谱”。关于脸谱的来源，一般的说法是来自假面具。

脸谱的颜色是对他们角色特点的一种暗示。京剧脸谱的类型基于一定角色的性格，气质而决定使用各种颜色。红、黄、白、黑、紫、绿、金、银是面部设计用来代表不同的字符的主色调。红色表明正直和忠诚：白色表示巧妙和狡猾。蓝色表现为苍劲，勇敢和进取，而黄色则体现的是一个足智多谋的角色，但不是那么外向的人。黑色表示忠直和务实的角色，而褐色通常是一个脾气倔强角色的象征，金色、银色代表神仙或鬼魂。

京剧的服装具有明朝服装的特点。道具包括布质墙壁、帐篷、斗篷、鞭子、桨和武器。道具是真实的，虽然不够实用，但丝毫不减低表现力。夸大和象征主义是京剧的特征。如拿着鞭子表明演员疾驰在马上；几位战士出现在舞台上就表示一支完整的军队；一位演员在舞台上来回转圈则表示一次长途等。

京剧有丰富的传统剧目，据统计达 1300 余个，并涌现出了许多著名的京剧表演艺术家：著名小生演员有谭鑫培、杨小楼、余叔岩、马连良和周信芳；旦角角色最著名的演员有梅兰芳、尚小云、程砚秋和荀慧生。虽然只有 200 年的历史，但它已成为一个博大精深的艺术代表，并在世界艺术林中占有一席之地。自 1919 年梅兰芳第一次赴日本演出以来，京剧不断地被传到国外，对促进国际交流做出了较大贡献。

实用词汇

梆子腔 clapper opera

采茶戏 tea-pickers' opera

彩旦 female comedian

唱白脸 play villain; pretend to be harsh and severe

唱独角戏 play a monodrama; go it alone

唱红脸 play the hero; pretend to be generous and kind

唱双簧 give a two-man comic show; collaborate with each other

潮剧 Chaozhou opera（popular in eastern Guangdong, Southern Fujian and Taiwan Provinces）

楚剧 Chu opera（a local opera popular in Hubei Province and part of Jiangxi Province）

串旦角儿 female character type in Chinese opera

戏（of amateurs）perform with a professional troupe

二人转 the provincial drama newly evolved from the song-and-dance duet, also known as Jilin drama

勾脸（in traditional Chinese opera）paint the face

旦角儿 female character type in Chinese opera

杭剧 Hangzhou opera

河北梆子 Hebei clapper opera

红净 red-face role

红生 red-faced young man role in traditional opera

花旦 one of the main divisions of the dan or female role in traditional opera（traditionally the role for a woman of questionable morals, notably a coquettish maidservant or an amorous young woman, bold, seductive, and charming; great emphasis being placed on acting)

花脸（戏剧）flowery-face role—a popular name for jing (so called from the elaborate facial painting)

花腔 ①florid or ornamentation in Chinese opera singing; coloratura, ② guileful talk

回戏（of an opera troupe, etc.）cancel a performance offhand

京韵大鼓 Peking musical storytelling

科白 actions and spoken parts in classical Chinese drama

老旦 part of an elderly woman

老腔 type of shadow play popular in Tongguan and Huayin in Shanxi Province

老生 one of the main divisions of the male role in traditional opera

脸谱 types of facial makeup in operas

龙套 ①costume with dragon designs worn by actors playing a walk-on part in Chinese opera, ②actor playing a walk-on part in traditional opera

念白 spoken part of a Chinese opera

青衣（戏剧）one of the main divisions of Dan or female role in traditional opera

髯口 artificial beard or whiskers worn by traditional opera

武丑 acrobatic clown

武旦 actress playing a martial role

武行 acrobatic actor playing a supporting role

武花脸 actor with a "painted face", playing a martial role

戏班 old-style theatrical troupe

戏眼 most interesting scene or part of a play

戏子 player

小旦 young female character

小花脸 clown

行头 actor's costumes and paraphernalia; clothing

压台 present a theatrical performance as the last item on a programme

压台戏 the last item on a theatrical programme

样板戏 model Peking opera, term used during the Cultural Revolution to refer to Peking operas with a modern, revolutionary theme

正旦 main female character

花朝戏 local opera popular in the countries of Zijin, Wuhua, Longchuan and Huiyang in Guangdong Province

名言俗语

好戏在后头。

The best is yet to be.

唱空城计

Perform The Stratagem of the Empty City—present a bold front to conceal a weak defence.

有音乐的地方就有爱。

Where there's music there can be love.

生活如一出戏：重要的不是其长度而是其演出精彩与否。——赛内加

Life is like a play: It's not the length, but the excellence of the acting that matters. —Seneca

世界是个大舞台，所有的男男女女只是表演者。——莎士比亚

All the world's a stage and all the men and women merely players. —William Shakespeare

俗语注解

扮戏：在传统剧中扮演角色

(of Chinese traditional opera singers) make up / put on a play

唱红脸：扮演英雄，或指有的人假装善良、大方

Play the hero / pretend to be generous and kind

唱白脸：扮演无赖角色，或指人假装严厉

Play villain / pretend to be harsh and severe

唱对台戏，唱反调

Put on a rival show

唱高调

Make high-sounding statement

唱老调

Sing the hackneyed tune

唱独角戏，个人孤立做事

Play a monodrama / go it alone

唱念做打：传统剧目的技巧

Singing, gesticulating, elocution and acrobatics—elements of the art of acting in traditional opera

唱双簧：两人配合完成表演

a two-man show; collaborate with each other

中西合璧

京剧集音乐、舞蹈、杂技艺术为一体，被称为中国的国剧，是中华文化的最高体现， 同时也是世界三大最精美的戏剧之一。与西方歌剧相比，主要区别在于京剧丰富的表现形式：舞台上不仅有音乐、歌舞，而且有表现人物性格和角色的脸谱、特别的服饰、哑剧、杂技和武术，充分体现了中国的传统文化。演员的手势、面部表情和动作特点表现出角色彼此间的关系。与西方歌剧和音乐剧比，京剧的伴奏乐器奇少。舞台上主要的乐器是唢呐和京胡。京胡可以说既是弦乐器也是独特的打击乐器。京剧的唱腔和西方歌剧的咏叹调可以媲美。

Peking Opera, a synthesis of music, dance, art and acrobatics, is known as China's national opera and widely regarded as the highest expression of the Chinese culture. It is the most refined form of operas and one of the three main theatrical systems in the world. In comparison with musical dramas of other cultures, the Chinese opera distinguishes itself with its rich forms of expression. Events on the stage are reflected not only in the music, singing and actions, but also the masks, the costumes, pantomime, dance, acrobatics, the martial arts and sometimes local traditions as well. The symbols pervade all aspects of Chinese opera and achieve very precise characterizations by combining symbols. Gestures, facial expressions and movements characterize their behaviors and demonstrate their relationships with each other. Unlike Western operas and musicals, instrumental accompaniment of the Chinese opera is sparse. The two main instruments are the suona and the jinghu, the latter of which could be described as both string instrument as well as a diverse percussion instrument. The difference between aria and recitative is however comparable with western opera.

UNIT 35

Sichuan Opera—Face Changing

川剧变脸

题记

中华文明源远流长，饱浸着东方魅力的中国戏剧更是名冠五洲。目前，全国有 300 多个枝繁叶茂的戏曲剧种在神州大地上摇曳生辉，竞展风流，其中，许多剧种在表演上都有自己的“绝活”。在林林总总的绝活中，若论神奇诡异，则首推川剧的“变脸”，其惊心动魄的艺术表现力往往令观者目瞪口呆。

Chinese civilization has a long history, with the famous oriental charming drama well-known in the wold. At present, there are more than 300 operas flourishing in our vast land, among which many of the performances have “unique skills”. The magic one among them is the “Changing face” of Sichuan opera, its soul-stirring power of artistic expression tends to stun viewers.

Sichuan opera is popular in Sichuan Province, Chongqing and Yunnan, Guizhou, Hubei Province, and it is the greatest among the local operas in southwest China. As far as Sichuan Opera is concerned, I believe that everyone thinking about it will remember the world-famous “Face Changing” which is quite unique. Face Changing is one type of Chinese opera performances used to show sentiment. The performance presents sudden changes in mood, such as fear, despair, or anger by changing the colour of faces. It used to be used in a fantasy role during the Ming Dynasty. Actors went off the stage to change the make-ups at that time. The later generations developed the skill and changed faces on the spot, and it was spread to acrobatic troupes, and other local operas, but Sichuan Opera is the best.

Face Changing is an artistic feature in Sichuan Opera, shaping the character to reveal the inner thoughts and feelings of the characters in a beautiful way. It was said that "Face Changing" was adapted by people to fight against ferocious beasts in ancient times in order to survive, and that they outlined different forms on the face in different ways to frighten the beasts. The skill of "Face Changing" has moved onto the stage and evolved into a unique art. There are two ways to change faces: a total change and partial change of the face. There are three changes, five changes, as well as nine transitions; Total Face Changing is divided into three types: "wiping the face", "blowing the face", and "pulling the face". In addition, there is a kind of "Qigong" change of face.

Wiping the face: To paint the particular part of the actor's face, the performer changes his makeup by wiping his face with his hand while performing. If you want the whole face changed, then you apply the paint on the forehead or eyebrows or if you only want to change the lower half of the face, then the paint can be painted on the face or on the nose, in this way the performer can change their face easily. If you only need to change a certain part of the face, then only paint the needed position.

Blowing the face: This kind of skill is only suitable for powder cosmetics, such as gold powder, graphite powder, silver powder and so on. A small box of various powders is placed on the ground of the stage, the actor moves with dance movements and takes the opportunity to put his face close to the box and blow the powder box, immediately the powder from the box changes his face to a different color. Another way is to hide the powder needed in the palm of the actor's hand as Xiaoqing who changes her face several times in the play "The Broken Bridge". The third method is to hide the powder in a wine glass, the actor blows into the glass, and his face changes while drinking. When blowing, the performers should pay attention not to blow unless the eyes, and mouth are closed, and to hold their breath.

Pulling the face: It is a more complex method of Face Changing. They put the painted Lianpu (masks) on pieces of silk which are cut clearly, with a thread attached to each mask, and then put them onto the face one after another. The silk thread is tied in a certain position of the performer's clothes where it is easy for him to reach without being noticed (such as the belts and the like). As the story progresses, the actors tear the masks off one by one with the dance movements. For instance, the actor could change his face green, red, white, black and another seven different faces in the plays *White Snake*. Pulling face is of some difficulty, the glue which sticks the masks should not be too sticky, or it will be not easy to pull the masks off in time, or the masks might be ripped off at one time. Moreover, the action should be quick and exact, and the actor should distract the audience attention smartly so that he can finish the change without being noticed by them.

Face changing requires agile behaviors, which change closely with the mood of the character, without being noticed by the audience. In the development of improving skills of Face Changing, the famous Sichuan opera performers Kangzi Lin, Wei Xianglin, Sun Decai and others have made great contributions.

In short, Face Changing is definitely one of the unique skills of the Sichuan opera, which has now been learned by other local operas. It has even spread overseas. Drama lovers around the world admire it and show great interest in

Face Changing and they have become keenly interested in Chinese drama, fostering cultural exchange and an overall increase of interest in China.

段落译文

川剧流行于四川省、重庆市及云南、贵州、湖北省的部分地区，是中国西南部影响最大的地方剧种。提起川剧，相信每个人都一定会想起世界闻名的川剧“变脸”绝艺。变脸属中国戏曲的情绪化妆，用于表现剧中人物情绪的突然变化，或惊恐、或绝望、或愤怒等。它最先用于神怪角色，明代已有，当时的变脸是演员进入后台改扮。后世则衍变为当场变脸，成为一项表演特技，不少地方剧种都有，以川剧最为著名。

变脸是川剧艺术中运用的塑造人物的一种特技，是揭示剧中人物内心思想感情的一种浪漫主义手法。相传“变脸”是古代人类面对凶猛的野兽，为了生存把自己脸部用不同的方式勾画出不同形态，以吓唬入侵的野兽。川剧把“变脸”搬上舞台，用绝妙的技巧使它成为一门独特的艺术。变脸有大变脸、小变脸之分。大变脸系全脸都变，有3变、5变乃至9变；小变脸则为局部变脸。变脸的手法大体上分为三种：“抹脸”、“吹脸”、“扯脸”。此外，还有一种“运气”变脸。

抹脸：是将化妆油彩涂在脸的某一特定部位上，表演变脸时用手往脸上一抹，就可变成另外一种脸色。如果要全部变，则将油彩涂于额上或眉毛上，如果只变下半部脸，可以将油彩涂在脸上或鼻子上。如果只需要改变某一个局部，将油彩涂在要变的位置上就可以了。

吹脸：只适合于粉末状的化妆品，如金粉、墨粉、银粉等等。有的演员在舞台的地面上摆一个很小的盒子，内装粉末，演员在表演时做一个伏地的舞蹈动作，趁机将脸贴近盒子一吹，粉末扑在脸上，立即变成另一种颜色的脸。比如《断桥》中小青的几次变脸，色粉都藏在演员的手心。还有一种方法是将色粉藏于酒杯之中，借举杯饮酒，用力一吹，脸色顿变。吹脸的秘诀是：吹时闭眼、闭口、闭气。

扯脸：是比较复杂的一种变脸方法。它是事前将脸谱画在一张一张的绸子上，剪好，且每张脸谱上都系一把丝线，再一张一张地贴在脸上。丝线则系在衣服的某一个顺手而又不引人注目的地方(如腰带上之类)。随着剧情的进展，在舞蹈动作的掩护下，一张一张地将它扯下来。如《白蛇传》中的演员，可以变绿、红、白、黑等七、八张不同的脸。“扯脸”有一定的难度：粘脸谱的黏合剂不宜太多，以免到时扯不下来，或者一次把所有的脸谱都扯下来；另外动作要干净利落，假动作要巧妙，能掩观众的眼睛。

变脸需要动作敏捷，密切结合人物情绪的变化，不露痕迹。在改进变脸技巧方面，川剧界著名的表演艺术家康子林、魏祥林、孙德才等作出了贡献。

总之，变脸在川剧中是很绝的一门技艺，现在已被其他兄弟剧种所借鉴，并且已经流传国外。世界各国的戏剧艺术爱好者们因喜欢“变脸”的奇幻而对中国戏剧产生浓厚兴趣，进而对中国有更多的了解，因此变脸也起到了促进中外文化交流的作用。

实用词汇

变脸（戏剧）turn hostile; face changing: change facial expression rapidly (to show extreme anger, fear, etc.)

猴戏 show by a performing monkey

花鼓 flower-drum, a folk dance

花鼓戏 flower-drum opera (popular in Hunan, Hubei and Anhui)

滑稽 funny; comic talk (popular in Shanghai, Suzhou, Hangzhou and their adjacent areas, similar to comic dialogue or cross talk in northern China)

话剧 modern drama

黄梅戏 form of regional drama popular in central Anhui province

徽调 Anhui musical style; old name for Anhui opera

徽诙谐曲 humoresque

徽剧 Anhui opera

基音 fundamental tone

吉剧 Jilin opera

江湖艺人 itinerant entertainer

江南小调 tune popular in the south of the Yangtz River

晋剧 Shanxi opera

昆腔 melodies which originated in Kunshan, Jiangsu province, in the Ming Dynasty

拉场戏 song and dance opera, a variety of traditional operas derived from *errenzhuan*

吕剧 an opera of Shandong province

傩戏 a kind of Anhui provincial drama featuring masked dancing; a provincial opera popular in the mountainous districts in western Hubei

瓯剧 Wenzhou opera, local opera popular in Wenzhou and northeastern Fujian province

评剧 a local opera of north and northeast China

蒲剧 a local opera popular in the southern parts of Shanxi province

祁剧 a local opera of Hunan province

陕西梆子 Shanxi clapper opera

绍剧 Shaoxing opera

婺剧 Wu opera

弦子戏 kind of Shangdong local opera

扬剧 local opera popular in Yangzhou

彝剧 yi opera

游春戏 one of the local operas in northern Fujian province

越剧 Zhejiang opera

粤剧 Guangdong opera

竹马戏 Zhuma opera, local opera of Fujian province

名言俗语

我宁可看到青年人脸红也不愿看到他脸色变得苍白。

I would rather see a young man blush but hate to see he turned pale.

世界是个舞台，男男女女，演员而已。

All the world's a stage and all the men and women merely players.

华丽的衣着不能为美人增色，且只能使相貌平平或丑陋的人更丑。

Beauty gains little, and homeliness and deformity lose much, by gaudy attire.

漂亮的面孔可能包藏着一颗龌龊的心。

A fair face may hide a foul heart.

人不可貌相。

Never judge from appearance.

外表常常骗人。

Appearances are deceptive.

好戏不厌百回看。

A good tale is none the worse for being twice told.

社会是个假面舞会，人人都掩饰着真实身份，而又因为这种伪装暴露了真面目。

Society is a masked ball, where every one hides his real character, and reveals it by hiding.

词语注解

梨园戏：福建省南部的一种地方戏

liyuan opera, popular in southern Fujian province

影调剧：河北唐山新发展成的一种地方剧

a newly developed local opera popular in the Tangshan area of Hebei province

苏白：在昆曲或京剧里用苏州方言

①Suzhou dialect, ②lines in Kunqu or Peking opera that are spoken in Suzhou dialect

野台子戏：在露天表演，非正规演员演出

performance given by itinerant entertainers (usually in the open air)

压不住台：吸引不住观众

be unable to hold the audience

拉场：故意延长表演时间等待主角出场

(of supporting actors in traditional opera) intentionally prolong one's performance on stage (before the leading actor or actress, who is late, is ready)

中西合璧

希腊的悲喜剧、印度的梵剧和中国的戏曲是世界上无可争辩的三个最古老的戏剧形式。中国的戏曲在传统戏剧舞台上一直唱主角，相当于西方的“莎士比亚”。然而，英语对戏剧的概念并不能充分反映中国戏曲的真谛，因为任何对中国戏曲稍有了解的人就都会认同“中国戏曲”中的关键东西与西方歌剧是完全不同的。变脸是川剧的绝艺。传说古人将脸部涂上各种颜色以吓唬入侵的野兽。川剧吸收了这一古老的技术，把“变脸”搬上舞台，用绝妙的技巧使它成为一门独特、完美的艺术。在西方，歌剧通常少有舞蹈，更不用说打斗场面。脸谱、头饰以及服装对刻画人物性格都有特殊作用。脸谱最初是作为一种手段，将男演员化装成女性展现给观众。从脸谱到面具的改变是非常小的一步，却形成了独特的变脸艺术。如今，高科技被应用于这一传统艺术。激光、闪光增添了其神秘感。像佐罗之类的现代面孔也出现在变脸节目中。

Greek tragicomedy, Indian Sanskrit drama, and Chinese opera are indisputably the three most ancient forms of drama in the world. In China, opera has traditionally been the main source of theatrical drama; it is the Chinese counterpart to the one in the West terms "theatre", as in "Shakespearean theatre". Yet the English language notion of opera does not fully capture the true essence of opera in China, as anyone even vaguely familiar with Chinese opera would agree. In fact, the term "Chinese opera" is itself not a bad jumping off point for talking about the phenomenon of opera in China, since the term suggests—and rightly so that there is something about opera in China that sets it apart from the western notion of opera.

Face changing is the highlight of Sichuan Opera. It is said that ancient people painted their faces to drive away wild animals. Sichuan Opera absorbs this ancient skill and perfects it into an art. In the West, opera usually has little or no action。

The Painted Face involves not only facial makeup, but also headdress as well as a specific costume to fit the specific role of the character. The Painted Face no doubt originated as a device to disguise a male actor as a female, as such provided important symbolic information to the audience. From the concept of the Painted Face to the idea of changing masks is a very small step, however a unique art of face changing has been formed.

Today high technology such as lasers and twinkling lights is used to enhance the traditional arts and adds a touch of mystery to it. And modern faces like Zorro are invited to the stage.

UNIT 36

Acrobatics

杂　技

题记

中国杂技是一种最古老的表演艺术之一，民间称为“把戏”或“杂耍”。杂耍的内容非常丰富和庞杂，主要有杂技、戏法和一些动物表演等。中国的杂技艺术以其绚丽多彩、古朴大方的特点博得国内外广大观众的赞赏和喜爱。

Chinese acrobatics is one of the oldest performing arts, and also known as "tricks" or "vaudeville". The content is very rich and heterogeneous, mainly including acrobatics, magic, and animal shows. Chinese acrobatic arts are popular with the audience home and abroad for its colorful, simple and ancient style.

Chinese acrobatics appeared in the Spring and Autumn Period 2,500 years ago, and were divided into six kinds, strength skills, juggling, juggling with the feet, driving skills and others. It is said that the earliest acrobatics came from battle experience of Chinese ancestors. Strength skill was one of the most basic skills and was developed firstly. The ancient strong men could throw and catch heavy cartwheels and lift big metal cauldrons of hundreds of pounds easily, showing that they not only had strong muscle, but also had mastered certain skills.

Chinese acrobatics was a kind of art that was evolved from daily life and production practice. The performers often made use of common items to show their skills. Most of the things they used were daily items, such as bowls, plates, cylinders, ropes, tables, benches, bicycles and so on. For example, in the traditional program, "juggling with the feet" the actors or actresses can juggle many daily objects, such as wine jars, water vats, tables, umbrellas, etc. It is really wonderful when some of actors sing while they are juggling.

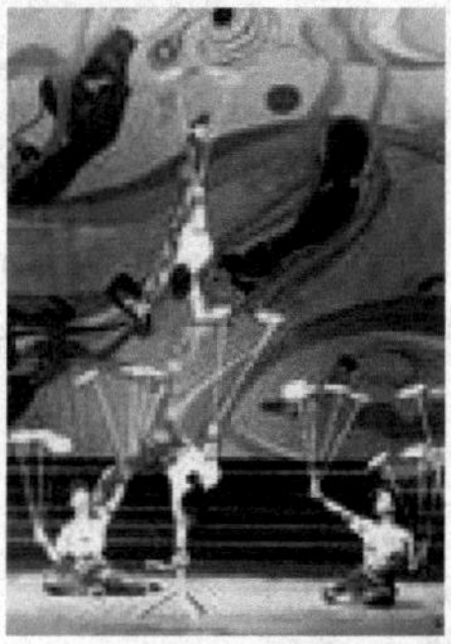

The acrobatics had formed into a complete art form in Han Dynasty and reached a considerable scale and level. According to records, in the spring, 108 BC, in order to entertain the envoys of Western Region States, the Han Emperor held a grand banquet in the capital Chang'an, and held an unprecedented, hundreds of acrobatic shows. Many foreign acrobatic troupes also took part in the shows.

The acrobatic arts of Song Dynasty were a turning point for the practice, away from the palace, and towards the ordinary people. The actors had to make a living as performers in the street because of losing their original position in the palace. So they created some new programs, such as kicking skills, covering up magic, and the skills of taming insects.

During Qing Dynasty, the content of the acrobatics was richer, and the skills improved greatly. They could be performed at any site, theatres, open-air sets, home celebrations, country markets, or temple fairs. Now we can still see the wonderful programs from that time, such as playing fork, dancing lions, playing jars and so on.

Magic is also a kind of acrobatics. Chinese magic paid a great attention to

the personal skills. A lot of traditional Chinese magic is often based on myths and legends. The performers like to create wonderful fantasy scenes. The excellent ones are the Phoenix delivering letters, card trick, and fishing.

At present, there are great changes in Chinese acrobatics. Many cruel and horrible programs such as sword swallowing, lying on nail-board have been cancelled. A large number of excellent programs, such as plucking up diabolo, bowl balancing, plate spinning, wire walking are still popular. Every year, a lot of acrobatic troupes travel abroad to participate in performances or international acrobatics competitions, and obtain many high-level awards.

段落译文

中国杂技大约出现在2500多年前的春秋时代，可分为力技、耍弄、足技、车技等六大类。相传最早的杂技是从古代战斗或生活演变而来的。首先发展起来的是力技。力技是杂技最基本的技巧之一，古时的大力士可以随手抛接沉重的车轮，也能举起重达几百斤的金属大鼎，他们不但臂力超人，而且还掌握了一定的技巧。

中国杂技是人民从日常生活和生产实践中创造出来的艺术。在杂技演出中，演员经常借物来展现技巧。所用的物件大部分是生活用品，如碗、盘子、缸、绳子、桌子、板凳、自行车等。例如传统节目“蹬技”，演员躺在特制的台上，以双足来蹬物。所蹬物品包罗万象，其中有很多生活中常见的酒坛、水缸、桌子、雨伞等。有些演员还可以边蹬边唱十分精彩。

在汉代，杂技就形成了完整的艺术形式，并达到相当的规模和水平。据记载，公元前108年春，汉武帝为了招待西域各国使臣，在都城长安

举行盛大国宴，并举行空前规模的杂技百戏汇演。很多外国杂技团体也参加了这次演出。

宋代是杂技艺术从宫廷走向民间的转折时期。由于杂技在宫廷里失去了原有的地位，艺人们常在街头巷尾卖艺，并创造出一些诸如踢弄技艺、藏掖幻术、驯虫蚁等小巧玲珑更贴近民间生活的新节目。

清代的杂技内容更加丰富，技术上也有很大的提高。演出场所也很随意，有的在杂耍馆和露天设场演出，有的在喜庆的日子里到富人家演“堂会”，也有的在集市或庙会上演出。如今我们还能看到耍钢叉、舞狮子、耍坛子等节目，就是当年庙会演出的精彩节目。

魔术也是杂技的一种表现形式。中国魔术历来注重演员的个人技巧，中国的传统魔术常取材于神话传说。演员总喜欢创造出一些适合人们幻想的奇妙情景。例如凤凰传书、变扑克牌、钓鱼等都是优秀的魔术节目。

目前，中国杂技在表演内容和形式上也发生了很大的变化，停止演出吞刀子、滚钉板等残忍、恐怖的节目，并推出了一大批优秀的节目，例如抖空竹、顶碗、转碟、走钢丝等。每年都有很多的杂技团体到国外参加演出或参加国际性的杂技比赛，并多次获得高级别的奖项。

实用词汇

杂技 acrobatics
杂技团 acrobatic troupe
魔术 magic
马戏 circus
滑稽戏 low comedy; mime
爬杆 pole climbing
蹬技 juggling with the feet
顶技 balancing act
口技 vocal imitation
鞭技 whipping act

柔术 contortionist act; contortion
钻圈 jumping through the hoops
耍坛子 vat juggling; jar balancing act
顶碗 bowl balancing
转碟 plate spinning
走钢丝 wire walking; wire dancing
小丑 clown
力士表演 strong man act
魔术表演 magic performance
杂耍表演 variety show; variety entertainment
纸牌把戏 card trick
滑稽表演 comic performance
驯兽师 trainer; animal tamer
魔术演员 magician
吞剑 sword swallowing
卧钉板 lying on nailboard
飞刀 flying knife
江湖艺人 stroller
空中飞人 flying man
高台定车 bicycle balancing on an elevated stand

名言俗语

百艺不如一艺精。
A hundred tricks are not so good as one well-learned trade.
一项技艺是取之不尽的财富。
A useful trade is a mine of gold.
技艺高超
superb skills
技艺精湛
highly skilled

表演从容

performing in a relaxed manner

精彩表演

cracking show

身怀绝技

A person with unique skills

大显身手

Giving full play to one's skill talent, etc.

杂技艺术家的职责即在没有阳光时创造出阳光。

It's the artist's job to create sunshine when there isn't any.

生命短暂而艺术永恒。

Art is long, and time is fleeting.

词语注解

踩高跷：表演者踩着有踏脚装置的木棍，边走边表演。

Stilt walk or walking on stilts: the performer stands on two poles each with a rest or strap for the feet while dancing.

走江湖：指四方奔走，靠武艺杂技或医卜星象谋生。

Harnstorming or wander from place to place and earn a living by juggling or fortune-telling, etc.

叠罗汉：人上架人，重叠成各种形式，是杂技表演项目之一。

Pyramid or human pyramid is a kind of acrobatic performance where a group of people pile one on top of another in various forms.

竖蜻蜓：也称为倒立。顶端朝下地竖立。

Handspring; Stand upside down or hand stand.

走钢丝：杂技的一种，演员在悬空的钢丝上来回走动，并表演各种动作。

Wiring walking; One of the acrobatic shows, in which an actor or actress walks to or fro and performs on a suspended steel wire.

中西合璧

很多人认为中西方杂技各有千秋，中国杂技以技巧见长，西方杂技以编排取胜。但是在杂耍表演，特别是丢掷技巧方面中西方却有着很多相同之处，都有着悠久的历史和同样的丢掷物。例如在中国的春秋时期就已经开始有丢球和丢刀剑等的表演。而在古埃及一位无名王子的墓中，壁画显示一些杂耍演员也在丢球。现在中西方杂技表演无论是魔术还是杂耍或是马戏都在互相借鉴，有些甚至融合成了一体。

Many people think that there are some differences between western acrobatics and Chinese acrobatics. Chinese acrobatics is known for its skills and Western acrobatics is famous for its arrangements. But there are many things in common between them, and both have a long history in juggling. For example, in the Spring and Autumn Period, Chinese began juggling with balls and swords, and in an ancient Egyptian tomb of an unknown prince, the murals show circus performers juggling with balls, too. Now the West and Chinese acrobatics learn from each other and even mix together in magic or juggling performances.

UNIT 37

Cross Talk

相　声

题记

相声是曲艺的一种形式，也是我国十大类曲艺中最受欢迎的一种，它以语言为表现手段，并穿插歌、舞等表演。相声演出形式有单口、对口、群口几种。其形式活泼，语言幽默。源于北京，流行于全国。

Xiangsheng translated as Crosstalk, is a Quyi art form, which is the most popular among the ten ones. There are three kinds of Xiangsheng: Dankou, Duikou and Qunkou, of which are conveyed in vivid and humorous language with sometimes singing and dancing performances. It originated from Beijing and was spread nationwide.

Xiangsheng, crosstalk, is one of China's foremost performing arts and a Quyi art which is comedic and made up of speaking, imitating, teasing, and singing. The language, rich in puns and allusions, is used in a rapid, bantering style. It used to be performed in Beijing dialect, now mainly in Putonghua or mandarin and sometimes in local dialects. It is very popular all over the country and welcomed by the people of the world. Many foreigners have come to China to learn it and become successful, take Dashan,as a an example.

The earliest Xiangsheng was developed from folk ventriloquism. It emerged in the Qing Dynasty during the reign of Emperor Guangxu as an art of performance. Zhu Shaowen, a Peking Opera performer, whose stage name was Qing Bupa (Not Afraid of Poverty), used to perform in the entertainment quarter of Beijing known as Tianqiao. The imperial court prohibited performing because of the continual royal deaths including Empress Cixi's funeral. He always began his talk with a ragged verse and imitated the street hawkers' peculiar cries and sang some ancient songs with a pair of bamboo clappers, a fan, or a handkerchief, setting up a piece of cloth as a tent, or simply drawing a circle with white sand in the street. He later took on two apprentices, and they performed together, so it became crosstalk with a Dougen and Penggen.

Modern Xiangsheng performers must have four skills — speaking, imitating, teasing, and singing. "Speaking" refers to the storytelling, as well as speech and the way of speaking. "Imitating" refers to the imitation a variety of characters, dialects, and other sounds, learning to famous operas, songs and dance, etc. "Teasing" means to create humor. "Singing" is considered to refer to singing "Taiping lyrics".

There are three forms of Xiangsheng: Dankou Xiangsheng was performed by one-person and the one performed by two people was called Duikou Xiangsheng or "cross talk", while the third form performed by three or more people is considered as Qunkou Xiangsheng. In cross talk, one man was called Dougen, and the other, Penggen. When one is the primary talker while the other chimes in, this is called Yitouchen (heavy-at-one-end), and the subject of argument between them is called Zimugen. In Qunkou it calls for one artist to say funny things, while others chime in and yet another makes them stray from the subject. Of the three forms, cross talk is the most popular and widespread.

Xiangsheng is considered as "the art of laughter". Laughter is the aesthetic principle of crosstalk. "Edutainment" (education and entertainment) is the art of the comic dialogue which is the most important feature of the art.

The process of crosstalk performance and appreciation, and the communication between performers and audience is bi-directional. This characteristic is a unique art form—the form of traditional Chinese comedic dialogue. This form involves the audience's participation, which results in a unique artistic charm. The relationship between the audience and Xiangsheng is so close that "there is no misunderstanding". Xiangsheng draws wisdom and humor from people, playing on their unyielding pursuit for truth and their optimistic spirit, while being satirical towards evil. It became an excellent art form of the exquisite liveliness and its uniqueness.

The development of crosstalk has its characteristics, originated from all walks of the lower classes. Its main function is to satisfy people, and allow them to speak out their minds, enjoy the laughter and express their attitudes. With a history of more than 100 years, xiangsheng has developed into a unique form and a fixed model for shows from Dankou and Duikou, to Qunkou. We have a large number of crosstalk performers such as the first generation Zhu Shaowen, Zhang Sanlu to the fifth or the eighth generation Ma Sanli, Hou Baolin, Ma Ji, Tang Jiezhong, Jiang Kun, Zhao Yan... etc. Due to its humor, sarcasm and unique aesthetic effects, Xiangsheng has spread far and wide not only becoming popular in China but all over the world.

段落译文

相声是中国最重要的表演艺术之一，也是一种富有喜剧色彩的曲艺品种，以说、学、逗、唱为主要表现手段。相声语言往往显得节奏快而幽默，其中运用了双关语和隐射的表现手法。过去主要是用北京话，现在多用普通话，也有用方言表演的方言相声。相声在中国乃至世界深受欢迎，甚至有许多外国相声爱好者来中国拜师学艺并获得成功，大山就是一个很好的例子。

一般人认为，我国最早的相声是从民间口技发展演变而来。相声作为一项独立的艺术表演形式，始于清光绪年间。当时有个京剧演员叫朱少文，艺名叫“穷不怕”，因清朝皇室连年死人，特别是慈禧太后丧事，朝廷禁止演戏，朱绍文只得在北京天桥等处摆地摊演相声。他在街头简单地搭个布棚子，或者就用白色的沙子画个圈当场说起来，道具只是两块竹板或者是把扇子、手绢，边说边唱。后来朱绍文又收了两个徒弟，两人一起合说。这样就形成了现在的一逗一捧的对口相声。

现代相声包含四项技能：说、学、逗、唱，这是相声演员必备的四大基本功。“说”是指讲故事，还有说话和铺垫的方式。“学”是指模仿各种人物、方言、和其他声音，学唱戏曲的名家名段，现代也有学唱歌，跳舞等。“逗”意思是制造笑料。“唱”经常被认为是唱戏，唱歌。实际上“唱”是指演唱“太平歌词”。

相声有三种形式。单口相声是由一个人表演；对口相声是两个人合作完成；群口相声则是由三个或三个以上的演员一起表演。在对口相声中，一个人叫逗哏，另一个叫捧哏。如果其中一个占表演的主要地位，另一个附和，这种形式的表演叫“一头沉”。子母哏指相声表演时，两个演员(逗哏和捧哏)所承担的任务基本相同，如通过相互间争辩来组织包袱等。群口相声有一个演员逗哏，其他的则是捧哏。在这三种形式中，两人相声最流行。

相声被称为“笑的艺术”。笑是相声所追求的美

学原则；“寓教于乐”是相声艺术最根本、最主要的艺术特征。

在相声的表演和欣赏过程中，演员与观众的交流是双向的，十分密切的。这一特点与它特有的艺术形式——对话的形式分不开。这种形式满足了广大观众的参与意识，由此产生了独特的艺术魅力。相声与观众结成了“无话不谈”的朋友，它从群众中吸取智慧和幽默，表达了群众对真、善、美的追求和乐观精神，并对生活中的假、恶、丑进行揭露和讽刺。相声以其精湛的生活内容和独特的艺术形式，成为优秀的艺术之花。

相声发展有自己的特点，它来自市井和民间，主要通过笑来为底层群众解意、开心，表达一种对待生活的态度。相声艺术如今已经走过一百多年历史，旧时的相声通过岔曲说唱、喜剧小段、民间笑话，延伸出一种独立形式，从单口，到对口再到群口，呈现出固定的表演模式。我国出现了一大批著名的相声明星：从第一代的朱绍文、张三禄到第五、第六代的马三立、侯宝林等，到第七代的马季、唐杰忠等，再到第八代的演员姜昆、赵炎等。由于相声幽默、具有讽刺性和独特的艺术美，因此传播广泛，不仅在国内深受人们喜欢，也受到了世界的青睐。

实用词汇

对口快板儿(戏剧) rhymed clapper talk
对口相声 cross talk
多口相声 cross talk performed by more than two persons
即兴曲(音乐) impromptu
即兴诗 extempore verse
讲叫板 rhyme the last sentence of a spoken part to introduce a singing part
街头卖艺 perform in the street
说唱文学 narratives with tones
借古讽今 use the past to disparage the present
开口饭 profession of singing, acting, storytelling, etc.
开口跳 acrobatic comedian
侃大山 chat idly

侃星 chatterbox

侃爷 big talker

看把戏 watch a circus or an acrobatic show

口头文字 folk tales

口诛笔伐 denounce in both speech and writing

口技 ventriloquism

快板(音乐)allegro

快板儿 rhythmic comic talk or monologue to the accompaniment of bamboo clappers

快板儿书 rhythmic story recited to the rhythm of bamboo clappers

快书 quick-patter (rhythmic storytelling accompanied by bamboo or copper clappers)

模仿秀 imitation show—a show in which people mimic stars (usually singers)

捧角 try to build up an actor

曲牌 the names of the tunes to which qu are composed

曲艺 folk art forms including ballad singing, story telling, comic dialogues, clapper talks, cross talks, etc.

山东梆子 Shandong clapper opera

山东大鼓 local style of story-telling in Shandong province accompanied by a sort of semi-circular cymbals

山东快书 Shandong clapper ballad

书茶馆儿 teahouse with professional story-telling

书场 a place of entertainment where quyi performances are given

书坊 place serving as both a printing house and a bookshop

书鼓 small drum used to accompany versified storytelling

说书 storytelling

调嘴学舌 tell tales

脱口秀 talk show

笑星 comedy star

歇后语 two-part allegorical saying

名言俗语

笑一笑，十年少。

Smile makes one young.

只工作不娱乐使人愚钝。

All work and no play makes Jack a dull boy.

笑一笑而忘却，比愁眉苦脸地记住要好得多。

Better by far you should forget and smile than you should remember and be sad.

世界没有任何一种东西比艺术会给身处逆境的人带来更多的安慰与甜蜜。

There is no comfort in adversity, more sweet than art affords.

不要在一边等别人同你一起快乐，任何幸福都得自己去创造。

Don't wait around for other people to be happy for you. Any happiness you get you've got to make yourself.

笑，这个世界与你同笑；哭，独自去哭吧。

Laugh, and the world laughs with you; weep, and you weep alone.

愉快地笑，这是精神健康的唯一标记。

Happy laughters are the only mark of the healthy spirit.

词语注解

借古讽今

to use the past to disparage the present

笑破肚皮：大笑

to split one's sides with laughter

笑面虎：外表看起来善良，但内心残忍的人

smiling tiger—an outwardly kind but inwardly cruel person

调侃儿：用行话说

talk in professional jargon

说唱文学：用唱歌或讲故事的娱乐的方式

literary entertainment in a form of storytelling and ballad singing

中西合璧

由于文化背景、思维方式的差异，中西方喜剧也大有不同。在外国演讲的人常会发现听众对他讲的某个笑话毫无反映，然而在国内同一个笑话会使听众笑得人仰马翻。汉语言丰富精妙、富于智慧，因此中式幽默更多的是体现在语言上；而西方的喜剧色彩更多的是体现在肢体动作及表情上。但是真正的幽默可突破地域限制，比如中国的相声和西方的脱口秀都受到人们的喜爱。脱口秀是西方受欢迎的电台或电视喜剧节目，通常由一个或几个主持人和嘉宾谈论社会热门话题或其他议题。许多脱口秀(特别是在广播电台的)让听众通过电话、信件、电子邮件和互联网视频参与节目。这种节目的娱乐性很强，和中国的相声功能相似。尽管与相声的形式完全不一样，但它们的目的是一致的：让人们欢笑、给人启示。这就是为什么有那么多大山来中国学说相声。

Different people have different thought patterns due to different cultural background, and enjoy different comedies. Performers often find that the audiences have no reflection on their jokes in foreign lands, while they can make the listeners burst into laughter with the same joke! Chinese language is rich in words, and people are intelligent, and therefore Chinese-style humor is reflected in the language; and the Westerners are rich in body language. But all the people in the world are fond of humors such as the Chinese cross talks (Xiangsheng) and the Western talk shows. A talk show is a radio or television program where one or more hosts discuss current issues or other topics with guests. Many talk shows (especially those on radio) allow members of the public to join in, through telephone calls, letters, e-mail and internet to chat. All talk shows are meant to entertain, and many features of it are the same as Xiangsheng in China. Although they are completely different in the forms of styles, the aim is the same: to make people laugh and think. This is why there are so many foreigners like Dashan (a famous Canadian who has been famous for being a cross talk performer in China) who have come to China to learn to be a cross talker.

UNIT 38

Auspicious Culture

吉祥文化

题记

在绵延数千年的中国传统文化长河中，吉祥文化是一条十分重要的支流，它凝结着中国人的伦理情感、生命意识、审美趣味与宗教情怀。它的核心在于帮助人们更好地生活，激发人们创造美好的生活，凡是人们认为好的东西，都会表现在吉祥文化之中，构成吉祥文化永恒的主题和美好的画面。吉祥文化的影响从古及今，无处不在。

In the thousands of years of Chinese traditional culture, auspicious culture has been an important tributary. It condensed Chinese people's moral feelings, life awareness, aesthetic and religious sentiments. Its core is to help people and inspire people to create a better life. Whatever people think of will be reflected in auspicious culture, and it is constituted of the eternal theme of culture, auspiciousness, and beautiful imagery. Auspicious culture has influenced people from ancient times till now, and it still exists in every corner in China.

In the development of Chinese 5000 years history, people have expressed their wishes for a happy life by making good use of Chinese characters, beasts, flowers, birds, heavenly bodies, natural phenomenon, such as thunder and lightening by way of metonymy, personification, puns, homonyms, symbols and thus Chinese propitious culture has been formed.

Literally, auspiciousness means luck and peace. Good luck means good omen, thus everything is satisfactory and pleasant. We may see the life consciousness, the esthetic appealing and national qualities of our Chinese people through the decorative design, pattern and signs. There are man elements which carry good luck. The most common are here as the follow

Auspicious Animals

Chinese people think that animals can bring them good luck. Some of the animals which embody good fortune exist in the real world and some are imaginary. The unicorn, the phoenix, the turtle and the dragon were called, "The Four Spirits" by the ancient Chinese people. These are the intelligent and propitious animals. Among them only turtles really exist in the world. It symbolizes 'longevity' because turtles have a long life. The unicorn, the phoenix, and the dragon symbolize peace, nobleness, and braveness respectively. These three animals are in people's imagination.

In Chinese culture, "dragon and the phoenix" are most popular propitious symbols. You can see them everywhere, especially on the traditional bridle dresses, the patterns of dragon and phoenix are embroidered.

Auspicious plants are auspicious, meaning that people enrust. Flowers, trees, fruit carry auspicious meanings accordingly. Such as "the Three Friends in Winter (of the cold)", we people use plum blossom, bamboos and pine trees to express auspicious content. Red beans show "the thinking of somebody". It is a traditional habit for lovers to present as gifts. Orange, for instance in Chinese “桔” is a homonym of “吉”. People wish good luck to each other through presenting oranges. Pomegranate is a symbol of many children and happiness. And the orchid is famous for its unique delicate fragrance and it is regarded as “the noble among the flowers”, a symbol of elegance. Fragrance, color and elegance are all in peony.

Auspicious numerals

In our Chinese culture, numerals not only tell the quantities, but carry collocations of auspiciousness. “one”, “ten”, “hundred”, and “thousand” together with some other other numerals have collocations. Even numerals have the propitious meanings as well as odd numerals and they have been playing a very important role in the history of our culture. It is said there were 9,999 rooms in the Forbidden City! The most popular propitious numerals are “three”, “six”, “nine”, “eight”. If we have got these numerals in our telephone numbers, car numbers, room numbers, we would be specially happy because people think these number can bring them fortune.

Characters

Chinese characters themselves are great decorations. Therefore, people love to show the propitious writings in various forms of calligraphy. The commonly used four characters are “fortune”, “wealth”, “longevity” and “happiness”. “Fortune” means good luck while “wealth” means the success in career; “Longevity” represents a long life while “happiness” enjoyment and delight. Chinese people like to decorate all kinds of things with multiple designs of these characters to express their good wishes.

Auspicious language

China is a nation of etiquettes. People choose words to communicate whenever they talk to each other. For example, we Chinese people certainly say "Wish you a prosperous new year" during Spring Festival and a good wish to anyone to increase their wealth in the coming new year. When attending a wedding ceremony, we must say to the newly-weds to "Live together all their lives". When the old have their birthday, people must say "Be happy as deep as the South Sea and live as long as the mountain" to bless them with a long and a happy life. When a store starts its business, we say something to show our wish to make the store's business getting better and better. Many other words are used as "Everything goes well" or "Good wishes come true" or "Make progress in study" to express our good wishes to each other in our daily life.

Auspicious Behavior

In China, people would like to do anything propitious to express their good wishes. The most typical time is during the Spring Festival. Chinese people always put Chinese couplets or the character FU on the door to stimulate the hot atmosphere to show their wishes. All the family members have a rich dinner (Nianfan) together to show they are united; the older would offer money wrapped in red packets to the young people blessing the children healthy in the coming year; playing firecracker indicates to welcome the new year while getting rid of the old; having Jiaozi and Niangao symbolizes good fortune and wealth; relatives and friends pay visit to each other to bless them with good wishes.

It is obvious that Chinese propitious culture lies everywhere in the life. If you understand it, you can understand Chinese culture better!

段落译文

在中华民族5000年漫长的岁月里，先民们巧妙地运用人物、走兽、花鸟、日月星辰、风雨雷电、文字等等，通过借喻、比拟、双关、谐音、象征等等手法，来表达自己对吉祥美好生活的向往。透过这一个个纹饰、图案、符号，可以看到中国人的生命意识、审美情趣、宗教情怀和民族性格。

吉祥指“吉利”与“祥和”，是指美好、幸运的吉兆、行为、祈愿意识和形体表达。中华民族有许许多多被人们视为吉祥的元素，最常见的有如下几类。

吉祥动物。中国人认为，动物可以给人们的带来好运。一些动物含有好运的意思，有时体现在真实世界里，也有一些是人们虚构的。我国古人把麒麟、凤凰、龟和龙并称为“四灵”，即四种灵异的吉祥动物。这四者千百年来成为中国人生活中的恒定认同吉祥物。它们之中，龟是真实存在的动物。龟的生命很长，所以它是“长寿”的象征。麒麟为仁兽；凤凰为百鸟之王；龙是中华民族的象征。麟、凤、龙，都是按中国人的思维方式复合构思所创造的虚拟的。在中华文化中，龙和凤是最受欢迎的吉祥元素，在许多场合都能看到。例如在传统的新娘礼服上，一定会用金丝线绣着龙凤图案，寓意龙凤呈祥。

吉祥植物是被人们赋予吉祥意义的植物，有花草、树木、果实，它们表示吉祥意义多以组合图案构成。如岁寒三友，人们大都用梅、竹、松来表示来寓意。红豆象征思念，石榴象征多子多福，橘象征大吉，芙蓉象征荣华富贵等等。兰花和牡丹花都是中国的传统名花。兰花以其独特的清香著称，被称作“花中君子”，是高雅的象征。牡丹花兼有色、香、韵三者之美，形象雍容华贵，被视为繁荣昌盛、幸福、和平的象征。

吉祥数字在中国文化中，不仅表示多少，还隐含着吉祥意思。从一到十、百、千、万等数字都有吉祥含义。偶数有吉祥的含义，奇数也有吉祥的含义。吉祥数字一直以来在中国的文化中扮演着重要的角色，据说紫禁城就有 9999 个房间。最受中国人欢迎的吉祥数字是“三”、“六”、“九”和“八”。如果在自己的电话号码、车牌号码、房间码中有这几个数字，人们就会特别高兴，认为这样会给自己带来幸运。

吉祥文字是指那些基本涵义吉祥，或引申涵义吉祥，或在人们的生活习俗中赋予了某种特定吉祥意蕴的汉字。常用的吉祥文字有“福”、“禄”、“寿”、“喜”四个字。“福”代表幸福、福气；“禄”代表事业成功；“寿”代表长寿；“喜”代表快乐和令人高兴的事。人们喜欢把这些吉祥文字组成的图案用在各种各样的装饰品上，以表达美好的愿望。

中国是礼仪之邦。吉祥语言是人们见面时喜欢说的吉祥话语。例如，在春节见面时一定会说“恭喜发财”，就是祝对方在新的一年里增添财富；参加婚礼时，一定要祝新婚夫妇“百年好合”，就是祝他们幸福美满；给老人家祝寿时，要说“福如东海，寿比南山”，就是祝愿他幸福长寿；商店开业，要说“汇川纳海，聚福生财”，就是希望商店生意越来越好。还有“万事如意”、“心想事成”、“学习进步”、“工作顺利”等等，都是在日常生活中人们互相表示良好祝愿的话语。

吉祥行为，是指用行为来体现吉祥的内涵，可分为祈求吉祥的行为和包藏吉祥的行为两种。前者是为了达到吉祥的目的而专门实施的行为，后者则是某种行为中包藏着吉祥的内涵。在婚嫁、生育、开业、奠基、纪念……等等，人们在大部分的生产生活交往行为中，都有吉祥文化的渗透与影响。最典型的是在春节，人们会在门上贴春联、贴福字，表达自己的愿望，增添喜庆的气氛；所有家庭成员聚在一起吃团圆饭，表示家族的团结；长辈会给小朋友压岁钱，祝愿小朋友平安健康；燃放爆竹，表示辞旧迎新；吃饺子、吃年糕象征吉祥和富裕；亲戚朋友互相拜年，互道祝福。

总之，吉祥文化在中国遍及人们生活的方方面面，要想更好地理解中国文化，必须了解中国的吉祥文化。

实用词汇

大吉大利 good luck and great prosperity

福星 lucky star

福星高照 the lucky star shines high above

关帝 deified title for Guan Yu as good of war

关帝庙 Guandi Temple

关门大吉 close down for good

贺礼 congratulatory gift

洪福 great blessing

护心镜 chest plate (round metal piece on armour to protect the chest)

还愿 redeem a vow (as to the Buddhist); fulfill one's promise

黄道吉日 propitious (or auspicious) date

火树银花 fiery trees and silver flowers—dazzling displays of fireworks and lanterns (on a festival night)

吉期 wedding day

吉庆 auspicious occasion

吉日 auspicious day

吉日良辰 lucky day

吉祥 lucky

吉凶 good or ill luck

吉凶未卜 one's fate remains unknown

吉兆 good omen

嘉言懿行 educational noble words and deeds

佳话 deed praised far and wide

看日子 select an auspicious day

看相 read fortune (by face, palm lines, etc.)

龙凤呈祥 the dragon and the phoenix bringing prosperity—exercise good fortune

龙凤帖 marriage certificate or lines

龙肝凤髓 dragon's liver and phoenix's bone marrow—great or rare delicacies

桃符 peachwood charms against evil; Spring Festival couplets

万福 curtsy

万古千秋 throughout the ages
占卜 practise divination
占卦 divine by means the Eight Diagrams
占课 divine by tossing coins
占梦 prognostication by dreams
占星 divine by astrology

名言俗语

世上无难事，只怕有心人

nothing in the world is difficult for one who sets his mind on it

寿比南山，福如东海

may you live to be as old as Zhongnan Mountain and may your happiness be as deep as the Eastern Sea

万古长青

remain fresh forever

万古流芳

be remembered throughout the ages

龙凤呈祥

the dragon and the phoenix bringing prosperity—exercise good fortune

吉庆有余

auspicious happiness in superabundance

吉人天相

Heaven stands by the good man

大吉大利

good luck and great prosperity

福星高照

the lucky star shines high above

金玉满堂

Treasures fill the home

生意兴隆

Business flourishes

岁岁平安

Peace all year round

恭喜发财

Wishing you prosperity

和气生财

Harmony brings wealth

心想事成

May all your wishes come true

吉祥如意

Everything goes well

国泰平安

The country flourishes and people live in peace

招财进宝

Money and treasures will he plentiful

一帆风顺

Wishing you every success

步步高升

Promoting to a higher position

出入平安

Safe trip wherever you go

祝你新的一年快乐幸福

Wish you happiness and prosperity in the coming year!

事业成功，家庭美满

Wish you success in your career and happiness of your family

俗语注解

祈福：得到更多的好运

have one's good fortune compromised by having or getting more than one deserves

护身符：保护人免受惩罚或灾乱的东西

Amulet: protective talisman or a thing that protects one from punishment or censure

桃花运：恋爱方面的好运

luck in love

看手相：根据人的手相看其命运的好坏

Tell fortune: to tell someone's future by examining the lines on the palm of his or her hand

中西合璧

不同国家吉祥文化也不相同，例如，中国人根据发音认为有些数字是吉祥或不吉利的。6、8、9 被认为有吉祥的含义：6 顺，8 发，9 长久。数字 4 被认为是不吉利的数字，因为同音“死”（拼音 sǐ）。14 号被认为是最不幸的数字之一。因为 14 在普通话中通常说“是死”，十死“10 死”的声音；而在西方国家，13 则被认为不吉利，但 13 在广东话里意思是“要活”，是吉数 。又例如：无论是在英语国家还是在中国，“红色”有“庆祝”和“幸福”之意，中国有“开门红”，意思是“好运气”，英文也有“假日”的意思 。中西方也有很多不同地方，如“龙”在西方被认为是“邪恶的和不受欢迎的动物”，但中国人视其为“权力和幸运”的象征。在西方，“猫头鹰”指“明智和聪明”。在中国，“猫头鹰”指“坏运气”，如“夜猫进宅，后运将至”，甚至有人害怕听到它们的声音等等。

There are different auspicious cultures in different countries. For instance, In Chinese culture, certain numbers are believed to be auspicious or inauspicious. Lucky numbers are based on Chinese words that sound similar to other Chinese words. The numbers 6, 8 and 9 are believed to have auspicious meanings because their names sound similar to words that have positive meanings. Number 4（四; accounting; pinyin *sì*）is considered an unlucky number in Chinese, Korean, Vietnamese and Japanese cultures, because it is nearly homophonous to the word “death”（死 pinyin *sǐ*）. Number 14 is considered to be one of the unluckiest numbers. Although 14 is usually said in Mandarin as 十四 "shí sì", which sounds like 十死 "ten die", while in the west,13 is considered as unlucky, but number 13 sounds "yat sang" in Cantonese meaning "being alive". Another example, whether in English-speaking country or in China, "red" is related to celebrations and happy days. In China we have the phrase "开门红", which means "good luck". The same meaning in English is "red-letter days". On the other hand, "dragon" is thought to be evil and unwelcome animal in West, however, in China people regard it as power and luck and the kings regarded themselves as the sons of the dragon. There are many stories telling about the DRAGON. In the west, "owl" is wise and clever and just. Such as the English saying goes "as wise as an owl". But in Chinese，"owl"means " bad luck" . People are even afraid of their cries.

UNIT 39

Cultural Taboos

忌讳文化

题记

忌讳是人类的自然关系和社会关系的反映。从古到今，中国人凭借自己的智慧和经验，观察和总结出了很多禁忌。作为民俗的一种，它在人们的生产生活中占有十分重要的地位，并从多方面影响着人们的物质生活和精神生活。

Taboos reflect the nature of human and social relationship. Since ancient times, Chinese people observed and summed up a lot of taboos by virtue of their wisdom and experience. They play a very important part in our life and behaviors and influence people both physically and spiritually in many ways.

Taboos are the products of society and culture, and they appeared long time ago in Chinese history. With the development of society, generally taboos mean "not allowed", or "forbidden". As a product of traditional society, taboos exist in every corner of life and affect our life.

Name taboos. In ancient times, the names of the Emperor and Confucius were not allowed to be called or written directly. It was a national taboo. The ancestors' names (alive or dead) were to be avoided, which was a family taboo. For instance, the emperor was named Ying Zheng, so the first month was changed to be "zhengyue" in different sound. Sima Qian's "Shiji" was used instead of "Shi*tan*", just because his father's name was Sima *Tan*. By Tang Dynasty, in order to "respect the ancestors" and maintain the authority at home, people were not allowed to use the names of the monarchs for more than seven generations, even after they died. A mirror was a taboo in Song Dynasty, because the emperor's great grandfather's name was "Jing", the same sound as mirror. There are three ways to avoid taboos in ancient time: firstly, replace the word of the name of the monarch or the ancestor with other characters; secondly, keep it a vacancy, not to write the name of taboo; thirdly, fail to write the correct characters by missing some part of the word which was a taboo.

Digit taboos. Chinese people believe that figures are auspicious and ominous. Even number is auspicious. Generally speaking, there is an old saying "even means good", "66 Dashun", "Good luck begins from eight" and so on. Taking numbers as taboos reveals the avoided numbers which mean misfortune, for people think they represent danger, loneliness, departure, or death. If you give gifts to those who get married or have birthday, the gift should be in even number; but if you go to visit a patient or attend a funeral, an even number should be avoided, because nobody wants bad things in pairs. The number "three" pronounces "san" in Mandarin and it is homophonic with "san" which means "break up". However, Cantonese like "three", because "three" homophonic with "life". Another example , males do not celebrate their birthday at "thirty", while females don't have their "forty", for " 3" means to "break up" and "4" means "die". But how can women celebrate their "30", while men can have their "40"? In the old days, women had no position so they were in fear to "break up" ,when they celebrated "30", they were not afraid to "break up", and men celebrated "40", they believed they would not die. Here is another example. The Han Chinese avoided getting married in May, July and September, which were considered as inauspicious. And people should not get married at 18, for the couple would have 18 hardships. In Kaifeng and some other places people believe the old would die either at "73" or "84". These numbers are taboos, of course, which are lack of scientific justification, but the expressions of their loneliness, fear of death, the good wishes of longevity and human instinct to protect themselves.

Taboos for people and objects: women used to be taboos, they should not go out to the neighbors, the relatives or the friends in the first month of the New Year; women should not visit others at the houses in the month after they had given birth, for it was said that they would dirt others, or they would be unlucky; widows were considered to be ominous; the nuns and monks also were people avoided. In Hunan, it was said that if you encountered nuns or monks on New Year's Day, you would be unlucky a year. Those whose family member died should not pay any visit to others on the Spring Festival in the coming year.

Taboos for objects like animals, plants, artifacts are avoided by people. For instance, we call "Tiger" "Mountain Spirit" or "Beast"; "snake" as "long worm"; we were never allowed to point snakes with the fingers, or else your fingers would become a snake-head. It is also a taboo to hear cries of animals, such as the barking of dogs which sounded crying, or somebody would die in the vicinity. The cry of crows was considered as a bad omen throughout the country. And people didn't want to hear Owls at night too. Taboos for plants refer to the old trees beside the temple and the village, which should not be cut. Objects as umbrellas can not be pronounced as "san", because it is the homophone of "break up". A gift can not be a clock, because "clock" has the sound of "the end (of the life)". There are 12 taboos for chopsticks. For example, if you insert a chopstick into the rice at table, it was considered as a humiliation to others. In addition, you should not cross your chopsticks casually on the table which is a negative attitude to others.

Festival taboos. In language, people are not allowed to say "disease", "death", "ghost", "poverty" and other inauspicious words on the New Year's Eve and Chinese New Year in all parts of the country. In deeds, people should not break any bowls, and benches should not be made to fall to the ground on New Year's Eve, otherwise there would be something unlucky in the coming year. There was another old saying that if you had your hair cut in January, your uncle would die. In the past, people would never take porridge or meat as breakfast, we must eat cooked rice in the morning on New Year's Day so that the whole family would become very rich in the coming year. And people believed that we were not allowed to wash clothes, for the first or second day was the Water God's birthday!

In addition, there are a variety of other taboos in China, such as taboos of etiquette, and the body. At different times, different areas had different taboos. These taboos may now have changed in some ways, but the traditional Chinese taboos still remain. Some of the taboos have something to do with superstitions, and may not be very scientific, while others are the result of daily life and experience. They play a positive role to regulate man and society, and help people deal with interpersonal relationships.

段落译文

忌讳是社会与文化的产物。中国人忌讳观念的产生由来已久。随着社会的发展，忌讳一般指避讳、顾忌之意。作为传统社会的产物，忌讳存在于社会的每个角落，影响着人们的生活。

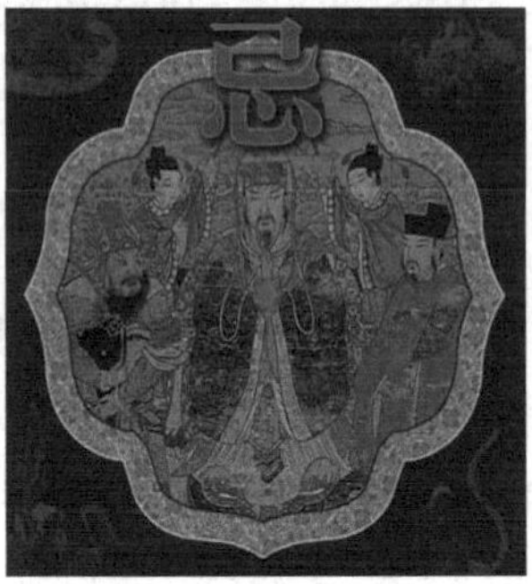

人名避讳 在古代，我国对某些人如皇帝、孔子的名字不许直接呼唤和书写，这是避国讳。凡遇祖先或先辈(活着的或死去的)的名字，全家共避之，这叫避家讳。如秦始皇名叫嬴政，就改读正月为“征月”或“端月”。司马迁著《史记》忌用“史谈”字，也是为避父名司马谈之讳。到了唐代，为了“尊祖敬祖”和维护家天下的权威，唐代要求对七世以内已死的君主必须避讳，到了宋代又规定七世以上的君主必须避讳。如宋代把镜子叫做“照子”或“铜鉴”，是为避宋太祖祖父赵敬的名讳。古代避讳的方法有三种。一是改字，对君主或所尊者之名改用其他字代表；二是空字法，将避讳的名字空而不写；三是缺笔法，对所避之字的最后一笔或几笔不写。

数字忌讳 中国人认为数字有吉祥与凶险之分。吉数一般为双数，有说“好事成双”、“六六大顺”、“要得发，不离八”等。忌讳数字是因为人们认为它对人有危险，不是孤独、离散，就是死亡，都是不吉利的。如果给结婚、祝寿的送礼，忌讳送单数；但给病人和丧家送礼，就忌送双数，因为谁也不希望坏事成双。忌“三”因为它与“散”谐音，但广东人喜欢“三”，因为在白话中“三”的谐音是“生”。又如：男不做“三”，女不做“四”，指年龄“三十”和“四十”。三和“散”，四和“死”谐音，不吉利，不应该做寿。但是女又能做三十，男也能做四十，这是为了破“散”和“死”。在旧时，妇女没有地位，怕“散”，做了“三”就不怕“散”了，男子做了“四”就破了法，就不会死了。又如若干年前，汉族人忌在五、七、九月结婚，认为不吉利。忌十八岁结婚，认为新人将受“十八难”；开封等地有“七十三，八十四，阎王不请自己去”的说法。这些数字忌讳，当然都没有科学道理。只是表达了人们对孤独、离散、死亡等的恐惧心理和对好事、长寿的愿望，也是人对自身本能保护的表现。

人与物忌讳 对人的忌讳，首先是忌讳女人。在新年正月初，妇女不能出门到邻居家、亲友家拜年；对产妇、寡妇忌讳更多。产妇未满月不能到别人家去，说是会脏了别人的门槛，人家会跑财；寡妇则被认为是不祥之人；尼姑、和尚也是被忌讳的人。在湖南，认为“元旦出行，遇到尼姑、和尚，一年里百事不利”。

家中死了人，来年春节就不能到任何人家去拜年。

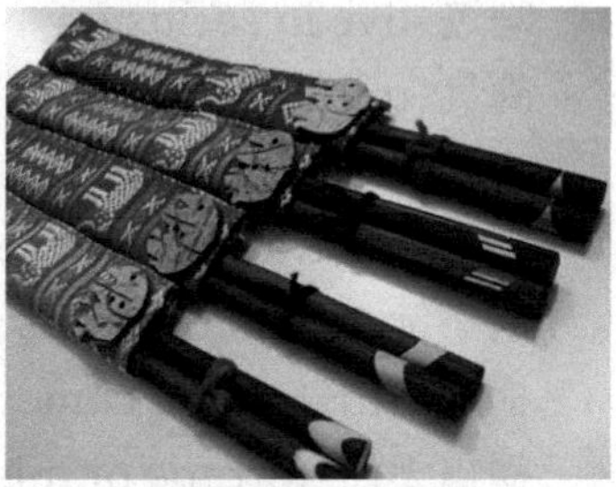

对物的忌讳较广泛，人们对动物、植物、器物、天体等都有忌讳。如称“虎”为“山神”或“大虫”；说“蛇”是“长虫”；忌讳用手指蛇的传说，否则手指会变成蛇头。人们还忌讳一些动物叫，如忌闻狗叫如哭，否则附近有人会死。忌闻乌鸦叫，其叫声在全国各地都被认为是凶兆。猫头鹰夜鸣也是被人忌讳的。对植物的忌讳是指忌砍伐庙旁、村后的古树。对器物的忌讳如雨伞不能叫伞，因为“伞”与“散”谐音。送礼不能送“钟”，因为“钟”的谐音是“终”。再如筷子禁忌有十二种。如在用餐时用一只筷子去插盘子里的菜品，被认为对同桌用餐人员的一种羞辱。另外，在用餐时将筷子随便交叉放在桌上，是对同桌其他人的全部否定等。

节日禁忌　在语言上，除夕和春节，南北各地都忌讳说“病”、“死”、“鬼”“穷”等一切不吉利、不祥的话。在行为方面，大年三十、初一忌打破碗盏，忌板凳倒地等，否则在新的一年里将有凶事。还有“正月不剃头，剃头死舅舅”的说法。另外在大年初一，早餐忌吃稀饭、荤食及药品：过去的常规穷人家才吃稀饭，所以在年初一的上午一定要吃干饭，表示家里整年都会很富有，还有一种说法，初一、初二忌洗衣：水有水神，水神的生日在初一初二，因此这两天不要洗衣服。

除以上所述，我国还有其他各种忌讳，如礼仪方面的许多禁忌、身体禁忌等等。不同的时代、不同的区域忌讳也不同，这些忌讳现在也许发生了一些变化，但中国传统的忌讳仍然保留至今。有些忌讳与迷信有关，很不科学，有些则是生产、生活经验的总结，起着调节人与社会、人与人的关系，有一定的积极作用。

实用词汇

避讳 avoid a taboo (on the personal names of emperors, one's elders, etc.)

顾大局，识大体 bear the overall situation in mind and put the general interest above all else

顾面子 save face

讳莫如深 not utter a single word about sth.

讳言 dare not or would not speak up

晦迹 live in seclusion

晦气 unlucky; pale and gloomy look

晦朔 from the last day of a lunar month to the first day of the next one

祸不妄至 woes never come without reason

祸不旋踵 misfortune is not far off

祸从口出 trouble comes out of the mouth

祸福无门 fortune or misfortune knows no doors—they are invited in

祸根 root of trouble; apple of discord

祸起萧墙 trouble arises behind the walls of the home—trouble arises within the family

祸水 person(especially a woman) who is the source of trouble

祸兮福所倚，福兮祸所伏 good fortune lies within bad, bad fortune lurked within good

积阴德 do good deeds to obtain one's credit in the next world

记言 recording words

忌辰 anniversary of the death of a parent, ancestor, or anyone else held in esteem

忌讳 taboo

忌口 avoid certain food for illness or some other reasons

忌日 date on which certain things should be avoided

忌食 ① avoid certain food for health reasons or because of medical treatment, ②avoid certain food out of religious beliefs

祭奠 hold a memorial ceremony for sb.

祭礼 sacrificial rites

祭品 sacrificial offerings

祭器 sacrificial utensil

祭扫 offer sacrifices and sweep the ancestral tomb

祭祀 offer sacrifices to gods or ancestors

祭坛 sacrificial altar

祭文 funeral oration

祭仪 sacrificial offerings; ceremony of offering sacrifices

祭灶 offer sacrifices to the kitchen god on the 23rd or 24th of the 12th lunar month

叫魂 call back the spirit of the sick

禁语（佛教）self-imposed silence

看风水 practise geomancy for selecting a site for a tomb, house, etc.

如意 an s-shaped wand or cepter, usually made of jade, symbolizing good fortune

隐讳 cover up

灾星 ill luck

早茶 morning tea

斋七（佛教）seven-week prayer for the dead

斋日（佛教）day of the Eight Commandments

隐士 recluse

走背运 have bad luck

名言俗语

入乡随俗。

When in Rome as the Romans do.

自己的命运自己掌握。

Every man is the architect of his own fortune.

呆人有呆福。

Fools has fortune.

禁果格外香。

Forbidden fruit is sweet.

机遇偏爱善断之人。

Fortune favors those who use their judgement.

风水轮流转。

Fortune knocks once at least at every man's gate.

坐失良机，后悔已迟。

It is too late to grieve when the chance is past.

谋事在人，成事在天。

Man proposes; God disposes.

福无双至；机会难得。

Opportunity seldom knocks twice.

俗语注解

回光返照：指人在去世之前短暂的意识恢复

last radiance of the setting sun: momentary recovery of consciousness just before death

如意算盘：聪明的想法

wishful thinking

送瘟神：意指离开或送走自己不喜欢的人或东西

send away the god of plague: get rid of sb. or sth. unwanted or unpleasant

祸不妄至：坏事发生总是有其原因

woes never come without reason

本命年：人出生后每个第 12 年

every 12th year after the year of one's birth

去晦气：赶走厄运

get rid of the ill-fortune

祭祖宗：献祭品给祖先

offer sacrifices to one's ancestors

压岁钱：在新年(春节)给孩子们作为礼物的钱

gift money; money given to children as a lunar New Year gift

中西合璧

忌讳是世界各民族之间普遍存在的一种文化现象，禁忌规范了人们的言语行为与社会交际。中西方在禁忌方面有很多相同点和不同点。如在西方国家，有些基督教徒对上帝非常虔诚，他们认为滥用上帝或上帝的名字是不敬的。这点和中国人一样，要尽量避免对“神”对祖先的不敬；中西方不愿或者不敢提及关于病和死。中西方忌讳也有不同的一面，如许多西方人忌讳 13，中国人忌讳 14，西方人忌讳提到龙，中国人则以龙为图腾等等。总之，了解中西方忌讳现象可以使跨文化交际更加得体。

Taboo is a commonly existing cultural phenomenon among nations in the world which regulates people's language and social communication. The great difference between Chinese and western culture directly results in the great difference between Chinese and western taboos. There are many similarities and differences between the Chinese and western taboos. In Western countries, some Christians believe that the misuse of the name of God is disrespectful. So do the Chinese people, one must try to avoid the name of "God" or even the names of the ancestors. In the West, people do not like to talk about the disease and death, neither do the Chinese. We have different taboos too. For instance, many Westerners take 13, as a taboo, while the Chinese have 14, Westerners avoid "dragon" while the Chinese take it as the totem, and so on. In short, to understand the phenomenon of taboo in different cultures can help us have a more decent cross-cultural communication.

UNIT 40

Chinese Fengshui

风水文化

题记

近年来，越来越多的外国人对中国的风水文化产生了浓厚的兴趣。而且很多大学开设了风水课程。人们正在用现代的科学方法对古老的风水学进行研究和探索。

In recent years, more and more foreigners have become interested in the Chinese Fengshui. What's more, Fengshui has been introduced into the school curriculums in many universities. Now people are studying the ancient Fengshui in conjunction with the modern scientific methods.

There are a lot of definitions of Fengshui in China. Generally speaking, it means the topography and the direction of the residential base and graveyard.

It can also be interpreted as a type of superstition because of the way ancient people connected it with destiny, and the good and bad fortune of their future generations. However, the common explanation is that Fengshui is a very useful technology to select the correct environment. Ancient people adapted their surroundings to create an auspicious site and layout, while adding artistic merit. Many people believe that there are a lot of coincidences between the considerations of Fengshui and modern science and technological truths, including the effects of light, water, and direction of the house. Of course the superstitious legends and explanations do not share much in common. Chinese Fengshui culture contains a lot of useful information about architecture, aesthetics, and ecology.

Fengshui influenced the location of villages in ancient China. A site surrounded by water or by a river, and in front of hills was the ideal site for many villages. Other villages were set up in front of or behind water or rivers because the villagers believed the river was their guardian.

Since ancient times, Chinese have paid great attention to choosing a place to dwell. It was believed that fengshui affected the prosperity of the family, and influenced the people's physiology, mentality, and

even emotion and ethics. Generally speaking, the best site to live should be a location facing water and with hills behind it. Also the gate or door is very important because according to fengshui it can pursue harmony and avoid harm. The mountain and water are the most auspicious things in nature for Chinese people, so the gate or door always opens towards them.

Although there is some superstition in Fengshui, people have studied it and found some scientific knowledge about environment, psychics, hygienics, and aesthetics in it. What is called "sha or evil" in Chinese Fengshui has turned out out to be disadvantages or things that are harmful to a living environment, such as direction, light, sound and even colour. According to the theories of the five natural elements of metal, wood, water, fire, and earth, all things on earth can produce and overcome each other.

In order to keep the balance, Fengshui is supposed to help people to promote harmony and avoid harm or "sha".

In daily life, people can change conditions, beautify the environment, and adjust their mentality to get the harmony. Chinese culture is developed with the belief of the middle course. So it is believed that it should be harmful for the people to live in a room, which is too bright or too dark, but you can mediate them with Fengshui.

Some Chinese people like to keep a bowl of fish or place some flowers and other auspicious things in the office to bring good luck in dealing with office politics, so some experts believe that it often helps, because if people have these psychological suggestions and a pleasant environment every day, they are more relaxed and more confident. Maybe Chinese Fengshui will become more scientific and perfect in the near future.

段落译文

在中国，人们对“风水”一词有很多的解释。一般来说，“风水”是指住宅基地、坟地等地理形势，如地势、山水的方向等。也有人认为“风水”是一种迷信，因为古人把风水和人的未来命运、子孙后代的祸福联系在一起了。而现在人们普遍接受的说法是：“风水”是一种非常实用的选择环境的技术，是古人为了适应生存环境，通过不断探索得到的经验总结，是中国古代居住选址与建筑布局的一门艺术。抛开那些迷信的传说和解释，很多人认为风水在选址时的很多选择条件，如对光的取舍、对水和风的考虑等都和现代科学技术相吻合。可以说中国的风水文化在建筑学、美学和生态学等方面都有着很多参考价值。

中国古代村落的选址一直受风水文化的支配和影响。许多村落的选址和布局都采用了“背山、环水、面屏”这种理想的风水模式。有些地区村落则采用“背水”的风水模式。当地的人们认为水是龙脉，水是一村的保护神，因此很多村庄背水或面水而建。

自古以来，中国人非常重视家居选址的问题，而且认为选址与家庭的兴旺是联系在一起的。同时还会影响到人的生理和心理，甚至会关系到家庭的情感、或伦理道德等。一般来说住宅建在背山面水处是最好的选择。另外门也十分重要。风水学认为大门为气口，起着避凶迎吉的作用。人们认为山和水是自然界最吉祥的，因此住宅的门往往朝向山口或水域。

虽然风水有些迷信说法，但是人们通过研究后发现，其实风水也包含了环境学、心理学、卫生学、美学等很多科学知识。在中国的风水学中，有些被称为“煞”东西其实是指住宅环境中的不利之处，如方向、光线、物体、声音、甚至颜色等。根据中国的金、木、水、火、土五行之说：一切事物都是相生相克的，风水学可以帮助人们趋利避害，达到一定的平衡。

在现实生活中人们可以根据风水学改变现状、美化环境、调节心理，使之达到和谐的目的。中国文化是基于中庸之道的，凡事不可缺也不可过。所以有人认为房间的光线太明或者太暗了，都会对人们产生不利的影响，可以运用风水学来调解。

有些中国人喜欢在办公室里放鱼缸或摆放某些特定的花草等吉祥的东西，主要目的是想化解工作中的不利因素，让工作更加顺利。因此有些专家认为如果人们每天面对这些心理暗示，他们情绪会更加放松，信心会更足，工作也许会真的越来越顺利。希望在不远的将来中国风水学会更加科学、更加完善。

实用词汇

风水 Fengshui
建筑学 architecture
美学 esthetics
生态学 bionomy; bionomics
鱼缸 a bowl of fish; fish tank
迷信 superstition; geomancy
中国文化因素 Chinese cultural elements
五行之说 the five natural elements
风水师 feng shui master
风水先生 geomancer
看风水 practise geomancy for selecting a site for tomb, house, etc.
趋利避邪 the pursuit of harmony to avoid harm
煞 evil, sha
中庸之道 the middle course
保护神 guardian
八卦 Eight Trigrams

名言俗语

风水轮流转。/ 人皆有得意时。
Every dog has his day, and every man his hour.
天有不测风云，人有旦夕祸福。
Fortune is fickle. Here today, gone tomorrow.
行中庸之道才安全。
Safety lies in the middle course.
没有因，哪有果。
Take away the cause, and the effect must cease.
无法预料的事往往最快发生。
That which one least anticipates soonest comes to pass.

十年风水轮流转。

The worse luck now, the better another time.

莫幸灾乐祸，风水轮流转。

Do not rejoice at my grief, for when mine is old, yours will be new.

俗语注解

风水：指住宅基地、坟地等的地理形式，如地脉、山水的方向等。迷信的人认为风水的好坏可以影响其家族、子孙的盛衰吉凶。

Fengshui or geomancy means selecting the location of a house, grave, etc. from the perspectives of the geomantic features of surrounding and nearly hills and waters. Superstitious people believe this could affect the fortunes of a family and its descendants.

风水宝地：各方面都比较好的地方

Place with good geomantic potency

煞气：迷信的人所指的邪气

Demon, evil emanations, or perverse trend according to the superstition

五行之说：指金、木、水、火、土五种物质。迷信的人用五行相生相克来推算人的命运。

It means the five natural elements of metal, wood, water, fire and earth. Superstitious people used the principle of the five elements producing and overcoming each other to tell the fate of a person.

中西合璧

风水学源于中国，是中国传统神秘文化的重要组成部分。20 世纪 80 年代以来，风水热席卷全球，形成一种令人深思的文化现象。风水文化盛行世界有诸多方面的原因，人类生态的大自然环境正在受到破坏：环境污染、人口膨胀、资源危机、水土流失、气候反常等。另一个重要原因是现代建筑往往忽略了人与环境的关系，而风水文化正是考虑了天、人、地的关系。不但从心理上满足了人的需要，而且有一定的实用价值。德国当前兴起了生物住宅热，这些土木结构的生物房屋对住宅环境的优选十分讲究，其标准竟是中国古代的风水学。美国人过去并不信风水，而据报道已有多所美国大学开设了风水课。日本已有 100 多所大学开设了风水课。

Fengshui originates from China and is an important part of Chinese traditional culture. Since the 80s of last century, Fengshui has prevailed throughout the whole world because of many reasons such as environmental pollution, population explosion, resource crises, soil erosion, climate anomalies and so on. Often the relationship between man and the environment is overlooked in modern architecture, however it is well considered in Chinese Fengshui. It not only meets psychological needs of the people, but also has a certain practical value. It is reported that biology houses are very popular in Germany, and the environment of the houses is selected carefully according to Chinese Fengshui. Although the Americans didn't believe fengshui before, now fengshui has been introduced into the school curriculum in many universities in U.S. It is also reported that there are more than 100 universities offering fengshui courses in Japan.